Linking Training to Performance

A Guide for Workforce Development Professionals

The editors wish to thank graduate research assistant Yeonsoo Kim for her assistance in following up on the copyright permissions sought for this book and to Sean Mahoney for his able assistance in reviewing an early manuscript draft.

Linking
Training to
Performance

A Guide for Workforce
Development Professionals

Foreword by George R. Boggs and James McKenney
Edited by William J. Rothwell, Patrick E. Gerity, and Elaine A. Gaertner

Community College Press®
a division of the American Association of Community Colleges
Washington, D.C.

The American Association of Community Colleges (AACC) is the primary advocacy organization for the nation's community colleges. The association represents 1,100 two-year, associate degree–granting institutions and more than 10 million students. AACC promotes community colleges through six strategic action areas: national and international recognition and advocacy, learning and accountability, leadership development, economic and workforce development, connectedness across AACC membership, and international and intercultural education. Information about AACC and community colleges may be found at www.aacc.nche.edu.

Design: Brian Gallagher
Editor: Deanna D'Errico
Printer: Graphic Communications, Inc.

Community College Press
American Association of Community Colleges
One Dupont Circle, NW
Suite 410
Washington, DC 20036

Printed in the United States of America.

ISBN 0-87117-361-1

CONTENTS

CONTENTS

America's community colleges have become the nation's premier providers of workforce education. However, like the colleges themselves, this essential role has evolved over time, defined by the colleges' responsiveness to community need and change. With the publication of *Linking Training to Performance: A Guide for Workforce Development Professionals*, community college workforce development practitioners now have the opportunity to examine this role in both its historical and modern operational contexts, seeing beyond the operation of one institution or system to compare and contrast disparate approaches in multiple states and communities. The book thus provides an invaluable frame of reference to stimulate strategic thinking about this critical component of the community college mission.

How did the evolution begin? Joliet Junior College, founded in 1901 and considered by most scholars to be the oldest community college, began with the sole mission of providing its students with the first two years of a university education, to enable the most capable of them to transfer to a senior institution. Many other community colleges began as teacher-training institutes. Still others began as community-based, manual learning divisions or citizenship schools to enhance the diploma programs at high schools.

Community colleges experienced their first period of dramatic growth in the aftermath of World War II. Thousands of American servicemen and women returning from the battlefields sought to build new lives and establish careers and families. On June 22, 1944, President Franklin D. Roosevelt signed the Servicemen's Readjustment Act of 1944, better known as the GI Bill of Rights. The GI Bill afforded thousands of service members access to vocational training and higher education formerly beyond their economic means. As veterans took advantage of this benefit, public and private two-year colleges responded by providing high-quality, reasonably priced education and training.

The rapid post-war growth of community colleges was, in part, a response to the demand created by the availability of this new and affordable higher-education option. Equally compelling was the demand from local business communities for better-educated workers needed for diverse economies generated by the war. Some states responded to training needs by creating technical colleges to fill specific educational requirements requested by the local business community. Students attending these colleges acquired skills that were immediately useable in the workplace. The initial associate degrees conferred by these colleges did not qualify students for transfer to nearby state colleges or universities; however, most states eventually authorized their technical colleges to provide transfer courses and programs. In the states where community colleges began as junior colleges, officials responded to local labor market demands by adding occupational programs to their offerings.

Thus, even though the colleges may have begun with different missions, they have evolved to become what is now referred to as the comprehensive community college. In addition to offering transfer and vocational education programs, community colleges responded to rapidly changing student and community needs by offering noncredit community education courses. Many of these noncredit courses were designed to respond to the local demand for specific skills. Others were designed to provide remedial courses and citizenship and language courses for new immigrants.

The driving forces in today's ever-changing economy are information and technology. These forces are so dominant and the advancements so continuous that "lifelong learning" has become a requirement for continued employment. The fact that the average age of the 10.2 million students in community colleges is 29 reflects this continuous learning trend. Nearly half participate in noncredit courses, and 28% of noncredit students already have a four-year degree or higher. Nearly 50% of all students taking credit and noncredit courses work full time. In both function and scope, many adults now use community colleges as a local graduate school—one that provides competencies and certificates in addition to degrees.

Comprehensive community colleges have evolved to provide multifaceted education for an increasingly complex economy and society. Because of the diversity in local needs, size, and state systems, colleges have developed many different strategies to serve their communities. However, it is rare for community college educators and professionals to have a view beyond their own state systems. Many operate with a limited appreciation of how their colleagues in other states and communities solve problems similar to those they face.

Linking Training to Performance: A Guide for Workforce Development Professionals is intended to significantly broaden that view. Early chapters present a history of structure and practice and an analysis of research on community college performance, describing practice against the backdrop of the major community, economic, political, and technological forces. Two other overview chapters draw attention to some of the internal tensions created by the evolutionary development of community colleges, particularly to how these developments affect the quality of workforce development delivery. One author concentrates on the elements that define a high-performance workforce development organization, while raising serious questions faced by most community colleges seeking to deliver high-quality services and suggesting that a highly insulated workforce development operation may be the most reasonable way for colleges to function. Another author offers the alternate view that a separate operation may keep workforce development from benefiting from other economies of scale within an institution.

These overview chapters will help readers examine how workforce development operations fit within their colleges and help them gauge how to drive change in a desirable direction. Practice-oriented chapters on public relations, partnering, finance and budgeting, needs assess-ment, and evaluation offer readers numerous hands-on strategies and tactics and real-world examples. And, in the appendixes, newcomers and seasoned practitioners alike will find a wealth of information and material to assist them day to day.

Given the anticipated high retirement and turnover rates among community college administrators and faculty, this book fills a decided void for professionals in the workforce development field. Although a guide like this cannot replace local institutional or program experience, the range of knowledge and skills that it covers will be invaluable to educators seeking to better respond to local workforce needs. We congratulate the authors and thank them for this important contribution to community college literature. ❧

George R. Boggs
President and CEO
American Association of Community Colleges

James McKenney
Vice President for Economic Development
American Association of Community Colleges

PREFACE

William J. Rothwell, Patrick E. Gerity, and Elaine S. Gaertner

A s U.S. employers struggle to maintain their productivity edge in the face of increasingly fierce global competition, community colleges have emerged as one key—and perhaps *the* key—network of providers to meet national workforce development needs. The challenges that community colleges face are daunting: a growing number of competitors, increasingly savvy and sophisticated customers who demand (rather than just ask for) what they want, expanding technological options for instructional delivery and performance support, and growing demand for services that go beyond the traditional educational or training services and include a full-range of performance improvement and management consulting services. Recent research conducted among 40 states has revealed a potential prioritized list of challenges facing community colleges (see Table P.1).

Despite these challenges, the community college role in workforce development is likely to intensify rather than diminish. The question is whether everyone is prepared for the challenges—and the opportunities—that the future will be present.

Table P.1	Challenges to Responding to Workforce Training Needs

Survey respondents were asked to indicate what they see as the main challenges that community colleges in their state face in seeking to respond to the workforce training needs of employers and workers. Forty of 45 states responded to this question.

Challenge	Responses	States
Lack of funding	30	AK, AL, AR, CA, CO, CT, DE, IA, IN, KY, LA, MA, ME, NE, NM, NV, NY, OH, OK, OR, PA, RI, SC, TX, UT, VA, VT, WA, WI, WV
Lack of funding for training in high-demand, high-cost fields	12	AL, AZ, CO, DE, IL, IN, KY, NM, OH
Need for better coordination among workforce agencies	8	AR, CA, DE, MN, NY, PA, RI, TX, VA, VT
Community colleges not recognized for their role in workforce and economic development	6	IL, KS, MA, NJ, NM, NY
Need to improve responsiveness of community colleges to changing labor market needs	6	AZ, IL, MN, MO, PA, WV
Recruiting qualified faculty for high-demand fields	5	AL, DE, NC, NM, TX
Need for coordination among education agencies	4	FL, IN, MS, OK
Lack of state funding for noncredit workforce training	4	MA, PA, VA, WV
Serving rural areas where good jobs are scarce	3	IA, NM, NY
Improving preparation and flow of recent high school graduates into postsecondary career education	2	GA, WI
Increasing burden for funding of workforce training on student-supported tuition	2	CO, IA
Lack of financial aid for part-time, working students	1	AR

Note. Data are from Jenkins and Boswell (2002).

Consider these compelling statistics, gleaned from multiple sources:

- "The nation's 1,151 community colleges enroll some 10 million people during any given year, many of them—average age 29—trying to assemble some job skills after having worked at less-satisfying tasks in early adulthood. In many areas, the schools [community colleges] are also dedicated to working directly with individual employers, even small ones, to train existing workers and help find and train new ones. The colleges grant more than 450,000 associate degrees and nearly 200,000 two-year certificates annually" (Bailey, 2002, p. B2).
- Attendance at community colleges is 63% part time and 37% full time (Bailey, 2002).
- Community colleges help individuals prepare for employment—but also help employed individuals hedge their bets in case of unemployment. About 37% of all workers in the United States today are concerned with job loss, up from just 12% in 1981 (Greenspan, 1999).
- "Community colleges are becoming one of the largest segments of the training provider industry, often discounting courses as part of an economic development strategy to attract or retain local businesses" (Masie, 1999, p. 48).
- Although many people tout the social role of the community college as a centerpiece for attracting jobs and bringing culture to otherwise rural areas, globalization is an issue of growing importance to them that may not be recognized as much as it should be (Levin, 2001).
- "In 1988, the Nationwide Commission on the Future of Community Colleges recommended that these colleges help build communities by creating partnerships with employers and making facilities available for workforce training" (Kasper, 2002/2003, p. 15). Many case studies have been published that document the impressive role played by community colleges in local employer partnerships to provide job training (see, e.g., Barista, 2000; Beck, 2001; Boehle, Stamps, & Stratton, 2000; Bowers, 2001; "Community College/Police Training Partnership," 2003; "Dearth of Workers," 1998; Frey & Kuhne, 2000; Hays, 1999; Holmes, 2003; Leung, 2003; Mayadas, 1997; Overman, 1999; Palumbo-Holland, 1997; Reis, 1996; Ruggless, 2000; "San Antonio Rolls Out," 2001; Siegel, 2000; Smith, 1996; Tejada, 2000; Theibert, 1996; Turpin, 2000; White, 2000; Wong 1999).
- "The growth of certificate programs [in community colleges] is an important trend, even though the number of certificates earned remains smaller than the number of associate degrees conferred. Most certificates involved specific, work-related training. [Later] During the decade from 1989–90 to 1999–2000, [short-term and noncredit] certificates awarded in computer-related fields were among those that had the largest percentage growth. For example, certificates granted in computer and information sciences grew 631 percent, increasing from 435 to 3,180. Other fields that saw gains in certificates conferred during the same period were vocational home economics (179 percent), precision production (152 percent), construction trades (142 percent), mechanics and repairers (121 percent), business management and administrative services (118 percent), and protective services (101 percent)" (Kasper, 2002/2003, p. 19).
- About 75% of the U.S. workforce is predicted to need job retraining over the coming decade. About 50 million workers will need technical training; about 5.5 million workers will need training for executive, management, or supervisory work; about 11 million will need customer service training; about 17 million will require basic skills training; and about 37 million new workers will require education and training to meet entry-level employer expectations (Quinley & Hickman, 2003).
- Employers are increasingly willing to outsource training to save money and gain the advantages of tapping outside expertise. "Training programs were outsourced last year at more than half of 225 employers in a survey by Buck Consultants Inc., a human-resources consulting concern. In 1999, 58% turned to outsiders, compared with 22% in 1996" (Tejada, 2000, p. A-1).

So what does this all mean? The answer seems clear: Community colleges are key providers of worker training. Their role in providing a comprehensive range of human performance improvement strategies is growing. And workforce developers have taken center stage in the provider—and sometimes the consulting—role. The work they do is increasingly professional—and sometimes even uniquely specialized—in approach, and their future role in community colleges has moved from marginal to central to strategic.

Linking Training to Performance: A Guide for Workforce Development Professionals provides the basic information necessary for the many workforce developers who work in community college and branch-campus settings. For those with experience as workforce developers, it is intended to be a useful handbook. For those new to their roles as community college workforce developers and who are expected to hit the ground running to generate revenue for their institutions, this book could be regarded as a survival manual.

This book is written for workforce developers in community colleges and branch campus settings. College administrators, public officials, and employers may also find it helpful because it will give them a frame of reference for directing—or judging the quality of—community college workforce developers, the functions they oversee, the results they obtain, and the services they offer. This book can also serve as a text for the many students who are preparing themselves for careers in the challenging world of workforce development in community colleges. The book is intended to cover key issues in workforce development. References are provided for readers who want to pursue key issues in greater depth.

The book begins with a big picture overview of the role of workforce development in community colleges. It then drills down to more specific issues. A summary of major topics is as follows:

- how community colleges respond to the nation's workforce needs
- the importance of strategic planning
- standards set by high-performing workforce development organizations (WDOs): service offerings, customer orientation, the organizational structure and relationship of the WDO to colleges, staffing methods, operations
- institutional requirements for integrating WDOs within the community college context
- how colleges cope with key challenges facing workforce development
- what *competency* means and why workforce developers should care about it
- competencies essential for success in workforce development
- navigating the barriers to building partnerships for successful workforce development programs
- transforming unorganized and fragmented collections of stakeholders into partners who produce change
- harnessing the potential that lies in stakeholder groups and forming productive collaborations
- applying basic marketing concepts to workforce development programs and services

- using a consultative sales approach to marketing workforce development
- finance and budgeting
- establishing and maintaining effective relations with faculty, staff, and administrators for WDOs
- conducting needs assessments for training and non-training projects
- project planning and integrating multiple projects
- evaluating WDOs
- reasons for outsourcing training and criteria used to select training providers
- key lessons learned and predicting the impact of important trends

Readers will also find wealth of useful resources in seven appendixes. The appendixes contain numerous templates, models, and tools (see page 129 for a complete list) that the 22 contributors to this volume have used and refined in their own work. These resources are also provided as separate PDF and WORD files on a companion CD, so that readers can readily adapt and print the resources for their own use. ※

References

Bailey, J. (2002, February). Community colleges can help small firms with staffing—Programs with two-year institutions aid in developing skills in short supply. *Wall Street Journal*, p. B2.

Barista, D. (2000, September). From mall to school hall. *Building Design & Construction, 41*(12), 22–23.

Beck, B. (2001, September). The next generation of steelmakers. *Iron Age New Steel, 17*(9), 14–17.

Boehle, S., Stamps, D., & Stratton, J. (2000, July). Teaching pronunciation online. *Training, 37*(7), 30.

Bowers, J. (2001, June). Banking consortium cashes in on rewards of state funding. *Texas Banking, 90*(6), 16–17.

Community College/Police Training Partnership. (2003, March). *Public Management, 85*(2), 22.

Dearth of workers with technical skills prompts employers to create labor pool through school alliance. (1998, March). *Workforce Strategies, 16*, 15.

Frey, B. A., & Kuhne, G. W. (2000). Workforce education: A staff development program. In J. Phillips (Ed.), *In action: Performance analysis and consulting* (pp. 67–74). Alexandria, VA: American Society for Training and Development.

Greenspan, A. (1999, March). The interaction of education and economic change. *The Region, 13*(1), 6.

Hays, S. (1999, April). Basic skills training 101. *Workforce, 78*(4), 76–78.

Holmes, C. (2003). The CATT's meow. *Business and Economic Review, 49*(3), 19–22.

Jenkins, D., & Boswell, K. (2002). *State policies on community college workforce development: Findings from a national survey.* Chicago: Center for Community College Policy Education Commission for the States.

Kasper, H. T. (2002/2003, Winter). The changing role of community college. *Occupational Outlook Quarterly, 46*(4), 14–21.

Leung, L. (2003, January). Community minded curriculum. *Network World, 29*(1), 47.

Levin, J. S. (2001). *Globalizing the community college: Strategies for change in the twenty-first century.* New York: Palgrave.

Masie, E. E. (1999, February). Yesterday's training channel is gone with the wind. *Computer Reseller News, 829,* 48.

Mayadas, A. F. (1997, October). Online networks build time savings into employee education. *HR Magazine, 42*(10), 31–35.

Overman, S. (1999, July/August). Maytag makes the grade on employee development. *Human Resource Management International Digest, 7*(4), 24–26.

Palumbo-Holland, G. (1997, July). Business experts and college faculty collaborate to design Instruction. *Performance Improvement, 36*(6), 38–41.

Quinley, J. W., & Hickman, R. C. (2003). *The need for workforce development: What research tells us.* Retrieved July 19, 2003, from http://www.ncwe.org/workplace/needworkforcedevelopment.htm

Reis, R. (1996, January). The right prescription. *Vocational Education Journal, 71*(1), 44–45, 61.

Ruggless, R. (2000, December). "Gringo Lingo": Operator taps TV to teach Hispanic staffers. *Nation's Restaurant News, 34*(49), 82.

San Antonio rolls out learning academy for public housing residents. (2001, September/October). *Journal of Housing and Community Development, 58*(5), 39.

Siegel, J. J. (2000, December). Flexibility is the key to training, recruitment. *Air Conditioning, Heating & Refrigeration News, 211*(16), 14.

Smith, V. C. (1996, February). School mates. *Human Resource Executive, 10*(2), 37–39.

Tejada, C. (2000, May 30). A special news report about life on the job—and trends taking shape there. *Wall Street Journal,* p. A1.

Theibert, P. R. (1996, February). Train and degree them—Anywhere. *Personnel Journal, 75*(2), 28–38.

Turpin, J. (2000, January). Partnership with training school benefits everyone. *Air Conditioning, Heating & Refrigeration News, 209*(3), 9–10.

White, C. (2000, November/December). Collaborative online course development: Converting correspondence courses to the Web. *Educational Technology, 40*(6), 58–60.

Wong, N. (1999, June). Job-readiness program is a "win-win" in Atlantic City. *Workforce, 78*(6), 152.

CHAPTER 1

The Role of Workforce Development Organizations

Laurance J. Warford

For those who wonder about the impact of America's community colleges on our national workforce system, an article by Crissey of the Associated Press provides convincing evidence that it is significant. The article, "Colleges Fill the Gap," provides personal examples of Americans across the country seeking new careers with the help of community colleges—institutions Crissey defined as "schools that have evolved from their junior college beginnings into the mainstay of America's work force" (Crissey, 2003, p. F2).

Crissey cited colleges that are experiencing double-digit enrollment increases, such as Harrisburg Area Community College in Pennsylvania and Gloucester County College in New Jersey. Montgomery County Community College in Blue Bell, Pennsylvania, Des Moines Area Community College in Iowa, and Lower Columbia Community College in Washington state are reporting enrollments at an all-time high. Crissey stated: "From their start in a Chicago high school with six students in 1901, community colleges have undergone a metamorphosis, adding vocational training, noncredit courses, and certifications, and, more recently, holding job fairs and contracting with companies to train workers" (Crissey, 2003, p. F2).

Crissey also cited examples of colleges adapting to changes to better aid their communities. Administrators at Copiah-Lincoln Community College in Natchez, Mississippi, are reportedly considering more afternoon and evening classes and more short-term training courses to counter a string of plant closings in their service area. Des Moines Area Community College is trying to help some 1,600 people who will lose their jobs because of a local corporation's decision to subcontract with a foreign company to make appliance components. The college will train people for new jobs in an expanding farm machinery company.

This story is one of many indications that community colleges are recognized as major players in workforce training and development. Community colleges are major recipients of federal retraining program funds; the bulk of the $1.6 billion spent in 2002 by the U.S. Department of Labor to retrain laid-off workers went to community college programs. High profile stories such as this one are only part of the comprehensive workforce training provided by community colleges. The American Association of Community Colleges (AACC) has estimated that nearly half of all people beginning a college career start out in one of America's community colleges (AACC, 2000, p. 4)—a surprising statistic when one compares the relative age of community colleges to that of other postsecondary training institutions.

THE EVOLVING MISSION OF THE COMMUNITY COLLEGE

The "metamorphosis" to which Crissey referred describes the journey of the community college from the junior colleges of the early 1900s to the present. Junior colleges provided the first two years of a college degree—what we now think of as the transfer function of the community college. As the need for postsecondary vocational–technical training increased, junior colleges became the common place to receive this training. From the late 1950s to the late 1960s, the junior college "grew up," according to Edmund Gleazer, former AACC president (Gleazer, 1973, p. 32). The junior college took on the responsibilities of providing programs and services geared toward vocational–technical education, and these institutions became known as community colleges. Community colleges sprouted up in nearly every state in the country; in a period of about 10 years, 500 had been established nationwide. Today there are approximately 1,300 community colleges in the United States. The original community college mission concept generally included four major components:

1. The first two years of college credit, transferable to a four-year college
2. Programs of vocational–technical preparatory education for entry into the workforce
3. Programs of adult education including vocational–technical supplementary programs as well as enrichment, general interest, and basic education programs
4. A comprehensive array of student services

Growth has become standard for the community college since the 1960s. Not only have the number of institutions and their enrollments grown, but so have their missions. Community colleges have become an important part of the solution for employee training, developmental education, and economic development. These institutions often play a strong role in community leadership as well, sometimes even becoming their area's cultural center. Today, community college campuses boast conference centers, high tech centers, theaters, and athletic facilities as they strive to meet the needs of their communities.

COMPREHENSIVE WORKFORCE TRAINING

The 1980s and 1990s saw a broad range of technical, social, and economic developments marking the threshold of a dramatic turning point in human civilization. By the end of the 20th century, communications, learning, and knowledge had replaced land, labor, and capital as the means for individual and national productivity and wealth (Warford, 1995). At that time, Stephen Daigle, senior research associate for the California State University system, suggested that there were at least three major areas of development worth watching:

1. Technological advances in computing and telecommunications
2. Beginning of a cultural revolution
3. Economic system of the industrial age diminishing in the wake of a massive structural realignment

Daigle predicted that integrated data, audio, and video signals would soon be available anywhere and any time and that technology would continue to make major changes in our lives. He also predicted that convenience, customization, and transience would increasingly characterize everyday lifestyles and that we would move into a "knowledge" or "information" economy in which the process of transmitting knowledge would hold the most importance. "Higher and continuing education—perhaps all of education—faces the challenge of accommodating the new paradigm steeped in the technology, culture, and the economy of our new age" (cited in Warford, 1995, p. 2).

As Daigle's predictions proved accurate, the American community college was faced with constant changes. Along with technological advances came competition, a global economy, and a knowledge revolution—all demanding that the community college focus on workforce training as a major portion of its mission. One major challenge community colleges faced was providing comprehensive workforce training programs. Providing initial training for workforce entry was no longer enough. The position of the United States in the global economy demanded sound entry training and strong programs of supplemental and continuous training. It is therefore worth examining why community colleges have been successful in meeting the challenges of workforce training needs in the United States.

A STRATEGIC PLAN FOR WORKFORCE DEVELOPMENT

Given the community college's predilection for shared governance and consensus-driven decision making, responding quickly and effectively to workforce issues can be especially challenging. Despite this challenge, community colleges have developed a comprehensive, institutional response to the workforce needs of the United States. This response begins with the community college analyzing its local workforce, identifying targeted segments, and then matching those segments with the most appropriate unit of the college to meet or exceed customer and stakeholder needs and expectations. A description of each major workforce segment served by community colleges follows, each of which supports the importance of maintaining a comprehensive view of workforce training.

Emerging Workers

Typically 22 years of age or younger, emerging workers are preparing for their first full-time jobs. They come straight from high school and often have few, if any, career plans. They experiment with courses, vacillate between transfer and occupational choices, and eventually settle on a prescribed program of study leading to employment. Members of this group are likely to be day students, hold part-time jobs, and lack the academic skills required to advance quickly to a four-year institution.

The need for training emerging workers is obvious, and rarely challenged, as a national priority. According to the U.S. Department of Labor, today's youth will find that slightly more than 20% of all jobs in the first decade of the 21st century will require a four-year degree, and 75% will require some postsecondary training. Certification and licenses accounted for about one fifth of all postsecondary credentials in 1997 (Carnevale & Desrochers, 2001), and it appears that certificates and licenses will play an even more prominent role in the future.

Transitional Workers

Moving from one career to another, transitional workers have been laid off from previous employment, are returning to the job market after time out for family reasons, or may be seeking challenging ways to spend their retirement years. This group also includes individuals attempting to improve their social and financial situation by switching jobs or careers. Motivation among these students is high, and their time frame for reentering or moving up in the workforce is short. They are likely to attend short courses and are often attracted to evening and weekend schedules.

Changing work patterns suggest that today's workers will make four to six career changes (not to be confused with job changes) in their lifetime. Thus, the pattern of working for the same employer for a period of decades is receding in favor of multiple employers, indicating that more people are staying in transition throughout their lives. Perhaps the most compelling current trend is toward postretirement job reentry. In a 2003 article published by the Associated Press, Armas noted that the 2000 census estimated that the number of Americans aged 65 or older either working or looking for jobs had grown by 50% since 1980. Finally, a major factor contributing to the need for training the transitional worker is that retraining will become necessary in most occupations as some jobs become obsolete and other jobs require new skills.

Entrepreneurial Workers

The entrepreneurial workforce consists of people who own or operate small to medium-sized businesses. These individuals have begun to use the community college as a substitute for in-house training, taking advantage of community services and continuing education programs. Community colleges often have Small Business Development Centers, and some states, such as Oregon, have well-developed state networks of these centers. With limited resources at their disposal, entrepreneurial workers often seek the quick and economical return on investment afforded by community colleges.

Small businesses are a vital economic segment, considering that 90% of businesses in the United States employ fewer than 20 people. It is estimated that some 850,000 new small businesses open annually, and their failure rate is high. The need for training for this segment of the workforce is great, because training and education have a direct, known impact on the success/failure ratio (Small Business Administration, 1997).

Incumbent Workers

Incumbent workers are currently employed but need additional training to maintain their present jobs or to qualify for promotions. They often rely on company-sponsored professional development programs to access educational opportunities. These workers have a strong desire to acquire new skills at an accelerated pace.

Although they often are provided with training by their employers, incumbent workers constitute the most commonly overlooked segment of the workforce. In the United States, 85% of the workforce for the next 10 years is already in the workforce. Plans for workforce improvement must include funding for workers' lifelong learning.

Organization is the primary challenge that many community colleges face in meeting the training needs of the four workforce segments. Community colleges have traditionally developed "silos" of learning based on curriculum content, credit/noncredit, and full-time/part-time students. Typically, community colleges deal with different types of workers and their diverse educational and training needs in varying ways. The following approach is typical.

One part of the college—*Division A*—has offered vocational programs for many years, providing an excellent foundation for emerging workers. Quality staff, up-to-date facilities, and strong advisory committees are its hallmarks. In addition, programs are constantly reviewed, revitalized, and reinvented to ensure that students receive training that will lead to success on the job. Supplementing classroom experience, cooperative education programs provide on-the-job training for hundreds of students in local businesses. These partnerships with the community are highly valued because they provide quality training to students and offer invaluable feedback about the college's programs to instructors and administrators. Programs linked with high schools, such as tech prep and dual enrollment, provide curricular ties between high schools and community college career programs. This enables high school students to begin career paths that they can follow into community college without duplicating course work, which consequently reduces the amount of time they need to spend in college.

Another part of the college—*Division B*—is sensitive to the local economy in a different way. Layoffs in the region have created a need for programs and services that can help people shift successfully from one job or career to another. Thus, the college provides career planning, job search assistance, and retraining to dislocated workers at little or no cost. The challenge here lies in taking workers who have spent their working lives in one industry, who are underemployed, or who have been laid off from their present jobs, and giving them adaptive skills to change careers and attain new occupational goals. In this situation, local employers see the college as a source of emerging workers and as a place that can provide expedient turnaround for transitional workers.

A third component of the college—*Division C*—provides programs and services to small-business owners and workers, including loan packaging assistance, resource materials, confidential business counseling, and educational programs that meet their schedules and needs. Faculty and staff members with business owner/manager experience are active in assisting the business community. Many people who are thinking of starting their own business use the college to find answers to their questions before making a commitment; they know that training can be the difference between success and failure.

The fourth component of the college—*Division D*—focuses on current worker training and retraining, offering customized programs designed to meet specific business and industry requests. In addition to programs focused on company needs, the college continues to provide open-enrollment continuing education opportunities. These offerings include hundreds of sections of classes, workshops, seminars, and institutes focused on providing job upgrade skills for workers. Many locations are available so individuals can access educational programs conveniently and at minimal cost.

Yet another part of the college—*Division E*—provides an array of student services. Community colleges provide many support services that enable students of all ages to participate and become successful in the academic community. These services include financial aid, counseling, support centers for women, child-care centers, and job placement services, to name a few.

Because of the large number of students requiring improvement in their basic skills to be able to benefit from college training, another part of the college plays an important role—*Division F*. This component is often called the developmental skills area. Unfortunately, a high percentage of students entering community college straight out of high school need some type of remediation. According to a report on Stanford University's Bridge Project, 40% of students in four-year institutions take some remedial education, compared to 63% at two-year institutions (Venezia, Kirst, & Antonio, 2003). Diverse populations, such as immigrants who need English as a second language courses or basic skills instruction, routinely enter community colleges. This diversity compounds the need for developmental skills training conducted with workforce training to help students succeed on the job.

The final component of the community college that often plays an important role in workforce training—*Division G*—provides general education development courses in all curricular areas. Perhaps the greatest value of the community college is its ability to provide transfer education and vocational–technical training at one comprehensive institution.

COMPREHENSIVE WORKFORCE TRAINING

A comprehensive workforce training program has many components. Table 1.1 provides a useful model, identifying workforce targets with typical programs offered by community colleges. The last column provides examples of the array of student services offered by colleges.

Simply possessing the components of workforce training programs does not guarantee that the community college will continue as the premier social institution in this country for workforce training. Some important questions have been asked (Warford & Flynn, 2000).

How well do the components mesh together to provide seamless responses to myriad workforce development trends, programs, and opportunities? Segmenting and then targeting the local workforce is a sensible way to meet workforce training needs. With a reasonably accurate analysis of the four workforce segments, identifying college programs and charging them with developing timely responses is relatively easy. Rather than responding as individual divisions, the college can respond collectively, aligned in a strong institutional commitment to meeting workforce needs.

How much impact do internal politics, history, and campus inertia have on the institution's ability to respond to national workforce initiatives and local company needs? Established, territorial institutional silos and roles will not help to meet workforce needs. The demands of workforce training have begun to blur the lines: New job titles are created, new programs are developed, and new funding streams can materialize.

For example, occupational education deans, instrumental in delivering technical and occupational education to students in the emerging workforce, are now asked to take over economic development and contract training responsibilities. Continuing education deans deliver training through noncredit fee-based programs, contract education, and economic development initiatives to meet the needs of both entrepreneurs and incumbent workers. These educators are increasingly asked to modularize credit curricula and deliver them in nontraditional modes. Student services deans are asked to absorb new groups of transitional workers into an already heavy

Table 1.1	Comprehensive Workforce Training Programs and Services at Community Colleges		
Workforce targets	**Programs**	**Services**
Emerging Workforce: People typically 22 years of age or younger who are preparing to enter their first full-time employment.	• Certificate and degree preparatory programs • Related instruction • Intensive, short courses • Basic skills and academic learning • Cooperative education • Tech-prep programs • Secondary credential programs	• Career counseling and advising • Job search and placement assistance • Labor market information • Assessment • Testing • Employment plan development • Child care • Financial aid and scholarships • Disability services • Transcripting • Work-study programs • Housing • Substance abuse services • Student multicultural associations • Veteran services • Women's programs
Transitional Workforce: Those who are changing from one career to another for a variety of reasons, including being laid off from previous employment, reentering the labor market as adults, and changes from underemployment.	• Dislocated worker and homemaker programs • Related instruction • Intensive, short courses • Basic skills upgrade • Injured worker programs—proficiency skills • Certificate and degree preparatory programs • Secondary credential programs • Continuing education • Post-retirement training	
Entrepreneurial Workforce: People who operate, and may own, small and medium-size businesses.	• Small business management • Farm business management • Continuing education • Seminars/workshops/short courses	
Incumbent Workforce: Those who are employed and need additional training for their current jobs or those who seek additional training for promotional purposes.	• Continuing education • Customized contract training • Apprenticeship • Seminars/workshops/short courses • Basic skills upgrade • Secondary credential programs	

Note. From Jenkins, Davis, and Boswell (2002). Adapted by permission.

caseload of undergraduates. Transfer and developmental deans are called upon to provide quality programs of general and developmental education, as needed, to provide certificate and degree graduates with marketable skills. If educators work in concert, no institution can match their combined strength.

Can community colleges meet the challenge? As community colleges are asked to provide training, education, and certification, questions about how to meet these challenges arise. What should a contemporary work-related curriculum be? Why do design, approval, and implementation take so long? Why are student service programs structured to serve recent high school graduates, when the average age is 30 for students in credit programs and 40 for those in noncredit programs?

The challenge is clear. Showing too much reverence for old market segments, clinging to outmoded organizational structures, and continuing campus turf wars must be replaced by an institutional strategic plan to meet *comprehensive* workforce development needs. The American community college is up to the challenge. ❋

References

American Association of Community Colleges. (2000). *Pocket profile of community colleges: Trends and statistics* (3rd ed.). Washington, DC: Community College Press.

Armas, G. (2003, May 21). More elderly staying in workforce. The Associated Press/ *The Register-Guard*.

Carnevale, A. P., & Desrochers, D. M. (2001). *Help wanted. . . credentials required: Community colleges in the knowledge economy*. Princeton, NJ: Educational Testing Service.

Crissey, M. (2003, May 18). Colleges fill the gap. The Associated Press/ *The Register-Guard*, p. F2.

Gleazer, E. J. (1973, December/January). After the boom…What now for the community colleges? *Community and Junior College Journal*.

Small Business Administration. (1997). *The annual report of small business and competition: The state of small business*. Washington, DC: Author.

Venezia, A., Kirst, M. W., & Antonio, A. L. (2003). *Betraying the college dream: How disconnected K–12 and postsecondary education systems undermine student aspirations*. Unpublished manuscript, Stanford University, Stanford University Bridge Project, CA.

Warford, L. J. (1995). Redesigning the system to meet the workforce training needs of a nation. *Leadership Abstracts, 8*(1).

Warford, L. J., & Flynn, W. J. (2000). New games new rules: Strategic positioning for workforce development. *Community College Journal, 70*(7), 31–33.

CHAPTER 2

Strategic Business Planning for Workforce Development

Frederick D. Loomis

Every moment spent planning saves three or four in execution.

—Crawford Greenwalt, former president of Dupont Corporation

The education sector has used strategic planning methods and tools for at least the past two decades. Today, most organizations do some type of strategic planning, as well as annual marketing or financial planning. However, critics of planning continue to question whether it is worth the effort. Why not just make up the strategy as we go along or merely improvise on a general sense of direction? In this chapter I present process guides, templates, and examples designed to assist administrators as they seek to develop a sound business strategy and effective performance measures for workforce education. Strategic business planning and performance management are essential tools for today's workforce education leader.

WHAT IS STRATEGY?

Strategy involves a planned course of action carefully designed to best align the organization with its environment so that it can respond most effectively to the forces that can positively or negatively affect the future (Rowley & Sherman, 2001). This definition is best understood in the context of viewing the organization from a systems perspective. All organizations must be responsive to their environments to thrive or merely to survive (Kast & Rosenzweig, 1979). As is depicted in Figure 2.1, organizations interact with the environment, obtaining "inputs" in the form of resources. The organization can be viewed as a network of people, structure, and processes that transform resources into products or services desired by customers or stakeholders in the environment. Feedback mechanisms (e.g., performance measures) allow the organization to adjust, improve, and achieve alignment with the environ-

ment. If the organization fails to produce at a rate that is valued externally, it will fail and possibly not survive. In this view, organizations that adapt quickly to changes in the environment have a competitive advantage. Strategy focuses on those activities in which an organization elects to excel, providing a unique value proposition (Porter, 1996).

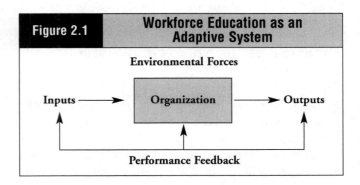

Figure 2.1 — Workforce Education as an Adaptive System

THE IMPORTANCE OF STRATEGIC THINKING

The ability to think and act strategically is a competency that managers need to develop in themselves and within their teams. Effective business strategy can emerge from a structured process of learning about the organization and its customers (Senge, 1990). It is important to note that this type of planning is not an isolated event. It does not happen because a retreat is held or a committee is appointed. Although strategic planning includes data analysis, *strategic thinking* involves synthesis, intuition, creativity, and seeing patterns and relationships—what Senge (1990) calls "systems thinking." Far too often, a strategic planning exercise will result in the documentation of goals that already exist. Strategic thinking, however, will allow the organization to

7

capture information from all sources and synthesize that new learning into a new vision or reinvention of what should be pursued. According to Mintzberg (1994), "real strategists get their hands dirty digging for ideas, and real strategies are built from the nuggets they uncover." To use an ice hockey metaphor, organizations that think strategically can consistently skate to where they think the puck is going to be.

In the business world, less than 10% of strategies are successfully executed (Bossidy & Charan, 2002; Kaplan & Norton, 2001). Therefore, building strategic thinking skills and the organizational capacity to implement strategy is as important as the strategy itself. Accordingly, Kaplan and Norton (2001) have advocated several key principles for becoming a "strategy-focused organization":

- Make strategy everyone's responsibility and translate it into operational terms so that everyone understands how performance is measured and how they contribute to the organization's goals.
- Make strategy a continual process, whereby employees and stakeholders meet regularly to discuss and review progress, take initiative, and help the organization adapt and change.
- Mobilize change through executive leadership by providing positive energy, focus, and direction to support strategy execution.

OVERVIEW OF THE STRATEGIC BUSINESS PLANNING PROCESS

Strategic business planning is a nonlinear, iterative process that involves both the organization and its stakeholders in arriving at a shared vision of future success. Stated simply, the planning process involves getting the right people around the table, getting them to focus on what is really important, and getting the organization to respond. Strategic business planning for workforce development involves mastering skills of strategic thinking, consensus building, and performance management.

The planning process should address five fundamental questions:

- Who are we as an organization (our mission)?
- What is happening in our environment (our issues)?
- What do we want to be in the future (our vision)?
- How will we get there (our strategy)?
- How will we know that we are making progress (our scorecard)?

Figure 2.2 illustrates a model and methodology for strategic business planning, which addresses these key ques-

tions. In the rest of the chapter, I will explain each step of the planning process model in detail and offer practical illustrations and useful templates for its implementation.

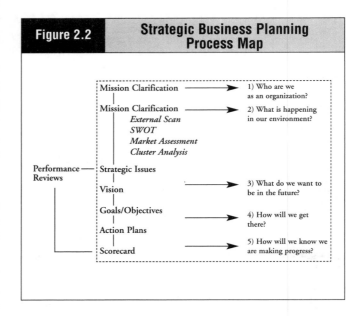

Figure 2.2 — Strategic Business Planning Process Map

MISSION CLARIFICATION: WHO ARE WE AS AN ORGANIZATION?

Yogi Berra, the famous New York Yankees baseball player and manager, once said, "If you don't know where you're heading, you're likely to end up somewhere else." Without a clear sense of purpose and values, organizations are lost. Missions provide meaning for an organization and its stakeholders.

The aim of the mission clarification phase of planning is to clearly specify purpose, philosophy, and values so that everyone inside and outside the organization understands who you are, what you do, and why you do it. It is the beginning of a strategy roadmap. Missions must focus on useful and desired ends. Otherwise, organizations cannot hope to command the resources they need to survive, including committed stakeholders and loyal, high-performing employees.

Mission statements vary in length, but they are usually short—no more than a page and usually just a sentence or paragraph. The development of a mission statement should be a team effort, following a Socratic process. The following questions can help guide the process of clarifying mission:

- Who are we—what business are we in?
- Who do we serve?
- Who are our key stakeholders and supporters?

- What social, economic, or political issues or needs are we in business to address?
- How do we recognize, anticipate, or respond to these issues, needs, and challenges?
- What is our philosophy? What are our values?
- What makes us distinctive or unique?

Formulating a mission statement should not be solely the work of the manager or executive. Adoption of a mission statement marks an important decision point in the strategic planning process and is usually memorialized in some way (e.g., the proverbial sign over the door).

Example: Mission Statements

Academic Department of a Major Research University: To promote excellence, opportunity, and leadership among professionals in the workforce education and development field, including, but not limited to, those employed in secondary or postsecondary education institutions, social services industries, employee groups, and private businesses.

Multinational Fortune 50 Technology Company: To enable people and businesses throughout the world to realize their full potential.

Local Workforce Investment Board: To develop and sustain a unified, customer-friendly, and market-driven workforce system through initiatives that support the productivity and growth of business and the economic self-sufficiency of our citizens.

STRATEGIC ANALYSIS: WHAT IS HAPPENING IN OUR ENVIRONMENT?

The analysis phase of strategic business planning focuses attention on the external environment (driving forces, market assessments) and the internal operations of the organization (strengths, weaknesses, opportunities, and threats, or SWOT). The outcome of this analysis should be a list of key strategic issues that will guide vision and strategy development.

External Scan

The external scan involves conducting an inventory of the political, economic, social, and technological (PEST) forces that can influence the way an organization functions. What trends most affect the workforce education field? Members of advisory boards are usually adept at

identifying and assessing external trends and issues. Published reports and data may also be helpful in this stage of the planning process.

A typical external scan is used to look at relevant trends in several areas, such as markets, customers, demographics, competition, economic indicators, and government mandates. For workforce education, an analysis of market and industry clusters is key to developing an effective strategy that aligns with local economic development strategies.

SWOT Assessment

Strategy fails when organizations are unable to support it. Therefore, you need to identify your organization's strengths and weaknesses, particularly those that affect critical success factors (those areas in which you must excel to remain competitive). However, simply creating SWOT lists is not enough—they must be discussed, analyzed, and compared (Bryson, 1995).

Strengths are capabilities that can be used to get an advantage over the competition. They may be human capital skills or competencies, facilities, or brand recognition. Weaknesses are barriers to success. They include processes that are not working or support functions that are underperforming. Key organization strengths and weaknesses can be identified through a combination of diagnostic questionnaires, confidential interviews, and internal focus groups with employees. Areas to probe for strengths and weaknesses include the following:

- Organizational structure
- Information systems
- Management practices
- Costs
- Quality
- Service
- Competencies
- Innovation
- Technology

External assessment should produce a list of opportunities and threats. Areas to probe include the following:

- Markets
- Industry clusters
- Customer needs
- Competition
- Legal mandates
- Economic conditions
- Technology

The SWOT analysis should provide four or five factors in each category, as is illustrated in Table 2.1.

Analysis of Industry Clusters

Workforce education and economic development professionals are increasingly turning to the industry cluster method to identify key areas for strategic investment and workforce development. An industry cluster is defined as "geographical concentrations of industries that gain performance advantages through co-location" (Doeringer & Terkla, 1995). Industry clusters allow for the identification of local industries that have concentrations of employment beyond the national average, which may indicate a local competitive advantage. Examples of clusters include pioneering technologies, diversified manufacturing, lumber and wood products, and health care. Cluster analysis can be used for redesigning or refocusing workforce education initiatives and aligning new programs with emerging economic development strategies. For some workforce development organizations, cluster analysis has provided a framework for increasing awareness of local economic opportunities and building consensus on broad-based community workforce and economic development strategy (Smith, 2003).

Market Needs Assessment

A market needs assessment can be conducted by mail or Internet survey, focus groups, or community meetings (including electronic town halls). Using the assessment should help you analyze your organization's competitive position by the following means:

- Dividing current and potential markets into customers whose needs are similar. This type of market segmentation allows you to develop competitive strategies that address the unique needs of each segment you target for emphasis.
- Rank ordering the needs of customers within each key market segment.
- Evaluating your organization's strengths and weaknesses against those of the competition in meeting customer needs. This competitive assessment points out areas where you might be underperforming in comparison to the competition.

Identification of Strategic Issues

Identification of strategic issues is at the heart of the strategic business planning process. Most organizations develop far more market needs and SWOT lists than they can address effectively and profitably with available resources. Therefore, it is essential to focus on three to five strategic issues that will be key to future success. A strategic issue is defined as a fundamental policy question or challenge affecting the organization's mission, mandates, structure, or management (Bryson, 1995). If selected correctly, these issues should have a profound effect on what the organization is, what it will become, and how it will get there. It is important to note that strategic issues are *not* current problems or crises and are not usually easily resolved.

Strategic issues can be identified through a SWOT or industry cluster or market assessment. As with every step

Table 2.1	A Sample SWOT Analysis for Workforce Development
Strengths • Commitment to quality • Targeted approach to business development • Delivery system infrastructure • Academic resources	**Opportunities** • Shift from training solutions to organizational development performance improvement • Need for workplace literacy skills • Computer-based training delivery • Outsourcing of training departments
Weaknesses • Lack of communication and coordination • Lack of job knowledge regarding performance consulting • Lack of office space • Lack of distance learning capabilities	**Threats** • Competition from consulting firms • Lack of collaboration within the organization and its partners • Bureaucratic delays with government-funded projects • Reduced funding to support programs

of the process, simpler is usually better. Strategic planning teams or advisory committees should not get bogged down in the analysis phase. Important and necessary actions should be taken as soon as strategic issues are identified. Strategic issues for workforce education may include the following:

- Program articulation with other education providers
- Adult literacy
- Workplace readiness
- Barriers to employment
- Performance monitoring and program evaluation
- Needs assessment and workplace performance
- Partnership development
- Rapid response program development
- Return on investment training

STRATEGY DEVELOPMENT: WHAT DO YOU WANT TO BE, AND HOW WILL YOU GET THERE?

As noted previously, strategy involves a planned course of action carefully designed to best align the organization to its environment. The mission clarification and analysis phases of the process are designed to shed light on the key issues that the organization must address to create the future state it desires. Once strategic issues have been identified, strategy development can proceed when you address the following questions for each issue (Bryson, 1995):

- What are the options to address the issue?
- What are the barriers to realizing each alternative?
- What major proposals might be pursued to achieve the alternative and overcome barriers?
- What major actions must be taken in the short term (with existing staff and within existing job descriptions) to implement each major proposal?
- What specific steps must be taken within the next six months to implement each major proposal, and who will take lead responsibility?

Articulating a Vision for the Future

A vision is a statement of a realistic, credible, attractive future for your organization (Nanus, 1995). It should represent a shorthand summary of the outcomes that can be expected if strategic issues are addressed and strategy is effectively executed. A well-articulated and widely communicated vision can jump-start an organization and motivate people to make change happen.

Example: Vision Statements

Academic Department: Offering a cost-effective program that is recognized nationally as being among the best of its type in scholarship, leadership, and professional preparation.

Workforce Development Organization: To engage our community, meet identified needs, and be acknowledged as a provider of choice for targeted, high-quality training and development programs and services.

Setting Goals and Objectives

Goals and objectives allow managers to close the gap between the present state and the desired future. Goals define where you want to be and often use general, more timeless language. Objectives are more specific, measurable targets to achieve the stated goals. Each objective should have an owner who is responsible for monitoring performance.

Example: Goal and Objective Statement

Goal: To increase outreach and engagement with the community by expanding relationships with business and industry and the public.

Objective: To increase programs and enrollments so that we serve 30% more part-time adult students by 2005–2006.

Developing Action Plans

Action plans allow for the integration of strategy to department and individual planning. Action plans are developed from business strategies, goals, and objectives. When actions are assigned to individuals for implementation, employees can relate their contributions to the vision and strategy of the organization in a tangible way. A key

Example: Action Plan

Action: Visit 25 companies and community organization to cultivate relationships, assess needs, and develop and deliver programs.

Responsibility: Workforce Education Manager

Timeframe: January–March

to executing action plans is the ability to prioritize issues and focus limited resources on the most important issues.

Scorecard: How Will You Know You Are Making Progress?

Kaplan and Norton (2001) have developed a "balanced scorecard" methodology to focus and align organizations to their business strategies. A scorecard method for tracking performance has its greatest impact when it is deployed to drive organizational change. The balanced scorecard approach focuses on four key performance perspectives: customer, financial, internal, and learning. Each measure becomes embedded in a chain of cause-and-effect logic that leads to strategic outcomes (satisfied stakeholders, delighted customers, effective processes, and motivated, high-performing employees). Scorecard variables can be summarized in a "strategy map" that describes the process for transforming assets into measurable outcomes. It can provide a useful framework for stakeholders to better understand the organization's business strategy and performance outcomes. (For an example of a balanced scorecard, see Table 2.2.) Four key questions guide the development of a balanced scorecard:

- **Customer**: To achieve your vision, how must you look to your customers?
- **Financial**: If you succeed, how will you look to your shareholders?
- **Internal**: To satisfy your customers, at which processes should you excel?
- **Learning**: To achieve your vision, how must your organization learn, innovate, and grow?

Managing the Planning Process

Strategic business planning needs to be carefully designed and implemented. It is not a substitute for leadership. It is important for leaders to sponsor the process, keep it on track, and commit the necessary resources to the effort. Leaders should also encourage and reward creative thinking and constructive debate and discussion.

Daily routines can absorb planning time, so leaders need to set aside time for the process and secure the services of consultants as needed. An off-site planning retreat is a good way to kick off the process. Concentrated and uninterrupted focus must be devoted to the process at various stages of the effort.

Leaders can assign champions within the organization to design the process. If resources permit, champions can work with external, neutral process facilitators who are often helpful in getting the process started and maintaining momentum because of their group-process and communication skills. Skilled facilitators can help build the level of trust in a group and assist in building consensus. They should also do the following:

- Know the organization's culture and tailor the process to the groups involved.
- Use brainstorming, dialogue, discussion, and voting as appropriate.
- Be prepared to help groups get unstuck, by encouraging action and responsibility.
- Congratulate people and celebrate a team's accomplishments.

Lessons Learned

The following "dos and don'ts" are lessons learned from over 20 years of experience in designing and facilitating planning processes in education.

Do

- Minimize the time demands of managers and staff by designing a carefully thought-out process. Obtain top

Table 2.2	A Balanced Scorecard of Performance Measures for Workforce Education	
Customer • Enrollment and retention • Placement rate • Participant satisfaction	**Internal** • Response time • Marketing and sales • Closure rate
Financial • Cost per participant • Contracted income	**Learning** • Professional development • Employee satisfaction

leadership commitment to the process at the outset.

- Involve those who must execute the plan.
- Keep it simple. Good strategy is often intuitive. The process should bring out the creativity of all involved.
- Use electronic tools, such as groupware, e-mail lists, and Web logs to record discussions.
- Communicate the process and the resulting plan at all levels of the organization.
- Allocate resources to strategic priorities.
- Use a scorecard or performance measures to ensure accountability.

Don't

- Don't rush—planning takes time. But do not put off until tomorrow what you can decide and communicate today.
- Don't overdo the analysis. Use data prudently to identify and address strategic issues. Keep reports short and encourage lots of face-to-face interaction, particularly in the early stages of the process.
- Don't avoid the tough decisions. You might need to let go of some programs and activities to move ahead on new priorities.
- Don't assume a straight path to success. There will be many detours and roadblocks along the way.
- Don't give up. Stick with it. Keep the process alive by communicating your strategy with passion and commitment.

PUTTING IT ALL TOGETHER: THE STRATEGIC BUSINESS PLANNING TEMPLATE

Kaplan and Norton (2001) proposed a strategy map as the optimal way to describe the organization's strategy and the interrelationships between the various perspectives (customer, financial, internal, and learning). Goals can be summarized and mapped on one page. This creates what Senge (1990) called a "mental model" for the organization and can serve as a useful way to communicate the complexities of the organization's vision and strategy. I conclude the chapter with a checklist for ensuring that your planning process is complete and that each element has been considered and documented in your final plan.

Why plan at all? Today's workforce education providers must cope with continual change in economic conditions, government mandates, and community needs. To thrive and survive, institutions and community-based organizations cannot be stagnant. Likewise, planning cannot be a passive exercise. To respond to the challenges of the 21st-century global economy, organizations must learn to plan well and think and act strategically. Otherwise, they will continue to fight the daily fires brought about by constant change. ❋

Example: Checklist for Strategic Business Planning

- **Strategy Map:** one-page summary showing relationships of major goals and scorecard indicators.
- **Executive Summary:** one- or two-page narrative summarizing mission, vision, values, goals, and strategic initiatives.
- **Strategic Analysis:** documents external scan, SWOT, market assessment, and cluster analysis.
- **Mission Statement:** defines the organization, values, and stakeholders.
- **Vision Statement:** defines a future state of the organization
- **Goals and Objectives:** defines gap between present and future. Goals can be timeless; objectives are targeted, measurable, and specific.
- **Action Plan:** assigns responsibility for major activities within specified time frames.
- **Scorecard:** performance measure that addresses areas in finance, customers, internal processes, learning, and growth.
- **Financial:** includes operating budget, revenue projections, and break-even analysis.
- **Marketing:** identifies customer segments and addresses promotion, price, and sales strategy.
- **Organization:** includes roles and responsibilities in chart of relationships.

References

Bossidy, L., & Charan, R. (2002). *Execution: The discipline of getting things done.* New York: Crown Business.

Bryson, J. M. (1995). *Strategic planning for public and nonprofit organizations.* San Francisco: Jossey-Bass.

Doeringer, P. B., & Terkla, D. G. (1995). Business strategy and cross-industry clusters. *Economic Development Quarterly, 9,* 225–237.

Kaplan, R. S., & Norton, D. P. (2001). *The strategy-focused organization.* Boston: Harvard Business School Press.

Kast, F. E., & Rosenzweig, J. E. (1979). *Organization and management: A systems and contingency approach* (3rd ed.). New York: McGraw-Hill.

Mintzberg, H. (1994, January/February). The fall and rise of strategic planning. *Harvard Business Review.*

Nanus, B. (1995). *Visionary leadership.* San Francisco: Jossey-Bass.

Porter, M. E. (1996, November/December). What is strategy? *Harvard Business Review.*

Rowley, D. J., & Sherman, H. (2001). *From strategy to change.* San Francisco: Jossey-Bass.

Senge, P. M. (1990). *The fifth discipline: The art and practice of the learning organization.* New York: Doubleday.

Smith, R. V. (2003, June 9). *Industry cluster analysis: Inspiring a common strategy for community development.* Unpublished White Paper, Central Pennsylvania Workforce Development Corporation.

Establishing High-Performance Workforce Development Organizations

Pamela Tate and Rebecca Klein-Collins

Community colleges have long been at the forefront of serving the needs of adult learners. The advance of community colleges into the area of contract training and other workforce services to employers is a natural expression of that receptivity to the nontraditional student. And the need for training and consulting assistance to business and industry is greater than ever.

Community college–based workforce development organizations (WDOs), sometimes referred to as business and industry training centers, have a great opportunity to provide corporate customers with both customized training programs and other services related to overall business performance improvement. Through the work of the Council for Adult and Experiential Learning (CAEL), we have seen how the efforts of WDOs provide many benefits to community colleges, particularly revenue and good public relations in the community. Colleges certainly recognize what can be gained from having a WDO, but only a handful know how to make the WDO a high performer in training and development.

Achieving high performance means that WDOs need to improve not only their business performance but also their customer service. In addition, the challenge for these organizations is to leverage the strengths stemming from their affiliation with colleges while keeping in touch with the market and meeting customer needs. As WDOs have taken root on or around campuses, and as they have begun to play key roles in economic development activities, it has become increasingly important to provide support to them and to build awareness of model practices. In short, we need to know what high-performing WDOs look like and what they do.

CHARACTERISTICS OF HIGH-PERFORMING WORKFORCE DEVELOPMENT ORGANIZATIONS

Currently, several organizations are committing significant resources to identifying the best practices of WDOs affiliated with community colleges; throughout this chapter you will find references to research led by CAEL under contract with the Ohio Board of Regents (Barber & Klein-Collins, 1998). In addition, organizations such as the American Association for Community Colleges (AACC), the League for Innovation in the Community College, the National Coalition of Advanced Technology Centers (NCATC), and the American Society for Training and Development (ASTD) have taken leadership roles in the effort to support WDOs. Many of their publications have highlighted best practices of WDOs.

From these sources, common themes emerge around what factors support the performance and effectiveness of college-based WDOs:

- Service offerings
- Customer orientation
- Relationship to the college
- Staffing
- Operating as a business

We now discuss each theme in greater depth, looking at what CAEL found in its national study, what other researchers have found, and what other observers have reported, both in publications and in more informal conversations.

Service Offerings

Any business interested in improving its performance is

CAEL is a nonprofit organization committed to improving access to education for adults through partnerships with business, government, labor, and higher education. Founded on the concept that learning is a tool that empowers people and organizations, CAEL has worked actively since 1974 to identify and remove the barriers encountered by adult learners attempting to reenter the educational system.

For the past two decades, CAEL has applied its expertise to the field of workforce education, pioneering the development of employee education and development programs in a collaborative framework. These partnerships draw the employer, its unions (if applicable), its employees, education providers, and CAEL together to design the best possible intervention for the workers in question. In this partnership, CAEL acts as a bridge between the employer and the educational community, providing support services and linking employees to available educational opportunities.

Several other organizational activities have emerged out of CAEL's experience in the arena of employee growth and development: (a) consulting services for community colleges and other postsecondary institutions, business, government, and organized labor, assisting them in effectively responding to the educational needs of working adults; (b) public and private sector policy initiatives promoting policies responsive to the needs of adult learners; and (c) research aimed at expanding knowledge about effective learner-centered programs and building educational institutions' capacities to provide them.

For more information about CAEL and its projects and services, visit CAEL online: www.cael.org

naturally concerned about its products and services and whether they successfully meet the needs of customers, both in quality and scope. Bassi, Cheney, and Van Buren (1997) discussed the top trends for professionals in workplace learning, noting that the "rapid pace of change requires that workplace learning occur on a just-in-time, just-what's-needed, and just-where-it's-needed basis" (p. 47). A work group of AACC's Commission on Workforce and Community Development similarly noted that key criteria for comprehensive workforce delivery models are flexibility, responsiveness, cost-effectiveness, accountability, and quality (Muse, 1996).

WDOs must add real value to their corporate customers by offering a full-range of high-quality services and by being fast and flexible. By observing CAEL's work with employers, we know that good WDOs do this by customizing training programs or by using advanced technology to aid or accelerate training. These customized approaches, however, must supplement, not replace, credit and degree options for business and industry clients, because providing credentials to employees can be very important to companies and their employees.

The definition of "full-service provider," however, can go beyond mere training. Successful WDOs do not assume that training is the only possible, or best possible, solution to business performance problems. Among private sector training and development organizations, a best practice is first to conduct a complete assessment of what a business needs—it could be training, but a business's performance problems might more easily and inexpensively be solved through job aids, Total Quality Management, or assistance with reorganization/change issues (Robinson & Robinson, 1995).

CAEL and other organizations that work directly with employers on workforce development routinely and formally help business clients assess their needs prior to offering training or other solutions. Front-end assessment, however, is a best practice that has been slow in coming to community college–based WDOs. In research that CAEL conducted for the Ohio Board of Regents in 1997, for example, most of the college-based organizations surveyed and visited throughout the country offered a range of training services and a handful of nontraining services such as individual skill assessments and curriculum design. But very few reported having formal processes for assessing business needs prior to providing any services. Nevertheless, some were making front-end assessment part of their core competencies and were emphasizing its importance to their business clients.

One organization that CAEL visited developed a process for front-end analysis (FEA) with the help of expert Dana Robinson. In this process, after extensive analysis, the staff of the WDO explains to the customer which problems the company controls, which problems the individual employee controls, and which problems can be solved using training. The WDO staff then helps the customer to implement both training and nontraining solutions. By acknowledging nontraining solutions, the approach avoids wasting the company's time and money by eliminating unnecessary training and addressing the root causes directly. Incidentally, this is an approach that is also encouraged in corporate universities (Meister, 1997).

Being a full-service provider can be a tough job for a WDO with limited resources, but many WDOs are able to provide a broader range of services by forming partnerships and alliances with other organizations (Alfred & Carter, 1997; Jacobs & Teahen, 1997; Rosenfeld, 1995; Stamps, 1995; Westra, 1997). Partnerships can be used not only to develop marketing and sales opportunities but also to expand the range of services offered to the business community.

For example, WDOs can use limited internal resources to focus on a relatively small number of core competencies in service delivery while forming alliances with other organizations to provide formal needs assessments, specialized training programs, and nontraining performance consulting. Speaking to CAEL in 1997, James Jacobs, then-associate vice CEO of Macomb Community College, noted that no WDO should try to do everything itself, but it can be effective as a "systems integrator" or intermediary for connecting businesses to other organizations and services.

Customer Orientation

In a corporate setting, a key indicator of high performance is a focus on satisfying the needs of the customer. Similarly, a WDO can claim to be playing an economic development role only if it understands the needs of local business and industry and if the WDO has an orientation toward serving those needs. Customer service, flexibility in content and scheduling (in particular, offering services and training at the workplace), quick responses, quality of services, accountability, and understanding customer needs are all best practices for WDOs (Muse 1996; National Coalition of Advanced Technology Centers, 1997; Stamps, 1995).

Some aspects of this customer orientation are common practice for college-based WDOs. For example, offering classroom work at the employer's site is a common practice that is often as desirable for space-challenged community colleges as it is for the convenience of the employer and students. Accountability for the quality of services, however, often requires significant investment of time and effort to evaluate the services provided. The question—did we accomplish what we set out to do?—is often answered by applying one or more levels from the Kirkpatrick evaluation model (Kirkpatrick, 1998). Almost every WDO that CAEL has worked with conducts some kind of customer satisfaction survey during or at the end of a training session (level 1 of the model). Less common, and more time-consuming, are pre- and posttest evaluations (level 2), which can help WDOs in making midcourse corrections in a training process and in monitoring the overall quality of the instruction. Evaluation of the training application (level

3) and evaluation of business results—or the return on the investment—(level 4) are rarely, if ever, conducted by college-based WDOs. These higher-level evaluations, however, are also infrequently applied by the average private-sector training organization.

A customer focus also involves marketing. Through the marketing process, a high-performing WDO not only can tell business and industry about its services, but also can learn about the companies in its service region and evaluate the environmental context of the area. The WDO can, therefore, anticipate issues that may confront its target market, such as a shortage of skilled labor and easy access to transportation and service routes.

One college-based WDO studied by CAEL was unique in that it had a well-researched marketing plan that showed it had a thorough understanding of the link between its information technology platform and marketing. Technology was used for recording data and decision making. Telemarketing was conducted regularly with existing customers. Formal surveys, informal surveys, and sales input were used to gain insight into service quality. The WDO contracted with an outside market research firm to do ongoing research on customer service and market needs. This constant circle of research and evaluation drove all decisions on marketing strategy. At this high-performing organization, significant human and financial resources were also dedicated to the marketing process. The WDO had a dedicated marketing person who used data to develop marketing strategies, who planned and worked closely with the sales function, and who was responsible for the marketing plan and continuous implementation and improvement.

Relationship to the College

The business community and the academic community have differing value systems, timelines, and paces of operation. Neither community is inclined to change its values for the other, and neither believes it to be practical to change its operational systems for the other. Straddling these two worlds, and attempting to work with both, is the college's WDO.

College policies and practices can impose significant burdens on the operations of a WDO, which makes the WDO's balancing act more difficult. (Such policies and practices are discussed in greater detail in chapter 4.) In this chapter, we discuss several best practices related to how a WDO operates within a given college's organizational structure. These practices involve creating some degree of distance—or separateness—from the college.

One way to achieve separateness is for the WDO to physically be a separate, dedicated unit apart from the college (Johnson, 1995; Stamps, 1995). CAEL has cited several variations of this separateness. Some WDOs may be on campus in their own buildings, across the street from the main campus, or even miles away. One WDO, for example, was geographically removed from any of the college campuses and positioned in an industrial park that had high visibility among local business and industry. Directors of WDOs located in separate facilities reported that the separateness gives them more control over the facility. It enables the WDOs to project a more business-like image. And it gives the WDO more control over access and more flexibility for WDO-related business.

A second way to achieve separateness is for the WDO not to adopt the same operating procedures and practices as the college (Johnson, 1995). Traditional instructional operations are structured to serve many individuals and, in the case of publicly funded systems, to ensure strict accountability to public funding sources. Traditional procedures for billing and registration and course scheduling may be appropriate for serving many students with disparate interests in a rational way. They are not, however, the best way to serve employers who have an expectation of just-in-time, just-what-is-needed services.

Often the accounting and billing systems are geared to a credit-hour system and are designed to serve individual students rather than employers. Although WDOs usually do have credit offerings, they also offer a wide range of noncredit instruction, and they serve employers, rather than individuals, as customers. Small things can become major ordeals, such as arranging for a customer to be billed at an interval other than that scheduled for regular college students. Difficulties may arise because the WDO needs unique services from the college office, but there is no one in the college office—or a reasonable system in place—to facilitate that process.

The importance of aligning appropriate business processes at the college with a WDO's customers is demonstrated in the following example. At one WDO, a business customer wrote a check to pay for services, and the check was forwarded to the business office. The check was returned to the WDO because the college office could not process the check without a student identification number. The software system used in the business office was incompatible with the type of work the WDO did. A 1992 national survey of workforce training units revealed that this is a common problem nationwide: More than 50% of the respondents reported that "business office accounting/budgeting practices" present an obstacle to meeting the needs of employers (Doucette, 1993, p. 15).

One WDO that CAEL visited noted that invoices occasionally have to be done twice: one copy to satisfy college requirements, and the other to be sent to the customer. Although dual invoicing is not ideal, it enables the WDO to maintain its alignment with the college while acting in concert with business and industry expectations. We observed an exemplary practice in the implementation of this dual role: One college's information systems division created reports and registration systems specifically for the WDO to use that were also linked to the college systems for reporting purposes. Such an arrangement is an important example of how to establish a business-oriented process and still maintain close alignment with the college. Separateness is important, but WDOs should remain closely aligned with the college for support and assistance (Stamps, 1995). Although there are drawbacks to working with the procedures of a traditional instructional model, WDOs nevertheless benefit substantially from the college's local presence and reputation.

Benefits can also derive from alignment with the college through the sharing of information and resources between the WDO and the college. This integration often takes the form of sharing faculty and professional development. Some WDOs even use part of their own budget surplus to train college faculty on the needs of manufacturers. A related best practice is the sharing of information, particularly about workplace practices and employer needs, between the WDO and the college.

WDOs we visited attempted these and other forms of integrated activities. One WDO, for example, took advantage of the college's marketing systems, and the WDO and college have shared planning and fundraising activities. Another organization coordinated with the other units of the college to ensure that there was no duplication of services. The WDO and college coordinate their offerings of computer-based training and distance learning, the development of an intranet, and the service to joint technology committees.

The relationship between the WDO and the college can often be strained because they have different ways of operating. WDOs can experience difficulties if there is not a strong commitment from the college CEO or if the faculty does not have a clear understanding of the role the WDO plays in the college mission. One expression of the college's commitment to the WDO is through the reporting structure. If the WDO has a high standing with the college, the WDO director will report to a high-level administrator—for example, the CEO or a vice president.

The WDO can use many strategies to fortify its relationship with the college. Integration activities such as those just mentioned can be useful in forming a stronger partnership with the college. Good internal marketing is also a helpful strategy. For example, one WDO issues in-house newsletters to share with the rest of the college about what the WDO is doing. This helps build constant awareness within the college for the WDO's activities, helping in the coordination of services and programs and also serving to build the internal reputation of the WDO. Informally, the WDO director is also able to promote the organization through almost daily contact with the college's CEO.

Staffing

As in any organization, staffing is a key influence on the performance of WDOs. One key indicator of WDO efficiency is employing staff with relatively unique skills appropriate for producing services for business (Johnson, 1995). Professional development for permanent staff can also be an important investment for WDOs to retain a core staff of trained individuals. (Core competencies of WDO staff are addressed in greater detail in chapter 5.)

However, because WDOs are expected to provide such a wide range of specialized services, employing staff with specialized skills that meet every delivery need is almost impossible. Customers can differ by industry, and customer needs also change over time. Having comprehensive subject-matter expertise requires a different approach.

A best practice of WDOs is to keep a core staff of full-time regular employees for operations, administration, sales and marketing, and limited service delivery. As service contracts with customers are developed, expert consultants are retained on a project basis to deliver the training and/or other services. Best-practice WDOs have a regular pool of part-time delivery staff (sometimes pulling from both within and outside of the college) that are used as needed, thereby increasing the flexibility that the organization can have in offering training and services whenever and however they are needed by a customer (Stamps, 1995).

One major complication for staffing is the often rigid salary structure of the college. The salary scales for most colleges are based not on work experience but on academic credentials. Well-experienced trainers often find that WDOs cannot pay salaries as high as those that can be earned at private corporations. Often, therefore, the WDO director must use less qualified personnel simply because they are the only ones who are willing to work for the salary offered. Being tied to an inflexible pay structure may result in WDOs being perennially staffed with less experienced and less qualified candidates, which limits the organization's capacity. This is indeed problematic, given Rosenfeld's findings that "The ability to hire and retain staff with industrial experience is perhaps the most important indicator of a successful program" (1995, p. 29).

Even the use of college faculty can be very difficult, because the personnel policies of the college may be restrictive. For example, the college may have limits on the number of hours or courses that faculty can teach in any given term, or the employer-responsive training schedule may conflict with the faculty's regularly scheduled courses and office hours. However, the WDOs studied by CAEL had developed rather unique arrangements with their colleges. The colleges established incentives for the faculty to take on additional work through the WDO. The faculty had the opportunity to earn more money, and the WDO benefited from a readily available pool of expert instructors.

Operating as a Business

Earlier in this chapter, we noted the WDO's challenge of straddling the worlds of business and academia, and that for a WDO to successfully serve the needs of business, it must operate as much like a business as possible. For business and industry, high performance has been very well defined. In addition to staffing and customer service, described earlier in this chapter, best practices include

- Leadership
- Information and analysis
- Strategic planning
- Process management
- Business results

These practices, along with customer focus and satisfaction, are captured in, among other places, the criteria for the Malcolm Baldrige National Quality Award (for a description of these criteria, see www.quality.nist.gov). We will discuss each of these best practices in turn.

Leadership. Strong leadership is key to the success of any organization, and those providing workforce development services in a college environment must also demonstrate it. What factors make a successful leader can vary significantly across sectors or organizations. In 1997, CAEL asked focus groups of directors from WDOs in Ohio institutions to share their views on what specific competencies of a WDO director contribute to high levels of organizational performance. Their responses (see the box on the next page) apply to all WDOs, although relevant behaviors linked to the competencies may differ among organizations and may be influenced by organizational size, structure, and other factors.

Information and Analysis. The management, analysis, and use of data and information are key to supporting overall business goals, managing processes effectively, and maximizing performance improvement. As a business entity itself, a WDO needs to establish reliable measurements of needed data and information—data that are aligned with the key goals and objectives of the WDO. Examples of data to be analyzed include the following:

- WDO service quality improvement indicators such as customer satisfaction and customer retention
- Cost-to-revenue ratio
- Relationships between service quality and operational performance indicators such as operating costs and revenues
- Comparisons with competitors
- Information on target markets

Once specific data needs are determined, the WDO needs to establish internal processes for managing, analyzing, and using the data. Appropriate use of technology

---

Core Competencies for Directors of Workforce Development Organizations

In 1997, CAEL asked focus groups of directors from WDOs in Ohio institutions to share their views on what competencies WDOs should have. The following is a summary of their responses.

Leadership
Providing Direction
- Provides WDO with a clear sense of direction
- Takes charge, organizes resources, and steers others toward successful task accomplishment

Interpersonal
Stress Tolerance/Coping
- Remains calm, objective, and in control in stressful, ambiguous, or changing situations
- Maintains stable performance under pressure; accepts criticism without becoming defensive
Building and Maintaining Relationships
- Able to establish and maintain relationships with people at all levels (internal and external to the WDO and college)
- Builds ownership and support and exercises effective interpersonal influence through formal communication channels, informal networks, and alliances

Analytical
Problem Solving/Analysis
- Identifies problem and gathers data
- Breaks problem into component parts and differentiates key elements
- Makes accurate use of logic and draws sound inferences from information available to arrive at an effective solution
Business Management
- Establishes clear priorities
- Schedules activities to ensure optimum use of time and resources
- Monitors performance against standards to achieve financial or nonfinancial work results

Setting Objectives
- Produces detailed project plans in which desired results are clearly defined and action steps for achieving them efficiently and effectively are clearly specified
Decision Making
- Makes rational, realistic, and sound judgments and decisions based on consideration of all the facts and alternatives available

Business Awareness
Organizational Awareness
- Has knowledge and experience of a range of different, interrelated functions
- Sees organizations as dynamic, political, economic, and social systems
- Takes account of all the different functions and their interrelationships in developing strategies and plans
Strategic Perspective
- Takes a long-term view
- Thinks beyond details to see overarching goals and results
- Entertains wide-ranging possibilities in developing a vision for the future of the WDO
Commercial Orientation
- Knowledgeable about financial and commercial matters
- Focuses on costs, profits, markets, new business opportunities, and activities that will bring the largest return

Operational
Execution
- Drives projects along, gets results
- Ensures that key objectives are met
Customer Service Orientation
- Concerned to provide a prompt, efficient, and personalized service to customers
- Ensures that customer needs are met

for data gathering and analysis is critical to help staff plan and forecast quickly, accurately, and effectively. A WDO needs to regularly review its performance and use the review findings to improve its own performance. Using information and data from past contracts and from the marketplace ties strategic planning and other management activities to what is actually going on in and around the WDO.

Most of the WDOs that CAEL visited did use information such as revenue and enrollments from previous years in developing budgets and business goals. Some organizations used information and data to develop pricing structures that recover the real costs of delivering services, whereas others used it primarily in the marketing function. In general, however, WDOs conceded that they needed to do more in this area to improve their performance.

Strategic Planning. A good business does not let the market "happen" to it but rather sets out to make good business results happen in the marketplace. Strong planning and organization are therefore vital for any business to be a high performer. Similarly, a WDO should devise a plan outlining its strategic approach to doing business.

A WDO differs from a traditional business, however, in that its strategic planning must also be aligned with that of the college. Some WDOs visited by CAEL had developed a high level of strategic planning for their own operations and alignment with their colleges' strategic plans. The college plan clearly identified the roles and importance of the WDO in the strategic plans and referenced or highlighted the WDO's own plans and strategies. Other best practice planning examples include developing marketing plans, a sales plan and projections, staff training plan, and annual business goals.

Process Management. Managing business processes is another important criteria for high performance, and an increasingly important aspect of process management is flexibility. *Flexibility* means the ability to adapt quickly and effectively to changing requirements. Flexibility might result in rapid design and development of new services or the ability to produce a broad range of customized services, but it also involves outsourcing, decision making, and partnering arrangements.

WDOs need to have autonomy in all customer-related processes to achieve full accountability of results. Processes such as hiring, acquiring resources for services, billing and invoicing, and contracting are directly related to the successful outcome of the service delivery experience. Where WDOs must use college systems, college process owners should be identified to work with the WDO. In those cases, colleges should be held account-

able for process success and outcomes related to WDO business issues.

Business Results. Business results such as growing revenues and expanding product and service lines are also important to a WDO. It should be noted, however, that strong business results can be beneficial to the WDO only if that organization can exercise some degree of control over the budget and expenditures. Many college-based WDOs struggle because they are not given full responsibility and control over their incomes. Many WDOs are required to turn over their revenue surplus to their colleges. Some are not afforded a revenue budget but are instead awarded a yearly expense budget. Limited control over the budget means that WDOs often cannot reinvest a portion of the resources to continue to develop as a business.

To reinvest any surplus, the WDO director often must request funds from the college. This procedure affects the WDO adversely by impeding or even halting the growth and development of the WDO. Product research and development do not occur, making it difficult for the WDO to maintain market competitiveness.

One college visited by CAEL has forged a working compromise: The WDO has an expense budget and a variable delivery account. The director pays for all personnel and office expenses out of the fixed expense account, but then she has the freedom to spend what is in her variable account as needs dictate. If and when she overdraws on this account there are no penalties, and the college replenishes the fund.

WHAT WORKFORCE DEVELOPMENT ORGANIZATIONS CAN DO TO IMPROVE PERFORMANCE

Given what we know about the characteristics of high-performing WDOs, there are clear steps that any college-based WDO can take to improve its performance. Following is a summary of performance outcomes that CAEL suggests a high-performing organization should target—first, in the areas of service delivery and second, in management and operations of the WDO.

Service Delivery

1. **Develop and maintain a full range of high-impact services to customers.** To accomplish this, a WDO needs to offer both training and nontraining services in formats that are responsive to an employer's needs. The WDO should provide credit and degree options when possible and use technology to enhance access to, and the cost-effectiveness of, services.

2. **Systematically approach the sales and marketing process.** The WDO needs to identify strategies and relationships that increase its visibility and positive image in the business community. Some best practices include tracking sales leads, monitoring the sales cycle, using a consultative selling approach, and dedicating staff to the sales function. The use of computerized sales databases is a technology-based best practice.

3. **Diagnose customers' needs.** WDOs need to develop and apply a systematic process to determine appropriate training and nontraining solutions.

4. **Promote a customer orientation.** Focusing on the needs of the client is paramount, and this includes making sure, through the evaluation of customer satisfaction, that products and services are meeting the needs of the customer. Needs should be anticipated using market analysis and other strategies, and technology should be used to improve communication between the WDO and its customers.

5. **Measure the impact of programs and services.** Accountability to the customer includes making sure that the programs and services are doing what the WDO says it does. Regular evaluation of program impact is key to improving services and customer satisfaction.

6. **Develop strong partnerships and alliances.** A high-performing WDO will be in a position to leverage its connections with other service providers and state agencies to better meet customers' needs.

Management and Operations

1. **Optimize the financial performance of the WDO.** Optimal financial performance can be reached by using financial data strategically, identifying dependable revenue streams such as "anchor" clients, developing a pricing structure that covers costs, and having flexibility in and control over financial operations. Appropriate technology systems should be used to track and analyze finances and to link with college financial data.

2. **Manage human resources.** A high-performing organization can be proactive in the management of instructors and staff by maintaining a pool of talent for fluctuating service needs, monitoring and adjusting work flow, promoting the continuous development of staff, and optimizing staffing patterns to facilitate the accomplishment of organizational plans and priorities.

3. **Apply strong strategic and organizational planning.** Strategic planning involves using analysis and strategic forecasting as management tools for the WDO. In addition, it also requires the WDO's involvement in the college's planning processes.

4. **Maintain responsive operational processes.** A high-performing WDO must plan, design, maintain, and continually improve processes to support the WDO's operational goals. These activities require well-defined performance standards for all organizational processes and regular measurement of performance against those standards. The organization should use high-tech processes wherever possible to meet the information, planning, and service delivery needs of the organization.

5. **Establish and maintain a productive relationship with the college.** The director and the staff of the WDO must work collaboratively with campus programs and staff to communicate the needs, values, activities, and accomplishments of the WDO, to minimize performance barriers to the organization, and to market the WDO's achievements and contributions to the other institutional departments.

6. **Demonstrate strong leadership.** A high-performing WDO needs a leader who will design an effective organizational structure, manage the business, manage change effectively, and maintain currency in the training and development field. Best practices include providing WDO staff with a clear sense of direction and a vision of the WDO's role in the college and the larger community.

By achieving the outcomes just listed, a WDO can progress toward becoming a high-performing organization. Appendix A provides a self-assessment instrument to help organizations understand what they can begin to do to achieve these outcomes.

The Role of Technology

Readers may note that in the outcomes listed here, the use of technology is not depicted as a performance outcome to be sought as an end in itself. Rather, it is a method or tactic to be used in achieving high performance in various service delivery or WDO management and operations activities. There are those who believe that technology is so critical in today's training and development arena that it needs to be highlighted as a separate outcome. We do not question the importance of technology. What we do question is the use of technology simply for technology's sake. In our view, technology should be used to serve the organization and its clients, helping the organization reach other more important goals, such as high-quality service delivery, improved communication with the client, and fast and efficient analysis of financial and performance data.

So, although technology is not listed as a singular performance outcome, its role in serving the needs of business and industry should not be underemphasized. *Technology is perhaps the single most important tool for performance improvement that WDOs can use.* For that reason, technology-driven best practices are indeed highlighted throughout the model and in the self-assessment instrument in Appendix A.

FOR FURTHER CONSIDERATION: CREDIT VERSUS NONCREDIT INSTRUCTION

Organizations do not exist in a vacuum; they exist in many-layered environments. There is a business environment, which requires the WDO to act both responsively and proactively to customer needs. There is an operating environment that requires a core set of competencies from both leadership and staff. There is a college environment in which the WDO must act. And there is also the state policy environment, which also helps to mold the activities and leadership of a WDO.

Perhaps the most significant way in which a state government affects a college-based WDO is in setting the rules by which a community college system is funded. Core funding for colleges is typically based on the delivery of full-time-equivalent (FTE), for-credit courses; the delivery of noncredit instruction does not figure prominently, if at all, in the funding formula in most states. The National Council for Continuing Education and Training (NCCET) found that only 17 states fund noncredit courses on an FTE basis, with only three states—Maryland, Oregon, and Texas—providing comprehensive coverage of noncredit programs. States that fund noncredit courses generally cover from 50% to 75% of the rate (Warford, 2002). Understandably, therefore, colleges tend to place a premium on the delivery of for-credit courses because they help generate revenue for the college. However, the expectation that WDOs will steer their business clients to for-credit courses whenever possible can run counter to the goals and competitive success of WDOs.

First, this expectation places the general needs of the college ahead of the specific needs of the WDO's business customers, who often require customized, noncredit training options. This dichotomy between what the college and the customer are expecting makes it impossible for the WDO to serve the needs of both. Because of the college's dependence on credit FTE generation, it may be giving priority to one method of revenue generation (FTEs) over another (fee-for-service), thus frequently putting the WDO in the position of marketing potentially inappropriate business solutions to customers.

Second, in terms of revenue generation, delivering credit courses to customers is not always economically viable for WDOs because they are not able to charge as much as they can for noncredit courses. The college or the state specifies the charges for a credit class, and this level is often below what the WDOs can charge for customized training courses. In several informal conversations and focus groups, numerous directors have expressed that offering standard for-credit training actually costs the WDO money. (However, it should be noted that some colleges need to charge more for these classes because there is no funding from the state for them.) For these reasons, the focus on credit-bearing courses and programs that generate FTEs may not serve the interests of the WDO or the business customer. In return for a small number of FTEs, these college policies can lead to poor customer service and minimize the chance for WDOs to be competitive in the market.

The solution, however, is not simply for WDOs to focus on noncredit courses to the exclusion of for-credit courses. After all, employers are not the ones who are getting the instruction—their workers are. And working adults, now more than ever, want to earn credentials even when their employers may only see the need for a noncredit training package.

To meet the needs of both employers and individual learners, colleges and their WDOs need to strive for greater integration between the noncredit training and the credit and degree programs available through the community college system. Meeting the needs of employers need not mean that the learners themselves are unable to count instruction toward a meaningful credential. College-based WDOs offering customized or specialized instruction to businesses need to find ways to go beyond the transaction-based service to an integrated system in which more of the WDO instruction is assigned college credit or is at least linked to credit courses, credentials, and degrees in clear ways. The Kentucky Community and Technical College System, for example, has established clear administrative guidelines for offering workforce development (or noncredit) classes for college credit. Contact hours, lab hours, and even special accelerated courses can be converted to credit, with final approval by academic deans. Through solutions like this one, WDOs can maintain their flexibility and independent operations while taking full advantage of their firm standing in the community college system.

CONCLUSION

In this chapter we have outlined the characteristics of high-performing WDOs, as well some of the barriers that these organizations face in trying to reach a high performance level. WDOs and their colleges, in working together to reach the same performance outcomes, can make their partnerships successful ones that benefit the WDO, the college, and, most of all, the local business community and its workforce.

WDOs play an important role in the support of local economies, yet they have the potential to play an even greater one. To truly excel in their economic development role, WDOs need to be proactive in managing their business, their clients, and their services. But their place in the community college system is essential to provide a link to credit-based instruction that leads to formal degrees and credentials—the key to both economic and individual development and growth. ❈

References

Alfred, R. L., & Carter, P. (1997, April/May). Strategies for building high performing colleges. *Community College Journal*, 41–47.

Barber, R., & Klein-Collins, R. (1998). *Best practices of college business and industry centers: A self-improvement guide.* Chicago: Council for Adult and Experiential Learning.

Bassi, L. J., Cheney, S., & Van Buren, M. (1997, November). Training and industry trends 1997. *Training and Development*, 46–59.

Doucette, D. (1993). *Community college workforce training programs for employees of business, industry, labor, and government: A status report.* Phoenix, AZ: The League for Innovation in the Community College.

Jacobs, J., & Teahen, R. (1997). Shadow college and NCA accreditation: A conceptual framework. *NCA Quarterly, 71*(4), 472–478.

Johnson, S. L. (1995). The effectiveness of contract training operations in American community colleges. Retrieved June 4, 1997, from http://users.aol.com/stevesj243/contract_training

Kirkpatrick, D. L. (1998). *Evaluating training programs: The four levels (2nd ed.).* San Francisco: Berrett-Koehler.

Meister, J. C. (1997). *1997 survey of corporate university future directions.* New York: Corporate University Exchange.

Muse, C. (1996). *Model program development* (Report of Work Group II of the American Association of Community Colleges Commission on Workforce and Community Development). Washington, DC: American Association of Community Colleges.

National Coalition of Advanced Technology Centers. (1997). *Benchmarking report.* Palos Hills, IL: Author.

Robinson, D. G., & Robinson, J. (1995). *Performance consulting: Moving beyond training.* San Francisco: Berrett-Koehler.

Rosenfeld, S. A. (1995). *New technologies and new skills: Two-year colleges at the vanguard of modernization.* Chapel Hill, NC: Regional Technology Strategies, Inc.

Stamps, D. (1995, December). Community colleges go corporate. *Training*, 36–43.

Warford, L. J. (2002, December/January). Funding lifelong learning: A national priority. *Community College Journal*, 15–18+.

Westra, R. (1997). *Partnership improvement project* (Advanced Technology Centers and Manufacturing Extension Centers, Advanced Technology Centers Report Series, Vol. 1, No. 3). Waco, TX: Center for Occupational Research and Development, Inc. and National Coalition of Advanced Technology Centers.

CHAPTER 4

Integrating Workforce Development and Institutional Requirements

James Jacobs

s we have seen, one of the most significant contributions of community colleges to American society is their workforce development activity. About three fifths of more than 5 million credit-taking community college students are pursuing an occupational course of study (Dougherty, 2002). A recent publication of the National Assessment of Vocational Education (NAVE) indicates that the annual earning gains realized by community college students are very significant—15–36% higher than those realized by high school graduates (NAVE, 2002). Millions of other Americans have received continuing education and noncredit job training at community colleges. Equally significant are the ties community colleges have forged with local businesses. By taking advantage of institutional strengths such as organizational flexibility, close proximity to private sector enterprises, low cost, technical expertise, and experience with teaching adult learners, community colleges have become a major force in workforce development activities within the communities they serve.

The workforce development function emerged in the 1950s, when community college leaders sought to define their institutions more comprehensively than did traditional two-year junior colleges. These leaders sought to emphasize the "community" part of the name, working toward a modern community college that could serve the diverse learning needs of local populations, including workforce training (Cohen & Brawer, 1996). Consequently, the mission of community colleges broadened from serving individual students to companies within their service districts. Ten years ago, 96% of all community colleges indicated that they provided some form of workforce training for employees of local businesses (Doucette, 1993). A review of workforce development programs at seven major community colleges conducted by the National Center for Research in Vocational Education noted the emergence of three trends in the community college landscape: workforce development, economic development, and community development. The authors labeled this convergence "the entrepreneurial community college" (Grubb, Badway, Bell, Bragg, & Russman, 1997).

Community colleges represent a national system capable of developing a trained workforce (Batt & Osterman, 1993). After months of discussion and debate, in 2000 the American Association of Community Colleges (AACC) produced a summary of community college missions titled *The Knowledge Net*. According to this document, "Community colleges should view the preparation and development of the nation's workforce as a primary part of their mission and communicate to policymakers the uniqueness of this community college role" (AACC, 2000, p. 8). Workforce development has emerged as a major activity in community colleges, and virtually every major trend within higher education indicates that we can expect continued growth. Although this book focuses on community colleges, it is worth noting that in the last 30 years, four-year postsecondary institutions have witnessed a shift away from the humanities and hard sciences and toward business, technical, and health fields (Hudson, 2002).

Considering the significance of workforce development, surprisingly little attention has been paid to the skills needed to achieve this mission within individual institutions. The purpose of this chapter is to explore and discuss the institutional requirements of modern community colleges committed to workforce development. I will outline some of the current challenges facing workforce development and discuss the ways in which colleges have begun to cope with these challenges. A good deal of the information presented in this chapter is the result of academic research conducted by the many talented individuals at the Workforce Development Institute. The two leading community college organizations dealing with workforce development have also been instrumental: the National Council for Workforce Education (NCWE) (www.ncwe.org) and the National Council for Continuing Education and Training (NCCET) (www.nccet.org). A visit to their Web sites can yield rich practical information on the workforce development function of community colleges.

THE INSTITUTIONAL EVOLUTION OF WORKFORCE DEVELOPMENT

The impact of workforce development on the modern community college has evolved dramatically in the recent past. From 1950 to 1975, when the majority of community colleges were created, most employed a traditional college model, viewing instruction as the core of the institution. Instructional activity was subsequently divided between academic and vocational education. Ties with outside business and industry, such as apprenticeship education, were normally arranged through the vocational dean. Occasionally, a continuing education department extended its noncredit offerings into contracts with existing local companies, and some community colleges in midwestern urban centers maintained apprenticeship programs under local union and management agreements. However, these activities were typically coordinated by individuals who were not senior administrators or who were not part of the core operations of the institution (see Cohen & Brawer, 1996).

Relationships began to change in the early 1980s, when the post–Cold War economy began to unravel. Significant global competition and new information technologies created a massive dislocation of workers from traditional mass-production industries. Community colleges consequently found themselves at the center of efforts to revive the economic conditions of their communities (Davis & Wessel, 1998). Many of these efforts were implemented directly by college presidents, who created units separate from the traditional community college organization to respond quickly to plant closings, layoffs, and other forms of dislocation. These units, often named "Customized Training Departments" or "Centers for Business and Industry," were directly responsible for arranging specialized incumbent and displaced worker

training with local firms. Much of this work was performed through noncredit instruction. In many instances, these were considered "entrepreneurial units," meaning they needed to operate as for-profit centers (Dougherty & Bakia, 2000). Tensions often arose between units, leading to the term *shadow colleges*, which reflected that their activities were not considered central to the community college mission (Jacobs & Teahen, 1997).

Community colleges in general refused to validate the importance of these programs, but state economic development policies began to recognize their significance to workforce preparation. By the late 1980s, most states were using training and educational incentives as both business attraction and business investment strategies (Batt & Osterman, 1993; Office of Technology Assessment, 1990). Community college systems became central delivery pathways for state programs. Millions of dollars of state training monies began to flow through these customized training units, and firms began to seek out relationships with community colleges to obtain state grants.

In addition to these activities, the Job Training Partnership Act (JTPA) brought many contracts to colleges for the training of displaced workers. The employment shortages of the 1990s added yet another dimension as workforce development programs developed into job assessment and training organizations, responsible for securing appropriately skilled workers for the labor force. Many maintained significant contracts with their local workforce development boards to train new workers for local firms (Jacobs, 2001).

Workforce development programs became centers of grant management, adept at "making things happen" within the community college—even if it meant going outside to secure training and educational services from private vendors. In addition, because many units operated to fulfill contracts with business and governmental training programs, they were forced to learn how to complete projects on time and within budget. Some of the units were even charged by their presidents to earn "profits" beyond their costs to share with the general fund of the institution. Further analysis, however, suggests that the financial impact on institutions was minimal, and, at best, the units paid for themselves (Grubb et al., 1997). Finally, because of their work with state training grants, workforce units became rich sources of knowledge about the activities of local business, aiding the expansion of their partner networks.

In the mid-1990s, as their mission expanded, workforce development programs grew in size and influence within institutions. By the end of the 1990s, these once small and marginal organizations became multi-mission centers with large staffs, often led by a senior administrator such as a vice president of workforce development. A recent survey of community college administrators conducted by AACC indicates that large numbers of colleges have altered their administrators' titles from deans of occupational or vocational education to vice presidents of workforce development. Forty percent of the individuals who lead these units were the first to occupy them (Armey & VanDerLinden, 2002).

INSTITUTIONAL CHALLENGES OF GROWTH

The primary challenge faced by a community college workforce development program is similar to that encountered by many of the clients they serve: inability to manage rapid market growth. Rapid growth in size and significance within community colleges often outstrips their ability to manage and develop the core units of their business or their impact on their own institutions. In other words, as their significance within the institution grows, they are faced with the challenge of trading their relative independence for a more central institutional role. As workforce development units move out of the margins of the institution, they are faced with all of the challenges typical to a community college department. In particular, this has created issues around who develops and teaches curriculum, who defines and evaluates the success of the program, and how credit and noncredit activities are connected and transcripted. In all cases, the future efforts of workforce development units will bring them into greater contact with the rest of their institutions. This integration will prove beneficial in terms of clarifying the role of community colleges in future efforts toward workforce development.

Although workforce development has emerged as an important function of the community college, many traditional sources of funding—such as state and federal contracted training funds—are diminishing significantly. In addition, new competitors abound as more four-year public and private educational institutions enter the marketplace. The challenge is to shift the orientation of workforce development programs from the types of contract training they formerly performed to emerging markets in administrative and technical occupational ranks. Workforce development programs are beginning to see a stronger need for appropriate skill sets to match local economic development efforts. Thus, these units are not programming for the needs of a firm, but for a cluster of single firms or a group of individuals within a particular area (Rosenfeld, Jacobs, & Liston, 2003).

COMMUNITY COLLEGE MULTIPLE MISSIONS

The initial success of workforce development unit can be largely attributed to its isolation from the culture of the institution in general. Often, this was a conscious strategy initiated by the CEOs of colleges to ensure that the rest of the institution did not encumber units, enabling them to respond quickly to the needs of local companies. If the units were to be effective, they needed to spend much time and energy relating to businesses outside of the institution. Not only did the lack of internal institutional ties permit them to concentrate on one mission and develop specific technical competence, it also insulated units from various educational fads and organizational initiatives that often drain energies and dissipate the focus of an academic institution (Bailey & Averianova, 1998). In addition, because workforce development programs were often formed as separate entrepreneurial enterprises to keep costs low, they were staffed with temporary employees or part-time workers. This permitted them to develop with fresh sources of staff, many of whom came in from the private sector and were relatively unfamiliar with community college practices and procedures. These units generally remained outside of the general community college organizational culture, which is often heavily unionized and controlled by the interests of full-time instructional staff.

Today, these units are *not* marginal to their institutions and face the challenge of interrelating with, and providing leadership for, the entire institution. For example, noncredit customized training programs must now relate to the traditional vocational administrators in the performance of joint projects. Issues such as full-time faculty loads being met through customized training activities become central. Other challenges include determining who will select faculty for these assignments, who will develop the curriculum, which standards will be used, and who will evaluate the teachers. Most class selection issues are traditionally determined based on seniority within the institution; workforce development units used other criteria, which created the potential for friction. The more the units became immersed within the entire college, the more they were forced to deal with various parts of the institution—such as full-time teachers, union contracts, and institutional vestigial organs such as campus curriculum committees. Where avoidance of these issues was the appropriate strategy for success in the past, these units now need to confront or collaborate on institutional issues to determine appropriate solutions.

This challenge was exacerbated by the lack of skill sets appropriate for working within a new institutional paradigm of teaching and learning. Not only were the unit staff members often marginal to the institution at large, their skill sets were commonly highly specialized and inappropriate for governance in the rest of the institution. Little concern existed for the educational dynamics of the learning college as the firm replaced the individual as the programs' primary customer. A good deal of the expertise of the workforce development staff related to state government training programs and specialized procedures to access state monies to meet the training needs of companies. The daily tasks of individuals within the units were to administer grants, maintain records, and determine the training needs of companies, and to hire teachers and other training deliverers to complete projects. Curriculum content, standards of validation, and assessment of learning were not functions practiced within the unit. The major concern was client satisfaction—defined as the satisfaction level of a firm's management.

In some community college business and industry units, the person responsible for these activities was called the account manager. Workforce development programs tended to become masters of particular state processes, but these skill sets did not prepare them to function effectively within the academic culture of the community college. Because of this specialization, however, their familiarity with the real needs of firms became a valuable source of intelligence for regular college programs. In addition, their skills in developing grant proposals and managing projects in a timely fashion were very useful to the rest of the institution. In this age of accountability and efficiency, every organization needs to learn how to work effectively with fewer resources.

THE CHANGE IN MARKETS

Size and significance were not the only motivators for workforce development programs to move closer to the mainstream of their institutions. Decisive changes in the markets they faced also played a key role. At the time this book goes to press, almost all states are experiencing fiscal pressures that are leading them to scale back significantly workforce development training programs. This means that workforce development units simply cannot sell state monies to firms to obtain their training business. In addition, the post-"dot.com" recession has resulted in little domestic business expansion and reduced the corporate resources devoted to training. Thus, the very reasons for the expansion of workforce development units—increased demand for training and education on the part of companies—is now on hold, forcing retrenchment and redevelopment of new and different workforce development programs.

Three major trends have emerged in this market. First, the training market for frontline hourly employees is diminishing as the number of these jobs in the United States continues to decline. Much of the training budgets of firms has shifted to white-collar and technical training; more training and education are being invested in workers with significant postsecondary experience (Carnevale & Fry, 2001). One example of this extraordinary growth is the information technology (IT) certification programs in the past decade (Adelman, 2000). About 38% of adults who take noncredit occupational classes take them from business and industry, whereas less than 4% take them from community colleges (NAVE, 2002). This is caused by the decline in the number of frontline workers in manufacturing, the ability of computers to take over manufacturing functions, and the shifting training budgets of firms.

The second trend is the tremendous pressure on manufacturers to cut costs, which has influenced how much training is offered. In particular, small and medium-sized employers faced with major competition have begun budgeting less for training. Also, companies increasingly perceive continuous upgrading and training as the responsibility of the individual worker rather than that of the company. This is especially true in "new technology" firms that provide funds for employees to develop skills but prefer preexisting skills in the workers they hire. The proliferation of IT certifications is a means by which employers could demand specific validation of new information skills from individuals as a condition of advancement or hiring (Bartlett, 2002). The responsibility for education and training is clearly shifting from employers to employees.

Many community college workforce development units have little experience marketing to individuals. Moreover, it is unclear whether this is solely the prerogative of for-credit, occupational programs. Indeed, analysis of IT certification programs indicates that colleges often deploy these programs in more than one part of the college, creating internal competition between academic and workforce units. In some instances, colleges recruited private firms who established and delivered IT training when there was none at the college (Jacobs, in press).

It is important to note that new competitors exist in the marketplace. In the 1990s, many public and private four-year institutions began to offer programs to firms, successfully competing on price and quality with community colleges. Organizations such as the University of Phoenix target specific large firms as markets for obtaining degrees for their technical workers. Technical schools such as the DeVry Institute of Technology consistently expand their activities with direct ties to IT firms. Unlike community colleges, these private institutions tend to offer highly focused credit programs for their students. They are particularly good at helping minority students earn technical degrees (Bailey, Badway, & Gumport, 2001; Davis, 2003).

The third trend is the shift in public training emphasis. Many states use large public subsidiaries to support corporate training to lure new industry into their communities, but state economic development programs that target specific companies and sectors have decreased. Many states, such as Michigan, eliminated their modernization service and substituted more general training funds that provide considerable discretionary powers to the governor. Other states, such as Illinois and California, eliminated their customized job training programs altogether.

The 1990s did see some growth. That growth resulted from the development of both welfare and training programs under the Workforce Investment Act and Temporary Assistance for Needy Families (TANF). Even though these programs contain considerable funding for training recipients, their training tends to promote a "work first" approach to the handling of clients and jobs. Training is de-emphasized in favor of job placement, resulting in many workers falling off the welfare rolls. Most of the work they obtain, however, is low income and does not promote career pathways or provide a means to a better-paying job. In only a few states have TANF rules been interpreted to permit attendance at community colleges as a means to meet training requirements (Grossman & Gooden, 2001). Policymakers in these states emphasized the development of programs by which community colleges could become pathways to high-paying jobs for low-income people. Yet, on the whole, these programs were smaller and less directed at firms' needs than were many previous state expenditures, which targeted specific priority industries.

It becomes easy to see that the traditional markets for customized training departments have begun to evaporate. Workforce development programs must scale up their offerings, appealing to the professional development of individuals. Indeed, their current clients are primarily individuals seeking to upgrade their technical skills, often on their own time and at their own expense. Being a low-cost provider may not be as important as being a competent technical source of information. Reliance on state training programs is less an option as workforce units confront new challenges, both inside and outside of their institutions. The remainder of this chapter is devoted to a discussion of these challenges, and what viable alternatives might open up for workforce development units.

WHAT COLLEGES NEED TO DO

Workforce development programs are faced with new challenges within their own institutions. They cannot afford to sit idly by and wait for the next good thing to come along. For better or worse, they need to participate with the rest of the institution, playing a role to ensure that community colleges become better institutions of learning and resources for their communities. There are five actions that the new units will be wise to take.

Share Institutional Intelligence

In a functional sense, workforce development units become the research and development arms for the community college. Because they maintain programs that are close to the needs of the adult education market, they are most keenly aware of emerging skill requirements and the needs of companies. They should be communicating these needs to occupational programs and to the community college as a whole. The units need to see themselves as providers of an internal educational function within the institution to help credit programs better serve their students.

It is important that this become part of workforce development programs' *function* and not be regarded as an afterthought. Rather than perceiving themselves as separate from the rest of the institution, workforce development units need to develop the capacity to summarize information regarding the marketplace and find ways to disseminate it throughout the institution. This includes liberal arts for-credit units, traditional curriculum units, and other parts of the college that could profit from the information. Workforce development programs could dictate the skill needs of firms in their community and generally scale up their programs to meet the needs of local employers.

Of special significance to this process is the introduction of skill standards, licensing, and other external validations of skills required by employers. This includes the rapid proliferation of IT certifications and the development of professional licensing in engineering and health care—something that has been described as a parallel universe (Adelman, 2000). These new standards have profound implications for community college students. Workforce development units can bring their substantive knowledge to relevant issues, becoming an important asset in helping the college understand and react to the community's needs. More so than other units of the college, the workforce development unit has its finger on the pulse of the business community.

Mesh Credit and Noncredit Offerings

As the role of workforce development programs becomes more instrumental in the training and education practices of their institutions, a reexamination of the distinctions between credit and noncredit becomes valid. Many of these distinctions are maintained by state reimbursement practices and institutional history. For firms and agencies, they are not relevant or useful—and these entities want to know if the student can perform the necessary skills. According to a national survey of adults, noncredit enrollments in public community colleges were about 90% of for-credit enrollments in 1995. By 1999, these noncredit enrollments exceeded credit enrollments by 8% (Bailey, 2002). Given the growth of outside forms of validation, it would be useful for credit and noncredit functions to be understood and coordinated as different forms of learning, both of which require appropriate rewards and validation. In the past few years, both NCCET and NCWE have produced policy documents that underscore the importance of developing this perspective (Flynn, 2002; NCCET, 2001; NCOE, 2000).

As the distinction between credit and noncredit becomes cloudier, the relationship between the two must be rethought. Specifically, it may be necessary to revise transcripts to determine the most appropriate way that workforce development programs can be transcripted. Many colleges are currently attempting to include information from the noncredit side of the institution on their transcripts. Workforce development units will need to discover ways to help others understand the transcription process so that the noncredit sector can be granted recognition (Carnevale & Desrochers, 2001). In Maryland, for example, both credit and noncredit work appears on transcripts (Stanley, 2002).

Use a Cluster Approach With Clusters of Firms

For the most part, community college workforce development programs work with more than one firm simultaneously—with the exception of the largest companies that may dominate their local economies. Most workforce development activities are not focused on a series of firms that share workforce needs. Strategic decisions in approaching groups of firms that are linked with one another, often referred to as *clusters*, are necessary. Examples of clusters are software development firms in Silicon Valley, metalworking firms around Detroit, or biomanufacturing firms in North Carolina. Developing education and training programs for the needs of these clusters is important for both economic development and workforce development interests. Adding to the economic viability of a company is important not only to supporting the local economy but also to securing job opportunities for students.

Working with clusters of firms may take many forms, including the development of new credit and noncredit

programs. In dealing with larger clusters of firms, colleges have developed various responses, from technology centers to industry-specific degree programs and corporate campuses. Working with clusters means more than simply assigning an account manager to service the firms. Colleges need staff members who have worked closely with these clusters, often with their specific firms, so that credibility has already been established within the cluster. They also need individuals who can follow an industry and respond to the specific needs of a cluster. Institutional relationships, developed with firms and driven by workforce development units, are of absolute necessity.

Not all community colleges have clusters of firms present, but many of the larger ones do. How well these units sustain work with clusters and develop both technical assistance and workforce development will be a test of the relevance of their work. This will place greater importance on workforce development units in community colleges and in the communities they serve (Rosenfeld et al., 2003).

Develop a Learning Perspective

In the past, workforce development units primarily developed training programs for firms. Today, as training becomes the individual responsibility of the worker, more emphasis must be placed on how programs can help the individual acquire new workforce skills. This means that colleges must be able to assess adult learners' technical and foundational skills. Many community colleges have recently initiated programs with ACT (American College Test) Work Keys that are designed to fill this role. Additionally, colleges must shift toward offering more learning in "bite-sized pieces" to fit the needs of adults. Modular curriculum development must become central to the new workforce unit. Given the career pathways of new occupational areas, many adults will eventually enter four-year institutions to earn degrees. How well workforce programs can develop career pathways that build on ties will be critical to the future of these institutions.

Workforce development units would be wise to monitor the growing use of the Internet and other forms of asynchronous learning techniques by the private sector. The widespread adoption of these techniques needs to be understood by community colleges. For example, one college found that welfare mothers with access to computers find time to do their class work at night after their children have gone to bed. Although the impact of these technologies clearly ranges across the entire institution, they may be particularly relevant to workforce development.

Another area of considerable importance to the entire college, but in which the workforce development unit might offer some specific skill sets, is the development of programs for new Americans—individuals who have recently arrived in the United States and speak languages other than English in their homes. Overall, workforce units must become centers of adult learning and leading implementers of these efforts within their institutions. This will help each unit fit within the basic framework of its institution and not just function along the margins.

Finally, workforce development programs must be concerned with the development of the public workforce. Too often, they are centered on their ability to function as entrepreneurial units, taking on only those projects and activities that can offer a profit. There are many areas of workforce development that may not be profit making but may play a crucial role in the local economy. For example, the development of public sector training of police, firefighters, and emergency response personnel may have an important impact on communities. Successful implementation requires individuals who are curriculum designers, assessment experts, and knowledgeable about the needs of adult workers. In brief, they need to be educators with specific skills that can be directed to the workforce education targets selected by their institution.

Tie Workforce Development to Low-Income Students

Community colleges can serve as a means of developing outreach programs for low-income populations. "Work first" concepts need to be supplanted with an examination of how community colleges can make a difference in the lives of low-income individuals, particularly during periods of labor shortages. Workforce development units hold substantive knowledge of specific hiring patterns and career pathways within local clusters of firms; they can develop specific programs that will lead low-income individuals to jobs and opportunities for advancement.

It is important not to overestimate the benefits of the economic growth period of the 1990s. Real wages for many did rise, but significant numbers of people fell out of the picture entirely. A 1999 *Business Week* poll indicated that almost half of all Americans did not feel that their economic lives had significantly improved as a result of the new knowledge economy (Osterman, Kochan, Locke, & Piore, 2001). As TANF and WIA (Workforce Investment Act) legislation continues to be redrafted, there is an enormous opportunity for community colleges to become the major centers for the education and training of low-income adults. This promise has been articulated in a number of important policy statements (Grossman & Gooden, 2001).

To play this role, workforce development units need individuals who are both expert in understanding the poli-

cies and procedures of federal, state, and local agencies involved in workforce development and sensitive to the needs of low-income adults. Some of this work will require individuals who are able to work with immigrant populations, understanding the cultural barriers that can prevent them from obtaining an education.

CONCLUSION

An astute reader will note that I have said little in this chapter about what many consider a key motivating force in workforce development activities: the institutional search for greater profits. The reason for this omission is very simple: Earning money for the institution has not historically been a driving force within workforce development units and is not likely to become one (Grubb et al., 1997). Specific amounts of contracts have never constituted a major percentage of the budget of the larger institution—although they may play a role on the margins of budget development. However, the roles outlined in the previous section would clearly be costly and provide even less new revenue for the institution from their implementation.

Moreover, there is reason to believe that thinking of workforce development as a "cash cow" is neither realistic nor wise. In a period of extreme competition, cost is only one dimension. Quality is often far more important to both businesses and individuals. Emphasis should be placed on outcomes and not on generating revenue. These institutions have a rich legacy that can sustain growth and innovation well into the future. ❊

References

Adelman, C. (2000). A parallel universe: Certification in the information technology world. *Change, 32*(3), 20–29.

American Association of Community Colleges (AACC). (2000). *The knowledge net: Connecting communities, learners, and colleges*. Washington, DC: Community College Press.

Armey, M. J., & VanDerLinden, K. E. (2002). *Career paths for community college leaders* (American Association of Community Colleges Research Brief No. 2, Leadership Series). Washington, DC: American Association of Community Colleges.

Bailey, T. (2002). *The integration and coordination of credit and non-credit activities at community colleges*. Unpublished manuscript, Columbia University, Teachers College, Community College Research Center.

Bailey, T. R., & Averianova, I. E. (1998). *Multiple missions of community colleges: Conflicting or complementary.* New York: Columbia University, Teachers College, Community College Research Center.

Bailey, T. R., Badway, N., & Gumport, P. (2001). *For-profit higher education and community colleges.* Paper prepared for National Center for Postsecondary Improvement (Deliverable #0400). Stanford, CA: Stanford University.

Bartlett, K. (2002). *The preconceived influence of industry-sponsored credentials in the information technology industry.* Minneapolis, MN: National Center for Career and Technical Education.

Batt, R., & Osterman, P. (1993). *A national policy for workplace training: Lessons from state and local experiments* (Working Paper No. 106). Washington, DC: Economic Policy Institute.

Carnevale, A., & Desrochers, D. M. (2001). *Help wanted. . . Credentials required: Community colleges in the knowledge economy.* Washington, DC: Community College Press.

Carnevale, A., & Fry, R. (2001). *The economic and demographic roots of education and training.* Washington, DC: National Association of Manufacturers Center for Workforce Success.

Cohen, A. M., & Brawer, F. B. (1996). *The American community college* (3rd ed.). San Francisco: Jossey-Bass.

Davis. (2003). *Access and completion of minorities in community college programs.* Presentation at the meeting of the American Association of Community Colleges, Dallas, TX.

Davis, B., & Wessel, D. (1998). *Prosperity: The coming boom and what it means to you.* New York: Random House.

Doucette, D. (1993). *Community college workforce training programs for employees of business, industry, labor, and government: A status report.* Phoenix, AZ: League for Innovation in the Community College.

Dougherty, K. J. (2002). The evolving role of community college policy issues and research questions. In J. C. Smart & W. G. Tierney (Eds.), *Higher education: Handbook of theory and research* (Vol. 17). New York: Agathon Press.

Dougherty, K. J., & Bakia, M. F. (2000). *The new economic-development role of the community college.* New York: Columbia University, Teachers College, Community College Research Center.

Flynn, W. (2002). More than a matter of degrees. *American Community College Journal, 72*(6), 16–21.

Grossman, L. M., & Gooden, S. (2001). *Opening doors: Expanding educational opportunities for low-income workers.* New York: Manpower Demonstration Research Corporation.

Grubb, W. N., Badway, N., Bell, D., Bragg, D., & Russman, M. (1997). *Workforce, economic, and community development: The changing landscape of the entrepreneurial community college.* Phoenix, AZ: League for Innovation in the Community College.

Hudson, L. (2002). Demographic and attainment trends in postsecondary education. In P. A. Graham & N. G. Stacey (Eds.), *The knowledge economy and postsecondary education.* Washington, DC: National Academy Press.

Jacobs, J. (2001). Community colleges and the Workforce Investment Act: Promises and problems of the new vocationalism. In D. Bragg (Ed.), *The new vocationalism in community colleges.* San Francisco: Jossey-Bass.

Jacobs, J. (in press) . Informational technology and skills certification programs in community colleges. In T. Bailey & V. S. Morest (Eds.), *Community colleges and their future.*

Jacobs, J., & Teahen, R. (1997). Shadow colleges and NCA accreditation: A conceptual framework. *NCA Quarterly, 71*(4), 472–478.

National Assessment of Vocational Education (NAVE). (2002). *Interim report to Congress.* Washington, DC: U.S. Department of Education.

National Council of Continuing Education and Training (NCCET). (2001). *More than a matter of degrees: Credentials, certification and community colleges.* Carlsbad, CA: Author.

National Council of Occupational Education (NCOE). (2000). *Towards new roles of certification and validation by community colleges.* Columbus, OH: Author.

Office of Technology Assessment (OTA). (1990). *Worker training: Competing in the new international economy.* Washington, DC: U.S. Government Printing Office.

Osterman, P., Kochan, T., Locke, R., & Piore, M. (2001). *Working in America: A blueprint for a new labor market.* Cambridge, MA: MIT Press.

Rosenfeld, S., Jacobs, J., & Liston, C. (2003). *Models for cluster-based workforce development systems: A community college approach.* Carrboro, NC: Regional Technology Strategies.

Stanley, P. (2002). Credentialing success story for Maryland community colleges. *Workplace, 13*(2), 12–13, 34.

CHAPTER 5

Competencies for Workforce Developers

William J. Rothwell and Patrick E. Gerity

Workforce developers come from all walks of life. Some have participated in graduate training to prepare them for this line of work, perhaps matriculating from one of the 300 existing graduate programs in the United States focused on training and development, human resource development, workplace learning and performance, workforce education and development, adult education, vocational education, or related fields. Others come from unrelated work in other fields such as sales or even nursing or social work. When setting out to fill a workforce development vacancy, college administrators often find themselves facing this important question: What should workforce developers do, and what kind of people will be most successful as workforce developers? Answering that question requires a discussion of the competencies for workforce developers—the topic of this chapter.

WHAT IS A COMPETENCY?

Say *competency*, and it will have an effect on people. But the effect will be different from that of shouting "fire" in a crowded theater. Instead of inciting panic, it is more likely to throw a group into confusion. The reason for that reaction is, quite simply, that *competency* has several possible meanings.

Educators hearing *competency* may associate it with the knowledge, skills, and abilities (KSA) essential to occupational entry or success. Because educators analyze occupations to isolate the essential KSAs for occupational entry and development, they can relate to it immediately. To them, *competency* is simply a shorthand way of saying KSAs. And, internationally, competency is some-times equated with minimum skill standards for occupational entry.

The problem is that business leaders, and others who work with them, sometimes use *competency* in other ways. For example, it could mean anything leading to successful work performance. Identifying competencies therefore involves doing more than pinpointing what people must know, do, or feel in their work. Instead, it starts with clarifying the measurable work results desired from an occupation, job category, department, or individual and then working backward to isolate anything—traits, inborn talents, and even motivation levels—that contributes to individual success in getting results.

It is profoundly different to associate competency with KSAs (on one hand) and work outcomes (on the other hand). The difference centers on the results to be achieved. Educators assume that improvements in knowledge, skill, and ability alone will yield improved productivity and performance. But many business leaders know that workers can possess essential KSAs but still fail in their performance.

Another issue that is sometimes misunderstood is that most organizations have long relied on job descriptions as a key, and even foundational, element in their human resource management systems. Traditional college human resource management textbooks usually begin with a discussion of job analysis (see, e.g., Bohlander, Snell, & Sherman, 2000; Dessler, 2001), pointing out that a job description (which identifies what people do) is one product and a job specification (which identifies minimum entry-level qualifications) is another product expected from such an analysis. But job descriptions focus on work activities and not on measurable work results. Rarely, if ever, does a job description supply measurable performance standards. And, in any case, since work activities change so quickly in today's organizations, job descriptions are often outdated before they are finalized.

Identifying competencies often takes an approach different from traditional job analysis. It looks for unique discriminators of superlative incumbents—the "best-in-class" performers called *exemplars*. The exceptional ability of exemplars to outperform others may have more to do with the people doing the work than with the work they carry out. Although Americans believe that all people are created equal, the reality is that people do not produce equally. Some people achieve results many times those of average performers in the same job category, department, or occupation. Indeed, it has long been recognized that, in any group of job incumbents, some people will simply get better measurable results than others do. The difference between the average output levels of a member of a group and the output level of the exemplar in that group is called the performance improvement potential, and that gap indicates a realistic assessment of just how much measurable performance improvement is possible in a group (Gilbert, 1978).

Why is all that important? To answer that question, think of it like this: If we could just figure out what makes some people dramatically more productive than others, and if we could figure out how to narrow that gap and get more people closer to that level, we could realize quantum leaps in productivity. If exemplars were 20 times more productive than their average counterparts, and if it were possible to close that performance gap, it would then be possible to get 20 times the work results with fewer—but higher-quality—people. Alternatively, it would be possible to get the same output levels with a factor of 20 fewer people. That is exactly why business leaders are so interested in competencies and why some advise reinventing human resource systems to make competencies, instead of traditional but activity-oriented job descriptions, the foundation (Dubois & Rothwell, 2003).

Competencies go beyond mere knowledge, skill, and ability and focus on the individual more than the work he or she does. Sometimes called KSAOs to refer to knowledge, skills, abilities, and other characteristics, competencies are closely tied to the unique qualities individuals possess that lead to successful work results. Some of the "other characteristics" might include levels of motivation, innate abilities, or personality traits.

Competency work brings a special nomenclature to occupational studies (Dubois & Rothwell, 2000). *Competency identification* means discovering what competencies individuals must possess to be successful or even exemplary. *Competency modeling* means preparing narrative descriptions of competencies for an occupation, job category, or department. Notably, of course, a competency model describes "what should be." *Competency assessment* means comparing individuals to a competency model and clarifies "what is." Common approaches to competency assessment may involve testing, certification, simulations, multi-rater assessment, or even assessment centers. *Developmental planning* means helping an individual narrow existing gaps between the individual's current profile (as measured by a competency assessment) and the competency model (Dubois & Rothwell, 2000). *Developmental strategies* are on-the-job, near-the-job, or off-the-job learning experiences that help individuals narrow developmental gaps and thereby build their competencies.

At the same time, it is important to distinguish between individual competencies and organizational competencies. *Individual competencies* are worker characteristics. *Organizational competencies* are strategic strengths (Campbell & Luchs, 1997). Much has been written on individual competency identification, modeling, and assessment in recent years. Some published works extol the value of competencies (Ashton, 1996; "Competencies Drive HR Practices," 1996; Jeffords, Scheidt, & Thibadoux, 1997; Kochanski, 1997; Lado & Wilson, 1994; Langdon & Marrelli, 2002; Meade, 1998), whereas others simply provide background information (Rothwell & Lindholm, 1999; Shippmann et al., 2000). Numerous case studies show how organizations have used competency modeling to achieve breakthroughs in productivity improvement (Dubois, 1998; Stark, Valvano, & Luther, 1996). Several books provide guidance on how to conduct competency identification, modeling, and assessment (Dubois, 1993; Dubois & Rothwell, 2000; Lucia & Lepsinger, 1999; Spenser & Spenser, 1993). Workforce developers will find themselves increasingly tasked to help organizations build and use competency models because of the promise they hold to achieve quantum leaps in productivity improvement (Dubois & Rothwell, 2003).

The Importance of Competencies for Workforce Developers

College administrators must know what to look for when they face the task of filling workforce development vacancies. Competency models supply that information. Leaders of workforce development organizations also need information about how to build staff capabilities. Competency models can give guidance on which staff capabilities to build. In other words, competency models describe the *what should be* that can then be compared to the *what is* of individual or collective staff capabilities. By using competency models, workforce developers also add an important weapon in their consulting arsenal.

Competency identification, modeling, and assessment are important for businesses seeking ways to achieve productivity improvement in their workforces and to attract, develop, use, and retain talent (Rothwell & Kazanas, 2003). Awareness of competency identification, modeling, assessment, and development can be that weapon in the consulting arsenal. Many businesses have begun to experiment with and use competencies as foundational to their human relations functions (Dubois & Rothwell, 2003).

What Competencies Have Been Identified for Workforce Developers?

Many research studies have focused on the competencies essential for success in training and development, human resource development, human performance improvement, or performance consulting (Rothwell, 2000) and workplace learning and performance (Rothwell, Sanders, & Soper, 1999) specifically within community college–based workforce development. Competency studies have also been conducted of learners in workplace settings (Rothwell, 2002) and the competency expectations for workforce developers of such a key stakeholder group as corporate CEOs (Rothwell, Lindholm, & Wallick, 2003).

Although occupational studies of any field are helpful, the greatest value is realized only when they are made specific to a unique culture or institutional setting. Cultural adaptation studies have been conducted to show differences—and similarities—of workforce developer competencies cross-culturally (see Al-Hamli, 2003; Chen, 2003; Ginkel, Mulder, & Nijhof, 1994; Lee, 1994; Marquardt & Engel, 1993; Odenthal & Nijhof, 1996; Peerapornvitoon, 1999; Rijk, Mulder, & Nijhof, 1994; Yang, 1994; Yoo, 1999; You, 1993). This section provides a broad summary of several recent studies with references to more comprehensive treatments of these topics.

Competencies for Human Performance Improvement (Performance Consulting)

Recent thinking has suggested that workforce developers have a broader role than merely providing training. ASTD, formerly the American Society for Training and Development, sponsored a competency study to identify the characteristics necessary for success as a performance consultant (Rothwell, 2000). The study defined human performance improvement (HPI) as "the systematic process of discovering and analyzing important human performance gaps, planning for future improvements in human performance, designing and developing cost-effective and ethically justifiable interventions to close performance gaps, implementing the interventions, and evaluating the financial and nonfinancial results" (Rothwell, 2000, p. 3). The HPI process model, introduced in this study, was defined as "a six-step model that describes the key steps in conducting human performance improvement work" (Rothwell, 2000, p. 13). The steps in the HPI process model included the following (Rothwell, 2000, pp. 13–15):

- *Step 1—Performance analysis*: The first step involves "identifying and describing past, present, and future human performance gaps."
- *Step 2—Cause analysis*: "The root causes of a past, present, or future performance gap are identified."
- *Step 3—Selection of appropriate interventions*: "Here people who do human performance work consider possible ways to close past, present, or possible future performance gaps by addressing their root cause(s)."
- *Step 4—Implementation*: In this step, "people who do human performance improvement work help the organization prepare to install an intervention."
- *Step 5—Change management*: "During this step, people who do human performance improvement work should monitor the intervention as it is being implemented."
- *Step 6—Evaluation and measurement*: "At this point, those conducting human performance improvement work take stock of the results achieved by the intervention."

In this competency study, the roles of those who perform HPI work are tied to the HPI process model. Four roles were identified:

- *Analyst:* "conducts troubleshooting to isolate the cause(s) of human performance gaps and identifies areas in which human performance can be improved"
- *Intervention specialist*: "selects appropriate interventions to address the root cause(s) of performance gaps"
- *Change manager*: "ensures that interventions are implemented in ways consistent with desired results and that they help individuals and groups achieve results"
- *Evaluator*: "assesses the impact of interventions and follows up on changes made, actions taken, and results achieved in order to provide participants and stakeholders with information about how well interventions are being implemented." (Rothwell, 2000, p. 17)

ASTD Models for Human Performance Improvement also listed 38 competencies and 95 terminal and enabling outputs linked to the work of HPI practitioners. Significantly, the study emphasized that anyone—from CEO to janitor—could enact the roles of HPI.

For workforce developers who work in community colleges, the HPI study is important because it suggests that they can—and should—play a broader role in improving performance for their clients than by merely offering training or other educational services. Human performance, equated with outputs or outcomes, is affected by many variables. HPI is focused on discovering root causes of performance problems and providing solutions, used individually or collectively, to rectify deficiencies and thereby address root causes.

Competencies for Workplace Learning and Performance

In 1999, ASTD published another competency study, *ASTD Models for Workplace Learning and Performance* (Rothwell et al., 1999). Its purpose was to reinvent the field formerly known as human resource development in light of thinking about HPI. Workplace learning and performance, or WLP, is defined as the integrated use of learning and other interventions for the purpose of improving individual and organizational performance (Rothwell et al., 1999). Like HPI, it relies on a systematic process of analyzing and responding to individual, group, and organizational needs. WLP creates positive, progressive change within organizations by balancing human, ethical, technological, and operational considerations.

A key difference between the HPI study and the WLP study is the focus on *who* is targeted. HPI can apply to anyone. WLP is uniquely focused on those who work full time to improve human performance. Moreover, WLP links together two concepts and thereby builds a key expectation: that professionals in this field know how to use any mode of learning—from informal to formal—to achieve performance improvement. In that respect, WLP professionals are unique because they are expert in applying all methods to facilitate learning. Of course, learning, which is what people do for themselves, is distinct from training, which is what trainers "do" to others.

ASTD Models for Workplace Learning and Performance is the current competency study of the field. Although it applies to workforce developers in community colleges as much as it does to corporate trainers, it is an occupational study that must be tailored to unique settings and individual work to be most useful. (Table 5.1 summarizes the roles of WLP professionals, and Table 5.2 lists the competencies associated with WLP.)

Competencies for Community College Workforce Developers

Much research has been conducted on the unique competencies required of community college workforce developers, but surprisingly few people in the community college world seem to be aware of it. In this section of the chapter, we present a summary of this research.

Weischadle (1984) completed a study to identify similarities between technical trainers in two-year community colleges and technical trainers in industry, with a focus on community college instructors as industrial trainers. The study's purpose was to determine which competencies were common to technical instructors in two-year colleges and technical trainers in industry and business in Ohio, as well as which competencies were unique to each group. A secondary goal was to clarify and contribute to the literature on the profile of these individuals.

The methodology used by Weischadle was to merge several competency lists to develop a final list of competencies (Andreyka, 1969; Balogh, 1982; Christensen, 1976; Davie, Suessmuth, & Thomas, 1986; International Board of Standards for Training, 1988; McCullough, 1987; McLagan & McCullough, 1983; National Center for Research in Vocational Education, 1975; Ontario Society for Training and Development, 1979). The instrument was taken from the work of Andreyka (1969) and modified to include the competencies identified from the sources just cited. The result was a 14-page questionnaire. The instrument was pilot tested with a group of 10 subject matter experts who reviewed the instrument for clarity and completeness and suggested revisions.

The questionnaire was then mailed to a sample of 150 people: 94 technical instructors and 56 industry technical trainers. Eighty-six questionnaires were returned, for a response rate of 57.3% (58.5% of technical instructors and 55.4% of industry technical trainers). A 10% sample of nonreturns determined that there was no significant difference between respondents and non respondents.

The survey results revealed that 74% of the two-year college technical instructors had more than 11 years of experience in postsecondary education; 26% had high school teaching experience. This group typically had three years or less of teaching experience. Ninety-five percent had some college teaching experience. Of this, 37% had 5 to 10 years of experience. Sixty-seven percent of the respondents had received a master's degree, and 14.3% had a bachelor's degree as their highest level of education. Forty percent of those with a master's degree had a degree in business, whereas 35% had degrees in education and 20%, in engineering. Fifty-three percent of the two-year college technical instructors had between 8 and 12 years of technical work experience. Fifty percent had been employed full time in their technical field prior to their teaching position.

The technical trainers' results, for the most part, were similar to those of the two-year technical instructors. Fifty-seven percent had more than 8 years of technical job experience and had been employed in a technical area prior to going into technical training. A master's in education (64%) was the most common degree. However, technical trainers were less likely to have taught in a college or high school than were two-year technical instructors. Overall, there were 119 competencies common to both groups. The top seven competencies, ranked by mean, were

- Knowledge of subject matter
- Ability to solve problems
- Effective communication skills
- Discussion and group facilitation skills
- Ability to write effectively
- Ability to set priorities and use time effectively
- Knowledge of adult learning theory

Another competency study was conducted by Cookson and English (1997) at the Pennsylvania State University (Penn State) to examine the competencies essential for continuing education professionals throughout Penn State's continuing education system. The study's research objectives were, first to identify the areas of responsibility and tasks associated with the administration of continuing education programs and, second, to develop a performance-based self-assessment tool that could be used by individual continuing education administrators to evaluate their own professional competence and to guide the planning of their own corresponding professional development activities.

Cookson and English conducted this research using five phases. Participants were identified as exemplary directors and area representatives for continuing education at Penn State University. Phase I of the study involved using focus groups of exemplary performers to create a list of performance dimensions. The DACUM process—where DACUM is an acronym for developing a curriculum—was used with the groups to refine the list of performance dimensions (Norton, 1997). During the

Table 5.1	Roles of Workforce Learning and Performance Professionals
Manager Plans, organizes, schedules, monitors, and leads the work of individuals and groups to attain desired results; facilitates the strategic plan; ensures that the WLP is aligned with organizational needs and plans; and ensures accomplishment of the administrative requirements of the function. **Analyst** Troubleshoots to isolate the causes of human performance gaps or identifies areas for improving human performance. **Intervention Selector** Chooses appropriate interventions to address root causes of human performance gaps. **Intervention Designer and Developer** Creates learning and other interventions that help address the specific root causes of human performance gaps. Some examples of the work of the intervention designer and developer include serving as instructional designer, media specialist, materials developer, process engineer, ergonomics engineer, instructional writer, and compensation analyst.	**Intervention Implementor** Ensures the appropriate and effective implementation of desired interventions that address the specific root causes of human performance gaps. Some examples of the work of the intervention implementor include serving as administrator, instructor, organization development practitioner, career development specialist, process redesign consultant, workspace designer, compensation specialist, and facilitator. **Change Leader** Inspires the workforce to embrace change, creates a direction for the change effort, helps the organization's workforce to adapt to the change, and ensures that interventions are continuously monitored and guided in ways consistent with stakeholders' desired results. **Evaluator** Assesses the impact of interventions and provides participants and stakeholders with information about the effectiveness of the intervention implementation.

Note. From Rothwell, Sanders, and Soper (1999, p. 43). Adapted with permission.

Table 5.2	Competencies for Workplace Learning and Performance Professionals

Analytical Competencies

Analytical Thinking
Inspires the workforce to embrace the change, creates a direction for the change effort, helps the organization's workforce to adapt to the change, and ensures that interventions are continuously monitored and guided in ways consistent with stakeholders' desired results.

Performance Data Analysis
Interpreting performance data and determining the effect of interventions on customers, suppliers, and employees

Career Development Theory and Application
Understanding the theories, techniques, and appropriate applications of career development interventions used for performance improvement

Competency Identification
Identifying the skills, knowledge, and attitudes required to perform work

Intervention Selection
Selecting performance improvement strategies that address the root cause(s) of performance gaps rather than treat symptoms or side effects

Knowledge Management
Developing and implementing systems for creating, managing, and distributing knowledge

Model Building
Conceptualizing and developing theoretical and practical frameworks that describe complex ideas

Organization Development Theory and Application
Understanding the theories, techniques, and appropriate applications of organization development interventions as they are used for performance improvement

Performance Gap Analysis
Performing "front-end analysis" by comparing actual and ideal performance levels in the workplace; identifying opportunities and strategies for performance improvement

Performance Theory
Recognizing the implications, outcomes, and consequences of performance interventions to distinguish between activities and results

Process Consultation
Using a monitoring and feedback method to continually improve the productivity of work groups

Reward System Theory and Application
Understanding the theories, techniques, and appropriate application of reward system interventions used for performance improvement

Social Awareness
Seeing organizations as dynamic political and economic systems

Staff Selection Theory and Application
Understanding the theories, techniques, and appropriate applications of staff selection interventions used for performance improvement

Standards Identification
Determining what constitutes success for individuals, organizations, and processes

Systems Thinking
Recognizing the interrelationships among events by determining the driving forces that connect seemingly isolated incidents within the organization; taking a holistic view of performance problems to find root causes

Training Theory and Application
Understanding the theories, techniques, and appropriate applications of training interventions used for performance improvement

Work Environment Analysis
Examining the work environment for issues or characteristics that affect human performance; understanding the characteristics of a high-performance workplace

Workplace Performance, Learning Strategies, and Intervention Evaluation
Continually evaluating and improving interventions before and during implementation

Business Competencies

Ability to See the "Big Picture"
Identifying trends and patterns that are outside the normal paradigm of the organization

Table 5.2	Competencies for Workplace Learning and Performance Professionals (cont'd)

Business Competencies

Business Knowledge
Demonstrating awareness of business functions and how business decisions affect financial and nonfinancial work results

Cost/Benefit Analysis
Accurately assessing the relative value of performance improvement interventions

Evaluation of Results Against Organizational Goals
Assessing how well workplace performance, learning strategies, and results match organizational goals and strategic intent

Identification of Critical Business Issues
Determining key business issues and forces for change and applying that knowledge to performance improvement strategies

Industry Awareness
Understanding the current and future climate of the organization's industry and formulating strategies that respond to that climate

Knowledge Capital
Measuring knowledge capital and determining its value to the organization

Negotiating/Contracting
Organizing, preparing, monitoring, and evaluating work performed by vendors and consultants

Outsourcing Management
Identifying and selecting specialized resources outside of the organization; identifying, selecting, and managing technical specifications for these specialized resources

Project Management
Planning, organizing, and monitoring work

Quality Implications
Identifying the relationships and implications among quality programs and performance

Interpersonal Competencies

Communication
Applying effective verbal, nonverbal, and written communication methods to achieve desired results

Communication Networks
Understanding the various methods through which communication is achieved

Consulting
Understanding the results that stakeholders desire from a process and providing insight into how they can best use their resources to achieve goals

Coping Skills
Dealing with ambiguity and stress resulting from conflicting information and goals; helping others deal with ambiguity and stress

Interpersonal Relationship Building
Effectively interacting with others to produce meaningful outcomes

Leadership Competencies

Buy-in/Advocacy
Building ownership and support for workplace initiatives

Diversity Awareness
Assessing the impact and appropriateness of interventions on individuals, groups, and organizations

Ethics Modeling
Modeling exemplary ethical behavior and understanding the implications of this responsibility

Goal Implementation
Ensuring that goals are converted into efficient actions; getting results despite conflicting priorities, lack of resources, or ambiguity

Group Dynamics
Assessing how groups of people function and evolve as they seek to meet the needs of their members and of the organization

Leadership
Leading, influencing, and coaching others to help them achieve desired results

Visioning
Seeing the possibilities of "what can be" and inspiring a shared sense of purpose within the organization

Table 5.2	Competencies for Workplace Learning and Performance Professionals (cont'd)

Technical Competencies

Adult Learning
Understanding how adults learn and how they use knowledge, skills, and attitudes

Facilitation
Helping others to discover new insights

Feedback
Providing performance information to the appropriate people

Intervention Monitoring
Tracking and coordinating interventions to assure consistency in implementation and alignment with organizational strategies

Questioning
Collecting data via pertinent questions asked during surveys, interviews, and focus groups for the purpose of performance analysis

Survey Design and Development
Creating survey approaches that use open-ended

(essay) and closed style questions (multiple choice and Likert items) for collecting data; preparing instru-

Technological Competencies

ments in written, verbal, or electronic formats

Computer-Mediated Communication
Understanding the implication of current and evolving computer-based electronic communication

Distance Education
Understanding the evolving trends in technology-supported delivery methods and the implications of separating instructors and learners in time and location

Electronic Performance Support Systems
Understanding current and evolving performance support systems and their appropriate applications

Technological Literacy
Understanding and appropriately applying existing, new, or emerging technology

Note. From Rothwell, Sanders, and Soper (1999, pp. 53–56). Reprinted with permission.

DACUM process, exemplary performers gathered in a group and discussed their daily tasks and responsibilities. A facilitator then organized the tasks into categories. The participants were given the opportunity to change the categories. During Phase II, a focus group was used to generate a list of exemplary behavioral statements for each task identified in Phase I. In Phase III the statements developed in Phase II were stripped of all identification and then reassigned to the areas of responsibility. If 70% of the participants assigned the statement to its original classification, the item was retained in its original classification. Phase IV involved the assignment of a scale to the statements by the focus groups. Finally, in Phase V, the focus groups placed the statements on the scale. The statements and scales were used to develop a self-assessment instrument for the directors and area representatives. The instrument was administered to 11 directors and 22 area representatives.

Cookson and English noted that the self-reported areas of lowest competence equated to the areas of proposed professional development among the group of directors and area representatives. The results of the competency self-assessment revealed that directors had low self-ratings in establishing relationships with prospective funding sources,

preparing funding sources, preparing funding proposals, obtaining financial support for public service programs, and developing job descriptions reflecting professional development needs. The area representatives rated themselves low in the competencies related to marketing and promotion, planning and implementing comprehensive marketing campaigns, preparing program brochures, building and managing project teams, coordinating course outlines for evening courses, and designing and maintaining tracking systems for certificate programs. A limitation cited by the researchers involved the duplication of this procedure. They noted that the creation of scales that unequivocally discriminate between levels of performance for all possible tasks was useful but also difficult and time-consuming.

One of the least studied aspects of the five major functions of the community college is community services/continuing education (Amunson & Ebbers, 1997), one function of the community college mission that appears to be experiencing growth in some colleges. A significant portion of the growth has been in economic development and contract training. These two areas have been included in the genre of community services because of the workforce training needs necessary for new or expanding business and industry (Maiuri, 1993).

In a dissertation study, Amunson (1993) attempted to identify the perceptions held by current directors of community services regarding the important competencies for success as community services/continuing education directors in the future. Amunson's (1993, p. 4) research questions included the following:

- What are the leadership competencies needed by community services/continuing education directors, as perceived by leading community services directors?
- What competencies are perceived to be the most important when rated by current community services/continuing education directors?
- What are the appropriate competency definitions identified by the community services/continuing education directors?
- Which competencies are perceived to be the most important for future community services/continuing education directors?

The methodology in this research involved a model used for competency identification created by Vaughan (1987) and Keller (1989). Respondents for this Delphi study were nominated by leaders of the National Council of Community Services and Continuing Education (NCCSCE). The leaders were asked to nominate representatives from each of NCCSCE's 10 geographical areas to establish a participant pool using the criteria of (a) leadership in the field of community services, (b) service to NCCSCE and its mission, and (c) service in their respective region. The three most frequently selected members were included in the pool. Each was contacted to determine his or her willingness to participate. Twenty-eight members agreed to be part of the study, which provided at least two representatives from each region.

Once chosen, the participants were asked to make modifications to the Keller (1989) presidential competencies model by deciding whether or not the competencies were appropriate, inappropriate, or appropriate with a suggested modification for community service directors. Next, revisions were made to the competency model. The revised questionnaire was then mailed to the 28 participants to judge the competency and to provide feedback about each definition. For each competency, participants were instructed to rate it as "extremely critical to possess," "very important but not absolutely essential," "would be nice to possess," or "not important." Revisions were made, and the questionnaire was mailed again. The researchers predetermined that 80% agreement on a response for each competency would be construed as consensus and, therefore, a fourth questionnaire was not required.

The results of the study indicated that the first round of responses determined that the presidential competencies identified by Keller (1989) were appropriate for community services/continuing education directors. Participants suggested additional competencies, definitions, and modifications specific to community services directors' duties. These new competencies included focus, collaboration, diversity, institutional change agent, and comprehensive organizational understanding. The second round of responses placed value on each of the competencies, with a consensus reached on four: collaboration, communication, decision making, and integrity. These four community services/continuing education competencies were identified as critical to director success in programming and working with the public. During this process, consensus was reached on 18 competencies and their definitions, 25 achieved some level of stability, and consensus or stability was not reached with five competencies.

A stability measurement is a method of mathematically analyzing the responses for each competency response so that stability or movement from the mode responses can be calculated. Amunson (1993) decided that "any competency that changed less than 15% was determined to have reached stability and that consensus was defined by 75% agreement on a response for each competency" (p. 46). Amunson (1993, pp. 112–115) presented the 18 competencies on which consensus was reached (consensus was defined as 80% agreement). These definitions appear in Table 5.3; the 25 competencies that reached stability—that is, those that were changed less than 15%—and their definitions are given in Table 5.4. The five competencies for which neither stability nor consensus was reached are given in Table 5.5. (All three tables appear at the end of the chapter.)

In conclusion, along with identifying the specific competencies, Amunson (1993, pp. 122–123) listed several other points emphasized in the study:

- The process used in this study identified competencies for a community college administrative group whose significance is often questioned on many campuses. More is now known about what competencies community services/continuing education personnel must possess to perform their duties.
- The process assists staff development experts in identifying educational activities that support community services professionals in the performance of their duties.
- The identified competencies will be useful in developing job or position descriptions for community services/continuing education directors.
- Prospective community services directors will have

an available list of competencies if they desire to develop the skills necessary for advancement.

- It is possible to use the Delphi process to identify competencies for cases in which existing literature and research on competencies for a specific group of professionals are not available.
- The Delphi process model used in a previous study could be modified for use with a different administrative group at a community college.
- The identified competencies provide parameters with which to structure staff development activities for community services/continuing education directors.
- Community college administrators have a selection of competencies that may be used in designing a position description for recruiting new community services/continuing education staff. Evaluation of candidate competencies during credential and interview assessments may be conducted using the competencies as a standard for selection.
- Curriculum specialists at universities that have graduate programs for community college professionals will have the competencies already identified when developing and designing future course objectives. Presidential competencies identified by Keller (1989) and community services/continuing education director competencies selected through this study provide a base for administrative competency enrichment for community college administrators.
- This study, along with the studies conducted by Vaughan (1987) and Keller (1989), confirms that there is a commonality of administrative competencies developed by a community services/continuing education director that can transfer to the community college presidency.

Another study was conducted to determine perceived professional competency levels needed and possessed by current community college workforce development professionals that lead to successful job performance (Gerity, 1999; King, 1998). A related purpose was to determine the perceived professional development needs necessary to build those competencies. An additional purpose was to analyze the relationships between professional competency levels needed and possessed by community college workforce development professionals and their perceived professional development needs. This study also showed respondents' perceptions about the importance of various work activities linked to the need for professional development.

A review was conducted of literature on community college workforce development professionals, community college continuing education competencies, and commu-

nity college workforce development programs. The review yielded little research on the unique competencies essential to success in community college workforce development. In a doctoral dissertation study conducted in 1993, Amunson provided a list of 50 competencies with definitions for community college community services/continuing education directors. Another competency study conducted at Penn State University in 1997 (Rothwell, 1997) also examined competencies of continuing education professionals in the university's continuing education system, including its two-year campuses. The competencies identified in these two studies served as the foundation for the study described here (i.e., Gerity 1999; King, 1998).

Data for the study were gathered for the assessment of perceived importance of professional competency levels that lead to job success and the perceived need for professional development through the use of a survey instrument. Likert scales were used for rating the importance of the particular competency and the need for professional development. Surveys were sent to all community colleges belonging to the American Association of Community Colleges (AACC). Both AACC and the National Council for Continuing Education and Training (NCCET) endorsed the study, and NCCET provided funding for it.

The essential competencies identified for community college workforce developers could generally be summarized into 14 categories:

1. Personal organization and office management
2. Communication skills
3. Internal relations
4. Program support
5. Financial management/budgeting
6. Client management and relations
7. Training/organizational development
8. External and community relations
9. Marketing and promotion
10. Programming
11. Recruiting, hiring, and orientation
12. Supervision and management
13. Leadership
14. Professional development

One version of the competency model appears in Appendix B in this volume. It can be used as a foundation for an individual assessment, as shown in Appendix C. Moreover, it can have further practical applications to guide on-the-job training of workforce developers through one-on-one training and coaching. Appendix E offers a checksheet designed to aid in that process.

CONCLUSION

Competency studies are eminently practical and can be used to guide all facets of human resources management—from work design through orientation, training, selection, rewards, appraisal, and more (see Dubois & Rothwell, 2003). Of course, no general competency model can be useful until tailored to the unique culture of an organization or the unique demands of a particular department, job category, or occupation. The same is true of the competency models described in this chapter. To be most useful, they must be tailored to the unique institutional setting of the community college and the workforce development organization.

Whenever college administrators set out to fill a workforce development vacancy, they face tough questions: What should workforce developers do, and what kind of people will be most successful as workforce developers? Defining competency can be difficult, but, as is argued in this chapter, it is important for people to care about workforce development competencies. Available research has made strides in helping to identify the competencies essential to success in the challenging field of community college workforce development. ❊

References

Al-Hamli, N. (2003). *An investigation of workplace learning and performance competencies and roles as perceived by HRD practitioners in the United Arab Emirates.* Unpublished master's thesis, Pennsylvania State University, University Park.

Amunson, D. A. (1993). *Community college community services/continuing education directors: Competencies needed for future leadership.* Unpublished doctoral dissertation, Iowa State University, Ames.

Amunson, D. A., & Ebbers, L. H. (1997). Community colleges, community services/continuing education directors: Competencies needed for future leadership. *Catalyst, 26,* 2, 3–7.

Andreyka, R. E. (1969). *A survey and analysis of the educational tasks of Ohio's post high school technical instructors: Implications for teaching education.* Unpublished doctoral dissertation, Kent State University, OH.

Ashton, C. (1996). How competencies boost performance. *Management Development Review, 9*(3), 14–19.

Balogh, S. P. (1982). A comparative study of business and industry trainers as adult learners. *Dissertation Abstracts International, 43.* (No. 2530-A-8300204).

Bohlander, G. W., Snell, S. A., & Sherman, A. (2000).

Managing human resources (11th ed.). Cincinnati, OH: South-Western College Publishing.

Campbell, A., & Luchs, K. S. (1997). *Core competency-based strategy.* Boston: International Thomson Business Press.

Chen, A. (2003). *Perceptions of Taiwan practitioners on expertise level and importance of workplace learning and performance (WLP) competencies.* Unpublished doctoral dissertation, Pennsylvania State University, University Park.

Christensen, P. A. (1976). *Competencies for technical education teachers.* Unpublished doctoral dissertation, Colorado State University, Fort Collins.

Competencies drive HR practices. (1996). *HR Focus, 73*(8), 15.

Cookson, P., & English, J. (1997). Continuing education program administration: A study of competent performance indicators. *Journal of Continuing Higher Education, 45*(2), 1–11.

Davie, L. E., Suessmuth, P., & Thomas, A. (1986). *A review of the literature and field validation of the competencies of industrial and organizational trainers and educators.* Toronto: Ontario Institute for Studies in Education.

Dessler, G. (2001). *A framework for human resource management* (2nd ed.). Englewood Cliffs, NJ: Prentice-Hall.

Dubois, D. (1993). *Competency-based performance improvement: A strategy for organizational change.* Amherst, MA: Human Resource Development Press.

Dubois, D. (Ed.). (1998). *The competency case book.* Amherst, MA: Human Resource Development Press.

Dubois, D., & Rothwell, W. J. (2000). *The competency toolkit* (Vols. 1–2). Amherst, MA: Human Resource Development Press.

Dubois, D., & Rothwell, W. J. (2003). *Competency-based human resource management.* Palo Alto, CA: Davies-Black.

Gerity, P. E. (1999). *A study to identify community college workforce training and development professionals' perceived competencies and their perceived professional development needs.* Unpublished doctoral dissertation, Pennsylvania State University, University Park.

Gilbert, T. (1978). *Human competence: Engineering worthy performance.* New York: McGraw-Hill.

Ginkel, K., Mulder, M., & Nijhof, W. (1994). *Role profiles of HRD professionals in the Netherlands.* Paper presented at the conference "Education and Training for Work." University of Twente, The Netherlands.

International Board of Standards for Training,

Performance, and Instruction. (1988). *Instructor competencies: The standards.* Evergreen, CO: Author.

Jeffords, R., Scheidt, M., & Thibadoux, G. (1997). Getting the best from staff. *Journal of Accountancy, 184*(3), 101–105.

Keller, L. (1989). Competencies of future community college presidents: Perception of selected community college presidents. *Dissertation Abstracts International,* 50, 8A. (University Microfilms No. 8925692).

King, M. (1998). *The relationship between community college education professionals' education and work experience and their professional development needs.* Unpublished doctoral dissertation, Pennsylvania State University, University Park.

Kochanski, J. (1997). Competency-based management. *Training & Development,* 51(10), 40–44.

Lado, A., & Wilson, M. (1994). Human resource systems and sustained competitive advantage: A competency-based perspective. *The Academy of Management Review, 19*(4), 699.

Langdon, D., & Marrelli, A. (2002, April). A new model for systematic competency identification. *Performance Improvement, 41*(4), 14–21.

Lee, S. (1994). *A preliminary study of the competencies, work outputs, and roles of human resource development professionals in the Republic of China on Taiwan: A cross-cultural competency study.* Unpublished doctoral dissertation, Pennsylvania State University, University Park.

Lucia, A., & Lepsinger, R. (1999). *The art and science of competency models: Pinpointing critical success factors in organizations.* San Francisco: Jossey-Bass.

Maiuri, G. (1993). Economic development: What is the community college's responsibility? *Community Services Catalyst, 23*(1), 7–8.

Marquardt, M., & Engel, D. (1993). HRD competencies for a shrinking world. *Training and Development, 47*(5), 59–65.

McCullough, R. C. (1987). Professional development. In R. L. Craig (Ed.), *Training and development handbook* (3rd ed., pp. 44–45). New York: McGraw-Hill.

McLagan, P., & McCullough, R. C. (1983). *Models for excellence.* Alexandria, VA: American Society for Training and Development.

Meade, J. (1998). A solution for competency-based employee development. *HR Magazine,* 43(13), 54–58.

National Center for Research in Vocational Education. (1975). *Performance-based post-secondary occupational teacher education.* Columbus, OH: Author.

Norton, R. E. (1997). *DACUM handbook* (2nd ed.). Columbus: Ohio State University, College of Education, Center on Education and Training for Employment.

Odenthal, L., & Nijhof, W. (1996). *HRD roles in Germany.* De Lier, The Netherlands: Academisch Boeken Centrum.

Ontario Society for Training and Development. (1979). *Competency analysis for trainers: A personal planning guide.* Toronto: Author.

Peerapornvitoon, M. (1999). *A survey of workplace learning and performance: Competencies and roles for practitioners in Thailand.* Unpublished doctoral dissertation, Pennsylvania State University, University Park.

Rijk, R., Mulder, M., & Nijhof, W. (1994). *Role profiles of HRD practitioners in 4 European countries.* A paper presented in Milan, Italy. Twente, Netherlands: University of Twente.

Rothwell, W. J. (1997). *A study of the professional competencies of continuing and distance education professionals on Penn State's branch campuses.* Unpublished manuscript, Pennsylvania State University, University Park.

Rothwell, W. J. (Ed.). (2000). *ASTD models for human performance improvement: Roles, competencies, outputs* (2nd ed.). Alexandria, VA: American Society for Training and Development.

Rothwell, W. J. (2002). *The workplace learner: How to align training initiatives with individual learning competencies.* New York: Amacom.

Rothwell, W. J. (2003). *The strategic development of talent.* Amherst, MA: Human Resource Development Press.

Rothwell, W. J., & Kazanas, H. C. (2003). *Mastering the instructional design process with CD-ROM: A systematic response* (3rd ed.). San Francisco: Jossey-Bass.

Rothwell, W. J., & Lindholm, J. (1999). Competency identification, modelling and assessment in the USA. *International Journal of Training and Development, 3*(2), 90–105.

Rothwell, W., Lindholm, J., & Wallick, W. (2003). *What CEOs expect from corporate training.* New York: Amacom.

Rothwell, W. J., Sanders, E., & Soper, J. (1999). *ASTD models for workplace learning and performance: Roles, competencies, outputs.* Alexandria, VA: American Society for Training and Development.

Shippmann, J., Ash, R., Battista, M., Carr, L., Eyde, L.,

Hesketh, B., Kehoe, J., Pearlman, K., Prien, E., & Sanchez, J. (2000). The practice of competency modeling. *Personnel Psychology, 52,* 703–740.

Spenser, L., & Spenser, S. (1993). *Competence at work.* New York: Wiley.

Stark, M., Valvano, S., & Luther, W. (1996). Jaguar cars drive toward competency-based pay. *Compensation and Benefits Review, 28*(6), 34–40.

Vaughan, G. (1987). Community services: Pathway to the presidency? *Community Service Catalyst, 17*(2), 3–10.

Weischadle, D. E. (1984). Teachers make excellent trainers. *Performance & Instruction, 23*(3), 22–24.

Yang, J. (1994). *Perceived competencies needed by HRD managers in Korea.* Unpublished doctoral dissertation, University of Minnesota, Minneapolis.

Yoo, J. (1999). *Korean human resource development (HRD) practitioners' perceptions of expertise level and importance of workplace learning and performance (WLP) competencies.* Unpublished doctoral dissertation, Pennsylvania State University, University Park.

You, S. (1993). *Perception of Korean human resource development practitioners toward selected roles and competency standards.* Unpublished doctoral dissertation, University of Maryland, College Park.

Table 5.3	Competencies With Definitions That Reached Consensus Among Community College Community Services/Continuing Education Directors

1. **Analysis**: The ability to identify relationships between variables, constraints, and premises that bear on a goal sought or the resolution of problem.

2. **Collaboration**: The ability to work jointly with others for the benefit of all parties involved, both inside and outside the college.

3. **Communication**: The ability to transfer information from one person or group to another person or group with the information being understood by both the sender and the receiver (includes speaking, writing, and listening skills).

4. **Creativity/Innovation**: The ability to introduce new concepts, ideas, and opportunities and to make changes, even with limited resources.

5. **Entrepreneurship**: The ability to see new opportunities, assume some risk, and initiate changes necessary to implement them.

6. **Focus**: The ability to function and manage multiple tasks.

7. **Institutional change agent**: The ability through collaboration to convert workforce standards and community needs to effect change in college curriculum and delivery systems.

8. **Integrity**: The ability to inspire trust in the veracity of your words and actions to be viewed as one who stands on principle and is devoted to what is right and just.

9. **Interpersonal skills**: The ability to interact effectively with others, both inside and outside the college.

10. **Judgment**: The ability to choose effectively among alternative courses of action (includes the ability and willingness to establish priorities).

11. **Leadership**: The ability to influence people so that they strive willingly and enthusiastically to help accomplish individual and institutional goals.

12. **Personnel selection**: The ability to attract and select quality people.

13. **Positive attitude**: The ability to be optimistic and to see positive aspects, even in apparently negative situations, and to communicate a positive attitude to others.

14. **Scholarly writing**: The ability to write for publication.

Table 5.3	Competencies With Definitions That Reached Consensus Among Community College Community Services/Continuing Education Directors (cont'd)

15. **Sense of responsibility**: The willingness and perceived willingness to assume responsibility for one's actions.

16. **Supervision**: The ability to monitor and evaluate the activities of subordinates and organization units to assure that institutional goals, objectives, and plans are being accomplished effectively.

17. **Visionary**: The ability to create and communicate visions of what should and can be.

18. **Decision making**: The ability to know when and when not to make a decision (includes the ability to gather, analyze, and synthesize the information necessary to make sound decisions).

Table 5.4	Competencies With Definitions That Reached Stability Among Community College Community Services/Continuing Education Directors

1. **Commitment**: The ability to demonstrate and communicate commitment to a course of action, principle, or institution.

2. **Comprehensive organizational understanding**: The ability to see beyond the boundaries of a continuing education program in the context of the total college.

3. **Conflict resolution**: The ability to resolve conflict by discussion and to reach consensus among individuals and groups.

4. **Delegation**: The ability to know when and when not to delegate, how to assign tasks, delegate authority, and hold people accountable.

5. **Diversity**: The ability to work with a population that is diverse racially, culturally, and gender-wise.

6. **Environmental balance/control**: The ability to control emotions and convey a sense of self-control even under extreme pressure.

7. **Empathy**: The ability to view circumstances from other perspectives while remaining objective.

8. **Finance/budgeting**: The ability to develop and administer budgets, acquire department operating funding, and formulate and prioritize future financial plans.

9. **Flexibility**: The ability to allow for change when the situation may call for it.

10. **Information processing**: The ability to develop and use formal and informal networks, find sources of accurate information, and evaluate information.

11. **Integrating**: The ability to coordinate and blend the various components of the community services department into a coherent whole (includes the ability to develop consensus among diverse groups).

12. **Introspection**: The ability to learn through self-examination of thoughts and feelings.

13. **Knowledge of and commitment to mission**: A thorough knowledge of the community services department mission and purposes, a commitment to that mission, and the ability to communicate the department's mission and purposes to various constituents.

14. **Motivation**: The ability to motivate individuals and/or groups to work toward goal attainment.

15. **Organizing**: The ability to establish department structure (policies, procedures, position descriptions, and others), group activities necessary to accomplish objectives, and coordinate horizontally and vertically within the organization.

Table 5.4	Competencies With Definitions That Reached Stability Among Community College Community Services/Continuing Education Directors (cont'd)

16. **Patience**: The ability to maintain composure and self-control while waiting (includes tolerance for ambiguity).

17. **Performance appraisal**: The ability to establish subordinate performance expectations and provide counseling for improved subordinate performance.

18. **Persistence**: The ability to persevere—to keep going even against continued resistance or change of direction.

19. **Planning**: The ability to establish short- and long-term goals and objectives and to develop strategies, policies, programs, and procedures to achieve or change them as circumstances warrant.

20. **Public relations**: The ability to convey information about all college aspects to external and internal audiences, including students, faculty and staff, community, and other special interest groups.

21. **Risk taking**: The ability to make an assessment and take a chance, including the ability to cope with pressure from within and outside the organization.

22. **Sense of humor**: The ability to see the humor in a situation (includes the ability and willingness to laugh at oneself).

23. **Time management**: The ability to manage self and responsibilities within the context of everyday life.

24. **Use of power**: The ability to influence the beliefs or actions of other persons or groups (includes knowing when and when not to use authority).

25. **Wellness**: The ability to maintain psychological and mental well-being, including the ability to separate personal life from professional obligations so that fatigue can be avoided and health and personal life maintained.

Table 5.5	Competencies That Reached Neither Consensus nor Stability Among Community College Community Services/Continuing Education Directors

1. **Charisma**: The unique personality traits and characteristics that make an individual capable of securing others' allegiance and cooperation.

2. **Energy**: The ability to maintain vigor and vitality in accomplishing routine tasks or new challenges.

3. **Peer networking**: The ability to enter into and effectively maintain relationships with other department heads and state, regional, and national persons (includes knowing how to develop contacts, how to build and maintain networks, and how to communicate on a formal and an informal basis).

4. **Professionalism**: The ability to keep up to date on issues relevant to job, personal growth, and development.

5. **Research**: Understanding the value of institutional research and having the ability to use the college research function.

CHAPTER 6

Building Community Partnerships for Workforce Development

Mary Gershwin

Workforce development has become a central concern for employers, employer organizations, elected officials, community-based organizations, and labor unions. Community colleges have begun to bring these diverse stakeholders together, demonstrating the potential to increase the level of skills available throughout a community. Many community colleges boast impressive programs, meeting the needs of employers and local communities, as well as increasing the economic opportunities for their graduates. Forming new alliances is not without risk for the community college leader, however. Interorganizational workforce partnerships create alliances with implications for many people. These bonds can bring about unwanted commitments, new pride of association, increased knowledge, new opportunities for learning, and unforeseen chances for growth. From the outset, building partnerships on behalf of a community college means exercising responsibility and engagement.

How do community college leaders navigate the barriers to building partnerships that can produce successful workforce development programs? How do they transform unorganized and fragmented collections of stakeholders into partners who produce change? How do they avoid the messy entanglements that can derail success? In this chapter I offer insight regarding how to harness the potential that lies in stakeholder groups and how to avoid the pitfalls of unproductive attempts at collaboration.

CREATING PRODUCTIVE COLLABORATION

Creating outstanding achievements in workforce development requires people from diverse organizations to come together, determine a shared vision, allocate resources to bring that vision to life, and define roles and accountability to get the work done. In this situation no single organization has the authority to tell everyone else what to do, which can necessitate significant shifts in the perspectives of those involved. Most organizations are accustomed to goals being established in the context of existing accountability structures; these structures are not typically in place when organizations join for a collaborative initiative. Over the course of building meaningful outcomes, participants in an alliance must negotiate both the priorities that will be addressed and the processes by which decisions will be made. It can be messy work, to say the least. Most people and organizations would probably pass on such collaborations if they were not economic imperatives.

The workforce development problem is complex, and it can only be solved by weaving together the needs, interests, and resources of many organizations and people. Fortunately, innovative community college leaders are managing to induce people to work together in this unstructured and unfolding process, drawing the finest efforts and support from each organization. There are three steps for paving the way to a successful community alliance for workforce development: being accountable to the community college, learning the interests of participating organizations, and developing the skill to overcome challenges. Successful collaborators know how to harness the power of their community colleges while remaining engaged with the overall vision. They create powerful partnerships through these steps, overcoming the pitfalls of traditional approaches to partnering.

Step One: Be Accountable to the Community College

Those who effectively bring to bear the power of their community college build strong workforce development partnerships. Research reveals that the best partnership builders do so with a clear understanding of what matters to their college. Unlike civic initiatives driven by individuals who are investing their personal time, workforce development initiatives are normally driven by people who are being paid by an organization.

Workforce development investments are unfolding in a competitive environment; dozens of worthwhile initiatives are competing for the resources of organizations. Successful college leaders are selective in the workforce development partnerships they pursue. They acknowledge that their organization is courted by many offers for collaborative action, such as arts initiatives, environmental initiatives, safety initiatives, and the like. Productive collaborators know the needs of their college, drawing on available resources without pushing them beyond what they can deliver.

What does this process look like in action? One successful college leader describes his approach to the process of committing his organization as such: "Every document I ever write is written with me thinking, 'How would this look in the newspapers?' I'm just careful about exposing my college. I'm never inflammatory. I choose my words carefully."

Consider a few key questions that can serve to protect and promote the interests of your college:

- Is there an important benefit for my employer—a potential to be realized—that justifies my involvement with this group of stakeholders?
- Can I anticipate where this partnership could create risks for my college?
- Can I identify the resources my college can bring to the success of this initiative?
- Can I identify champions within my college who will help engage the commitment of my organization in the success of this venture?

Step Two: Learn the Interests of Participating Organizations

Several years ago, I studied a workforce development policy aimed at forming an alliance among participants from business, government, education, and employer organizations. The group met for several months and finally focused on a plan to seek additional state funding for adult education. Once this goal was established, the individual interests of the organizations around the table became obvious. Two education agencies began to lobby for positions as administrators of new dollars. Maintaining authority over the administration of programs was the dominant interest of one organization. The alliance quickly deteriorated into a parochial squabble as participants from each interest group vied for their own benefits.

Experienced college leaders understand that collaborative initiatives will create new threats as they produce change. Successful collaborators learn as much as they can about others. (See Example on the next page for a model worksheet that can be used to plan a collaborative process that clarifies key issues for different stakeholders.) The process of getting to know the others in a group takes time, and it can be easy to misjudge intentions. The participants involved are rarely willing to simply lay their cards on the table; we must go through a slow and subtle process to learn who is serious, who seems to have resources, and who could pose a high risk. Outstanding college leaders possess a set of flexible strategies that can speed up the collaborative process. The best collaborators tend to engage in the following common practices as they build relationships across organizations.

Focus on understanding partners, not critiquing them. Successful collaborators seek first to understand other organizations and the individuals that represent them. As one experienced collaborator put it, "A very good example of destructive partnering is the educator who critiques the business partner…well, then they become immediately defensive…so we have this standoff. They aren't doing it our way, so they aren't very efficient. This posturing goes on, and soon, I'm defending my way and critiquing yours."

Teach others to work with your organization. Successful college leaders share the information necessary to making relationships work, including the goals of their colleges, priorities of leadership, and information about their roles within the organization. They provide this information in an honest way that justifies and enhances mutual trust. Most successful college workforce leaders understand that the collaborative process requires patience and, most of all, a commitment to the long-term partnership.

Expect to learn new languages to build solutions. The learning process involves paying close attention to language. It is important to learn the functional meanings of expressions laden with significance, such as "the board." Successful college leaders also attend to details of language by noting "the little things," such as preferences for titles or first names, the correct names of organizations, and the names of key leaders within partnering organizations.

Example: Worksheet for Planning the Collaborative Process				
Question	**Community College**	**Trade Association**	**Chamber**	**Employer 1**
What is the primary business of the organization?				
How is the organization funded?				
What benefits might this organization gain from the alliance?				
What risks might threaten this organization?				
What resources might this organization have?				
What champions (leaders at higher levels) might this organization engage?				

Engage external forces for mutual gain. Finding others to speak effectively on behalf of an issue is sometimes required of collaborators. Leaders understand that meaning is constructed not only by the content of a message but also by who carries it. For example, in communicating with key legislators, one partnership engaged community leaders from targeted legislative districts to build legislative support. Another partnership, focused on improving workforce opportunities for older workers, engaged a respected individual from the local community to lead the dialogue.

Remain sensitive to the different stages of collaborative development. The process of creating common sets of knowledge on issues is a fragile one. New members with limited knowledge require time to learn the issues and the process. This frequently requires knowledgeable members to go slow in developing solutions, bringing newer members up to speed at a reasonable pace.

Scout the territory and keep "bait on the water." Successful leaders characterize the process of building support as one of scouting out hidden assets in their communities. Rather than attempting to create new structures for workforce development, these agents seek to connect with what is already working. As one leader said, "Don't look

for what your community needs. Look at what it has—your assets. Find the associations that are out there and organized already." Workforce development leaders in a community college constantly bring workforce development opportunities back to their organization, "casting bait on the water." Rather than insisting that a college respond to each opportunity, they invite members to explore them in a nonthreatening way. By using e-mail to post opportunities on an ongoing basis, they keep workforce development innovation in front of their organization and open the door to participation.

Step Three: Develop the Skills to Overcome Challenges

Active workforce development collaboration takes place when college leaders develop mechanisms for achieving real value from partnerships. Successful workforce partners understand that breakdown and burnout are ongoing threats. Effective partners anticipate common barriers to partnership, which helps them build solutions as they move forward. Partnerships cite two common causes for failure: problems with the goal and problems with the process.

Goal-related challenges. Mediocre workforce development initiatives are often plagued by noncommittal goal statements, such as "to be leaders in workforce development." In contrast, successful initiatives engender commitment because their outcomes are clear. *Goal clarity* implies a specific performance objective, phrased in concrete language so that it is possible to tell whether the objective has been attained. Experts on the collaborative process often use the Apollo moon project as an example of goal clarity. By committing to "placing a man on the moon by the end of the 1960s," the leaders of the mission took a clear stand.

Lack of compelling goals. Strong partnerships for workforce development are characterized by their compelling, noble, and worthwhile goals. Members can point to real, substantive ways that communities will improve as a result of the work of the partnership. Loss of focus or concentration on elevating goals can stem from various causes, the most common of which are the following:

- Partnership members start worrying less about achieving goals and more about who is getting the credit.
- Members lose focus on problem solving and become embroiled in questions of who is in charge.

Unclear consequences. What difference would it make if your workforce development partnership disappeared tomorrow? How would its demise affect your college, the community, its businesses, and its families? The strongest partnerships have a clear, shared sense of how they are adding value.

Short-term objectives with long-term goals. Short-term goals are critical to sustaining momentum in partnerships. The goals of most collaborative initiatives are long term, but incremental objectives are especially important in maintaining focus and keeping members at the table. The goal clarity exercise at the end of the chapter can be useful in situations in which goals are the primary problem.

Process-related challenges. People involved in a partnership must be able to keep the process moving. The following are a few process guidelines for college leaders working in community workforce partnerships.

- Look for opportunities to play the role of facilitator when necessary rather than acting solely as an advocate of your college's particular position. By bringing the needs, interests, conflicts, and concerns of others to the surface, you can help to advance the work as a whole.
- Create forums for top leaders to come together. Leaders should not form an alliance and then leave its nurtur-

ing to others. When top executives of a partnership are in contact, they hear about joint opportunities, find ways to turn information into shared benefits, and increase the chances that the partnership will evolve in a complementary rather than competitive direction. If top leaders fail to sustain their shared work, then staff members charged with implementing collaborative workforce projects should work on ways to keep the leaders engaged, keeping top support visible.

- It is important to remember that partners come together on their own timetable. Differences in expectations regarding the pace of a venture are a common source of conflict. Effective collaborators understand that managing the partnership process is a subtle dance between pushing for outcomes and allowing partners to go slow enough to build broad-based support.
- Be ready to give more than you get. Workforce partnerships are not cold-blooded alliances based on impersonal exchanges; rather, they depend on the creation and maintenance of a comfortable, trusting relationship. Being ready to give contributes to a growing, future-oriented focus.
- Be generous in sharing the credit. Partnerships can produce exciting victories. How a partnership deals with success can lay the foundation for future work, or—when one partner hogs the credit—destroy the potential for it. Disputes regarding credit destroy a project's potential for success and can stain the reputation of the organization for future partnering work.
- Assist in integrating new players into the partnership. The best workforce development alliances are living, growing organisms, open to new ideas and new members. Unfortunately, old players in a partnership often fear new ones. When new members are integrated smoothly into a partnership, the overall workforce effort will remain creative and vital.

CONCLUSION

In the current climate of economic growth and prosperity, community colleges possess rare opportunities to solve workforce challenges and create new collaborative capacity. They can use this time to improve the quality of the workforce, expand new opportunities for underskilled workers, and increase the competitive abilities of employees. Working together—across business, government, education, and community-based organizations—requires an alignment of diverse, sometimes competing interests. It is undoubtedly difficult work, but the implications of successful collaboration are profound. ❊

Example: Goal Clarity Exercise

State the goal of the workforce partnership:

Assess your partnership's goal by responding to the statements below to rate the goal for its clarity, compelling appeal, member engagement, defined consequences, and presence of short-term objectives.

1. The goal is clear: There is a clearly defined need—a goal to be achieved or purpose to be served—which justifies the existence of our partnership.

    True   False
    1   2   3   4

2. The goal is compelling: Our purpose is noble and worthwhile.

    True   False
    1   2   3   4

3. The goal is not politicized: Our members are more concerned about achieving the goal than getting the credit.

    True   False
    1   2   3   4

4. The consequences of our work are defined: There are clear consequences connected with our partnership's success or failure in achieving our goal.

    True   False
    1   2   3   4

5. We have short-term objectives: We have established short-term objectives on the road to larger goals.

    True   False
    1   2   3   4

Marketing Workforce Development Organizations

Paul Pierpoint

—————●————————————————————————————————————●—————

Not too long ago, mentioning the word *marketing* in relation to a college or university's interaction with its environment was considered worse than anti-academic—it was crass. Things have changed, however. *Marketing* has not been a bad word on most college campuses for at least a generation. As the world became more competitive, colleges began to expand their services beyond traditional 18- to 22-year-old residential students. Academic institutions could no longer afford to wait passively for the best and the brightest to come knocking at the door of the admissions office.

Current college leaders will not be heard proclaiming that higher learning is above the proletarian work of advertising, sales, and customer focus groups. In fact, college and university leaders across the country have become quite comfortable with marketing. Phrases such as *product positioning, discount pricing, psychographic market segmentation, multiple target marketing,* and *image promotion* versus *product promotion* are regularly heard in college meeting rooms. Some particularly progressive institutions have even gone so far as to accept the idea that students are customers. That is an alarming concept for traditional academics, but it is a powerful concept for those engaged in attracting and retaining paying students.

Over the last few decades, workforce development has similarly evolved from a minor auxiliary enterprise at a few colleges and universities into a central part of the missions of most institutions of higher learning. The combined energies of these two developments in higher education—aggressive participation in marketing and promotion and a strong commitment to workforce development—have pushed many colleges and universities

beyond the traditional limitations of the academy. These institutions have consequently found themselves in the rough-and-tumble world of business.

I cannot fully address all aspects of marketing workforce development programs and services in this chapter, but there are many basic textbooks that provide a solid foundation for comprehensive marketing strategies. All of them cover the "Four P's" (product, promotion, place, and price) and provide strong research bases for marketing concepts and practices. What I can discuss is the specific application of basic marketing concepts to the unique challenges faced by workforce development programs. I will address product, price, and place only peripherally. My primary focus is on the promotion of workforce development services.

IT'S NOT WHAT YOU'RE SELLING: IT'S WHAT THEY'RE BUYING

In their classic textbook *Principles of Marketing,* Kotler and Armstrong (2003) discuss the historical evolution of marketing from product-oriented to sales-oriented to market-oriented. Workforce development marketing in a competitive environment needs to be market-oriented, beginning with how product is defined. Workforce professionals who think their job is to sell training do not understand what their real product is. They are stuck in an obsolete product- or selling-oriented mindset.

From the potential client's perspective, the product of workforce development is not training. For the employer, the product may be performance improvement; for the government agency, reduced unemployment; for the individual, placement in a secure job. All of these could involve training, but it is possible that none of them would. Chapter 8, on consultative sales, develops the concept that an institution's real product is not the services it creates and provides but rather the benefits that its customers seek.

PRICE: WHEN EVEN "FREE" IS TOO EXPENSIVE

Like product, price is best defined in terms of the client's perspective. In one state, a workforce development program provides free training money to manufacturing and technology-related employers across the commonwealth. This program means that the price of training is zero for many employers, yet millions of dollars go unused every year. Why? One reason is that the largest cost of training is not the price paid to the provider—it is the cost of taking employees away from their work for hours, or even days, to receive training. This cost is even higher than that of the wages paid to employees while they attend training. Quite simply, many employers cannot afford free training.

Institutions that rely on offering the lowest price as their edge in competing for training business are failing to understand the real value of their product. Although many institutions can discount their prices because of public subsidies, significant discounts may not gain greater market share and may actually damage the marketability of the institution's services. Employers are generally less price sensitive than they are cost sensitive and will pay more for a service that minimizes peripheral expenses. For the most part, it is the perceived value of services, in terms of performance improvement, that determines the price an employer is willing to pay. Not surprisingly, the price of a service has much to do with its perceived value. Low-priced services are often perceived as low impact—and high-priced ones as high impact.

An institution that is confident in its ability to effect substantive performance improvement for the client should price its services accordingly. This does not mean, of course, that clients are not price conscious. The challenge for the training provider is to minimize the *total cost* for the employer while maximizing the total benefit. Training programs and delivery systems that ensure maximum effectiveness and minimum time away from work will earn a considerable premium. Without these factors, no price will be low enough to make the product marketable in the long run.

A MARKETING OPPORTUNITY: PRICING FOR NONPROFITS

Community service is part of the mission of most workforce development institutions. This means that they are sometimes expected to provide training or other services to community-based nonprofit organizations at prices well below normal. This is not only a valuable contribution to the community, but it can also be a powerful promotional tool for the college. Progressive colleges think of their work with nonprofits as a key component of workforce development marketing. They frequently provide training for nonprofit organizations or facilitate planning retreats for their boards of directors, at prices up to 90% below standard rates.

The investment pays back quickly. Many community and business leaders—people who can influence training decisions in organizations with the resources to pay for quality services—sit on the boards of nonprofits. When discounting services for nonprofits, a college administrator is wise to indicate the full cost (what businesses would be charged) on the invoice and then indicate the discount. This communicates the real price of the program as well as indicating the college's commitment to community service. Put simply, it is wise to use nonprofit clients to demonstrate the college's training capabilities to key decision makers in other organizations. It is smart marketing and good community service, and it makes influential friends.

MY PLACE OR YOURS?

"Anytime, anywhere" training with "a minimum class size of one" is the approach of many training providers. Allowing clients access to training at their convenience speaks to the rapidly emerging distance-delivery market. Progressive workforce development institutions are already invested in Internet-delivered training, developing their own online programs, or brokering the online courses of other organizations. Distance delivery is a tool every workforce development institution should have in its armory, but it is not enough to meet the location needs of most workforce development clients.

Most people still prefer to participate in training delivered in a structured classroom or lab setting. The training provider that can deliver in locations beyond its campus, and at times outside of regular university work hours, gains a significant competitive advantage. Some training is easily portable, especially "soft" training that is not equipment-dependent. The more readily transportable a particular kind of training is, the more competition there will be in the marketplace. A major competitive advantage can be achieved by delivering specialized equipment-dependent training to locations away from campus.

In 2001, Northampton Community College in Bethlehem, Pennsylvania, decided that the biggest market for its advanced technology industrial maintenance programs was too far from campus to use its existing labs. The college invested in a truck and portable equipment and began to deliver specialized training to manufacturers that were formerly too far away to serve. As a result, the technical training program nearly doubled the excess revenue it generated for the institution in the first year. Although many colleges may not be able to invest in portable electromechanical maintenance equipment, many institutions do have portable computer training labs. Considering that the demand for most computer training is in a long and steady decline, portability can help maintain profitability.

Of course, institutions must also pay attention to their on-campus facilities. Clients coming to campus will judge the quality of the training at least in part by the appearance of the buildings and rooms, the comfort of the furniture, the quality of the lunch, the reliability of the instructional equipment, and even the cleanliness of the restrooms. Although seemingly trivial, all of these things can say a great deal about the professionalism and quality of an organization's programs.

PROMOTION: MUCH MORE THAN JUST ADVERTISING AND SLICK BROCHURES

If an institution designs its services to meet the needs of its clients, prices its products appropriately, and delivers high-quality service where and when the client desires, it will still have a difficult time attracting business without investing in effective promotion practices. Potential clients need to know what an organization has to offer, and they need to be able to learn it with very little effort. The purchase decision-making process for most clients is typically energy conserving and risk averse. In other words, clients do not want to spend more energy than necessary to make a relatively safe purchase decision. This presents two primary challenges for the workforce development marketer: (a) how to get the message out so that it is received and understood and (b) how to ensure that the message will establish credibility with the client.

Promoting workforce development differs from other college marketing in terms of target market, customer expectations, funding, competition, relative flexibility from academic processes, and various other factors. Realistically, it is closer to corporate marketing than to educational marketing. Most institutional marketing is image promotion, with an occasional special event or other isolated purpose (such as fund raising). Workforce development marketing can and should include some institutional image marketing, but it needs to focus on specific programs and services and the benefits to be derived from them. Institutional image on its own is not enough to market workforce development effectively to businesses and individuals. Customers must feel secure with the organization that is providing services, but the details of what is taught, times and locations available, and modalities used in training can be more important to the purchase decision than image is.

Community colleges in particular are in a strange situation when it comes to image marketing. For some target segments of the market, such as executive leadership development or advanced technologies, community colleges are often perceived as academically insufficient. Clients may wonder, "What can a community college teach to a senior executive with an MBA and a law degree, or to a materials engineer with an advanced degree from a prestigious university?" Conversely, community colleges can be perceived as too academic by some sectors of the market: "What can a community college teach to a senior maintenance technician with 25 years of experience maintaining automated manufacturing technology? Or to a welder who is certified in 12 different welding techniques?" When such target groups hear the word "college," they often envision ivy-covered walls and stuffy professors. When credibility is low due to preconceived notions about what a training provider is or can do, few promotional efforts will succeed.

How does an organization overcome this credibility gap? For most community colleges, the best way is through patient, consistent, relationship building. The colleges are not going anywhere. They will remain part of their communities for years. If they do not enjoy sufficient credibility with their desired market today, it is never too late to begin building it.

Every workforce development professional interviewed for this chapter indicated that one of the most important factors (and usually *the* most important one) in the success of their organizations is credibility. Creating confidence in clients' minds that the institution is the most appropriate provider of workforce development services should be the primary goal of any workforce development marketer. Specific ways of building confidence vary greatly, but the backbone of the process is simple: Promise only what you can deliver, and deliver everything you promise, every time. Start small if necessary. Begin by promoting training areas in which the institution has or can develop very strong competence. If the institution already has a comprehensive set of demonstrated capabilities, colleges have found numerous ways to help potential clients learn about it.

The Center for Applied Competitive Technologies

(CACT) at DeAnza College in Sunnyvale, California, enjoys strong credibility across its service region. Paullette Young, director of CACT, attributes much of the center's success to its close partnerships with many business and professional associations. Center staff regularly speak at meetings of professional societies, and the center cosponsors workshops and seminars:

> We tell them, "We will offer a workshop on your behalf and list you as co-sponsor. You choose the topic of interest to your members—say, Root Cause Analysis for an American Society for Quality chapter, or Lean Manufacturing for the local SME [small and medium-sized enterprise]—we'll bring a trainer to your dinner to speak about the topic, then present a one- or two-day workshop on it for interested members." We split the proceeds with the association. That way they serve their membership and strengthen the association's budget, and we get to work with a dozen or two potential new clients. (P. Young, personal communication, 2003)

Partnerships with associations have been the most effective promotional tool the center has, Young said. Companies get an opportunity to see what the center can bring to their organizations at a very low cost. Young added that most professional associations are eager to find speakers with a relevant message for their programs.

BRANDING: MARKETING THE ORGANIZATION, NOT JUST ITS SERVICES

In some cases, close association with a college can reduce credibility or cause confusion among potential workforce development clients. Many workforce organizations have created separate identities that are promoted in conjunction with the college name or, in many cases, completely independent of it. Branding is a powerful marketing concept that goes well beyond differentiating the workforce development arm of a college from the rest of the institution.

A "college" may be too academic, or not academic enough, and can actually decrease the credibility of a workforce development organization. One very successful example of a separately branded workforce development unit is the Pacific Center for Advanced Technology (PCAT) at Honolulu Community College. Don Bourassa, director of PCAT, recognized early in the center's development that to gain credibility in the higher-end advanced technology training market throughout the Pacific Rim, the center needed an identity that was separate from the college. "I was shameless in promoting the PCAT brand," Bourassa said. "We used the PCAT name and logo in all of our advertisements in the major magazines and journals that serve our target market" (personal communication, 2003). Today, Honolulu Community College is one of the leading information technology training institutions on the Pacific Rim, but most of its clients know their training provider as PCAT.

Similar branding efforts exist at most colleges that are leaders in workforce development. Branding allows the institution to establish an individual identity for its workforce development unit, and it can also help customers make their purchase decisions. If the organization is successful in establishing awareness of its brand in the marketplace, and if customers associate the brand with high quality and effective training, then introduction of new training services is far easier. The brand will convey credibility and give new programs stronger recognition among potential customers. That, of course, is the reason that large corporations guard their brands so diligently— positive brand recognition is one of the most valuable assets any business can have. Workforce development units in colleges need to be vigilant about how their brands are used and attentive to what the marketplace thinks of them. A strong brand with high credibility opens doors to potential clients. A weak brand or, worse, a recognized brand with a weak reputation, will close doors.

DIRECT SELLING

In many academically based workforce development organizations, the only direct selling is performed by program managers and faculty. A growing number of colleges employ full-time professionals whose primary responsibility could be classified as "selling." Regardless of who is actually having face-to-face discussions with potential clients, effective personal selling is an essential part of any successful workforce development marketing effort. A critical element in workforce development selling for academic institutions is keeping the focus on long-term customer relationships, not short-term sales revenue. A comprehensive marketing approach includes direct selling.

Relationships are not established between organizations; they are established between people. To say that a college has a good relationship with a large local manufacturer understates the real essence of the relationship. Of course, the successful salesperson is more than a friendly ambassador. Product knowledge and an understanding of the customer's needs are part of the credibility challenge that every aspect of marketing must address.

The salesperson needs to know the capabilities—and limitations—of the training organization he or she represents. "We can do that" sounds great to the potential client, and it becomes a ready response for the salesperson, but if the organization *cannot* do that, future credibility is placed at risk. Knowing when to say, "We can't do that, but you may want to try this other training provider—a competitor of ours…." can be a powerful way to forge a trusting relationship with the client.

For most sales processes, a formal proposal will eventually be required to close the deal. A standardized proposal format is very helpful. Learning Resources Network's (LERN) report, *Writing Proposals for Contract Training*, is an excellent handbook for workforce development sales professionals (McBride, 1993). It offers very concrete instructions for creating effective training proposals as the result of selling activity or in response to a request for proposals.

PUBLICITY

The public information office at a college can be more important to establishing the college's reputation than the marketing department. This office can aid in keeping the workforce development unit and the college in the local news. Everything from weekly press releases about upcoming classes to carefully courted feature articles on special successes at the college can be invaluable. If an institution does not have a public information office, various handbooks and professional continuing education organizations, such as LERN and the National Council of Continuing Education and Training, can help the workforce development administrator in designing effective press releases.

Another way to gain publicity (and credibility) for workforce development programs is to get into the local business reporter's Rolodex as an "expert source." Reporters need knowledgeable and articulate sources they can call for clarifying quotes about current events. When the issues involve workforce development, economic development, or related concerns, the local college workforce development director should be one of the people reporters call for an interview.

Finally, do not ignore the power of the rubber-chicken circuit. Getting on the speakers' list for local service organizations such as the Kiwanis or Lions Clubs, local chambers of commerce, professional associations, and other organizations that host speakers is a great way to promote programs and services. Offer to talk about issues other than the college's specific programs. Workforce issues and their impact on economic development are of great interest to many people. This can become a logical platform for introducing some of the things a college is doing to improve the workforce—without engaging in a pure sales pitch.

PERMISSION MARKETING

E-mail and faxes are low-cost ways to send marketing information to potential clients, but because they are inexpensive, they are overused to the point that the messages are nuisances. Ask Internet users what they like least about e-mail, and most will say "spam." Organizations that develop their e-mail distribution lists by obtaining permission from the receiver first, however, can build an effective communication channel. Godin (1999) coined the term *permission marketing* and published a hugely successful book by that name. Godin describes in detail how an organization can use direct electronic communication channels not only to communicate with customers, but also to build stronger relationships with them. Permission marketers use every opportunity to ask for potential clients' e-mail addresses and fax numbers—and secure permission to use them.

The most effective marketers use this permission very judiciously. They send messages often enough to maintain a top-of-mind recall but not so often that messages are deleted or ignored. In these all-too-common cases, the marketer trains the customer to expect irrelevant, self-serving messages. The goal is to send messages that are interesting enough that they are likely to be opened and given at least a cursory look. Smart marketers do not just send messages that focus on selling training. They send messages about relevant developments in workforce development funding opportunities, interesting articles, new regulations, recent court decisions, and other items that may be of value to the reader. They make the messages valuable to the receiver so that those messages are likely to be read.

FEED THEM AND THEY WILL COME: INFORMATION SESSIONS

The information that a client needs to fully understand a program is often too complex to communicate effectively by traditional promotional methods. It may require a tour of training facilities, structured presentations by college staff members, or other activities best delivered to a "captured" audience. Information sessions, especially breakfast sessions, are a common marketing tool for workforce development organizations. Whether invitation-only or publicly advertised, information sessions with any number of potential clients can be very effective if the attendees are treated well, the food is good, and the message is relevant.

REPEAT BUSINESS

Keeping good customers is more important than attracting new ones. Repeat business is the best business, so building long-term trusting relationships is central to any good marketing effort. The retention of business begins even before the first deal with a new client is closed. Before signing the first contract, it is useful to ensure that the client is committed to training over the long run. Ken "Chip" Patton, former director of the Center for Professional Development at Glendale Community College, stated that his institution has enjoyed over 70% repeat business year-to-year, with an annual corporate client list of over 300 employers. One of the keys to attaining this level of customer loyalty is being selective in the choice of customers in the first place. Patton continued:

> California had a program to provide free training funds to small manufacturers. We were very active in the program but too many companies came to us because they saw the word "free." We required the top people in any interested company to attend a Saturday information session about the program. We figured if they wouldn't commit one Saturday to this, they were unlikely to commit to using the funds effectively. It worked beautifully. We had strong commitment from top management and ended up with very strong relationships that meant we were the training provider of choice even when public funds weren't involved. (K. Patton, personal communication, 2003)

Programs should select clients that have a commitment to developing the skills of their employees. It is the first step toward establishing a long-term relationship, and it creates a stable base for repeat business.

Glendale's pre-contract orientation was only part of its effort to maintain repeat business. "The state regulations concerning the money meant employers were responsible if someone did not complete the training or left the employer," Patton said. "The College was able to eat that cost for our good clients and, of course, that made them even more loyal. Take care of the customer and the long-run returns will be terrific." An important way to generate repeat business is to remember to thank clients for their patronage. Northampton Community College hosts a "Client Appreciation Dinner" every two

years. It invites over a hundred of its best clients to an evening of fine dining just to thank them for the confidence they have placed in the college. The cost can easily exceed $5,000, but it has proven highly effective in generating overall business, repaying the investment in a matter of days.

THE CORPORATE COLLEGE

In a growing number of cases around the country, relationships between workforce development providers and their customers have resulted in a merger of sorts. Employers have entrusted their local community colleges with basically all aspects of the training function of the company. The "corporate college" is the logical result of a college and an employer working closely together for a long time as training partners. At Gateway Technical College in Kenosha, Wisconsin, a large local manufacturer had enjoyed a long and successful partnership with the college and eventually asked the college to become the training department of the company. Pat Flanagan, vice president and provost of Gateway's Open Learning Campus, obtained approval from the state to have the employer's facility certified as a campus. This has allowed the college to provide a full array of credit career-ladder programs that lead to degrees. Gateway has full-time employees housed permanently at the employer's facility. According to Flanagan (personal communication, 2003), "The partnership has been so successful that it was recently presented with the state's Workforce Development Bellwether Award." Corporate colleges are not for every employer or every workforce development provider, but they do signify the growth that can stem from careful nurturing of customer relations.

THE WEB PAGE IN MARKETING

Institutions are increasingly giving their Web sites a major role in marketing their programs and services. John Vukich (personal communication, 2003), manager of the Gorsich Advanced Technology Center at Pueblo Community College, offered his experience on turning a Web site into a helpful marketing tool:

> We use the Web for marketing our programs via a comprehensive Web site with metafiles and tag words to move us up the food chain when someone does a search for technical training. We also pay a fee to search engine companies that gets us on the first four or five pages of searches. We've had hits from Alaska, the East Coast, other southwestern states, etc.—several

of which we've provided training to. Some have traveled here; some we've traveled to depending on their needs and how many people are to be trained.

Web sites are passive, so it is critical to use advertising and public information messages to drive potential clients toward a site. Links that take users directly to the most relevant page—usually *not* the institution's home page—are the most effective. Of course, a site must be user-friendly and communicate the message that the organization is competent and capable. Although most colleges have a Web site, surprisingly few have sites that adequately serve the workforce development client. They may be useful for finding a specific class (although even this simple process can be surprisingly complicated), but

if a client wants to learn about customized training opportunities, available training funds, or other more complex issues, a poorly designed site can be worse than no site at all. ❋

References

Godin, S. (1999). *Permission marketing*. New York: Simon & Schuster.

Kotler, P., & Armstrong, G. (2003). *Principles of marketing* (10th ed.). New York: Prentice Hall.

McBride, S. (1993). *Writing proposals for contract training* (Research Rep. No. 239). River Falls, WI: Learning Resources Network. Available at http://www.lern.org

CHAPTER 8

The 5-S Consultative Approach to Sales

Wesley E. Donahue and John E. Park

The greatest ability in business is to get along with others and influence their actions.

—John Hancock

John Hancock recognized the importance of relationships in business more than 200 years ago. And the importance of relationships has not changed since then. This chapter focuses on a consultative approach to sales in higher education and how successful relationships form the cornerstone of sustainable client relationships.

It is valuable to understand that a consultative approach to selling is ideally suited to professionals working in higher education who focus on establishing and sustaining relationships with external constituents. A traditional hard-sell approach to sales that emphasizes features and benefits will meet with only limited success in higher education. In reality, the traditional hard-sell approach is growing less popular everywhere. Clients seek individuals and organizations that can provide them with the greatest value of services or products in a trustworthy, cost-effective manner. Organizations are seeking opportunities to collaborate with institutions of higher learning that can add value and sustain long-term relationships.

Institutions of higher learning have been undergoing a transition over the past decade similar to what banks and other financial institutions experienced in the 1980s. Banks in the 1970s and early 1980s focused on internal needs and, in most cases, were driven by the need to follow regulations and policies rather than to meet or exceed clients' expectations. Baby boomers remember *bankers' hours*, a derogatory term that referred to a brief 10:00 a.m.–4:00 p.m. workday—and also the limited hours that banks were normally open. It was no surprise that in most cases these hours did not coincide with the hours when most customers could do their banking. In the

early 1980s, competition in the banking industry began to intensify, and banks extended their weekday hours. Progressive banks opened branch offices in grocery stores and malls and offered Saturday hours. Tellers began to cross-sell other services, and suddenly customer service was a priority and not a mere afterthought. These are only a few examples of client-focused initiatives aimed at meeting or exceeding client expectations.

Similar attention to the needs of traditional and adult students, as well as businesses seeking educational programs, is occurring in higher education. Private, for-profit, higher education institutions have been gaining momentum. They pride themselves on being student- and client-centered in how they deliver educational programs. Student services and class delivery methods are built with students' needs uppermost in mind. Administrators in many higher education institutions have realized the importance of developing a consultative approach to selling workforce development programs to business.

Almost everyone in a business or service organization today is involved somehow in sales. We try to sell others on the value of our ideas, the importance of what we do, or the value that we can bring to a project or an organization. Workforce development professionals who represent two- or four-year institutions are also constantly presented with opportunities to sell the value of the services they provide to external and internal clients. How these interactions and relationships progress and develop can have a tremendous impact on individual and organizational success.

Relationships are the foundation of sales success. Successful relationships with clients, superiors, subordi-

Consultative Approach versus Traditional Hard-Sell Approach	
Consultative	**Hard–Sell**
• Focus on your knowledge, expertise, and strengths	• Focus on product or services
• Listen to client needs and situation	• Present features and benefits
• Add value by focusing on problems and opportunities and offering solutions	• Overcome objections
• Position yourself as a resource to help client be successful	• Use closing techniques to ask for the order
• Build relationships by providing ongoing follow-up and support	• Close the sale

Note. From Donahue and Park (2003).

nates, co-workers, and colleagues are critical to the effective performance of all sales people and sales leaders. This is especially true in higher education, where we are not selling a tangible product. We may be trying to help an organization improve the effectiveness of its managers through a performance management program or selling a health-care organization on the value of having its nondegreed nurses enroll in a degree completion program. Each of these activities can affect the bottom line of an organization. However, the impact of education can occur slowly and incrementally over time. Selling its value is different from selling a raw material or specific part required in the completion of a product.

The critical situations presented in this chapter will emphasize the importance of establishing a consultative approach for relating to different types of clients and offer solutions that meet their needs and solve their problems. These critical situations focus on the importance of self-development and the projection of a professional and trustworthy image. A consultative approach to sales is focused on delivering value to clients in a way that helps them to succeed and be more effective in their organization, whether it is a for-profit or nonprofit environment. In short, the consultative approach to selling responds appropriately with solutions to meet the needs, feelings, capabilities, and interests of clients.

How to Use the 5-S Consultative Approach to Sales

We developed the 5-S Consultative Approach to Sales (Donahue & Park, 2003) to offer sales and workforce development professionals a systematic process and road map to success. We summarize this approach by defining the five "S's," which we then examine in detail in the rest of the chapter:

- Strengths: Understand individual and organizational *strengths.*
- Situation: Focus on client relationships in the context of the *situation.*
- Solutions: Listen and identify performance gaps, needs, and *solutions.*
- Success: Collaboratively implement solutions for *success.*
- Support: Provide follow-up and *support.*

To supplement each aspect of the approach, we present critical situations based on our experiences. Each example follows a similar format that begins with a description of the management situation and needs, follows with an analysis of the learning needs and interventions, and concludes with tips for proposals. The purpose of this format is to offer learning applications to workforce development professionals who may encounter similar challenges in the future.

Workforce development professionals should recognize the positive impact that the services they provide can have on organizations and approach clients with confidence. Often, newer professionals lack sufficient self-confidence to follow a consultative approach, so they resort to the traditional hard-sell approach, as is illustrated in critical situation "Operation Brochure Dump."

Understand Individual and Organizational Strengths

Many successful sales professionals are driven by their desire to prove they can sell anything, and they disregard the needs and situation of the client. The problem with this type of approach is that it reflects a traditional hard-sell approach rather than a consultative, client-focused approach. A consultative approach to sales requires a high level of self-awareness.

Critical Situation: Operation Brochure Dump

Management Situation and Needs

"Every time I call on a potential client, I make sure that I have a large supply of all the brochures and pamphlets we have in the office. The first thing I do is to hand out the brochures and then walk them through all of the courses we have available. It just seems that I never have enough time to tell them about the great things we can do for them. I just don't understand. It seems to me after about five minutes, the client quits listening to me and just sits there and looks over the brochures. I don't seem to be able to hold the client's attention."

Learning Needs and Interventions

This approach is very common among those new to sales. Newer workforce development professionals who are unsure of their ability to have effective dialogue with a potential client use brochures and pamphlets as crutches. Seasoned workforce professionals will tell you that typical learning needs and intervention opportunities exist in most organizations in a number of general areas, including

- Basic communications and human relations
- Customer service
- Leadership and management
- Specialized computer and technical training

Tips for Proposals

- Proposals and brochures must be designed to support a consultative approach.
- Timing is critical and must be considered in the presentation of proposals and brochures.
- Personality styles of decision makers must be considered. Clients with analytical styles may prefer to read and reflect on information and must be given time to do so. Driver styles may be direct and impulsive. Clients with expressive or amiable styles may have difficulty keeping focused with a detailed proposal; an executive summary would be essential for working with this personality type.

Growth and development are difficult at both an individual and an organizational level. Without the establishment of a baseline from which to measure performance, it is difficult to identify developmental needs and to determine competence. With Rothwell, we identified a competency development framework for sales professionals that include three overarching developmental areas that can be helpful in guiding self-analysis: knowledge of self, knowledge of products and services, and knowledge of clients and business. These key areas are essential to developing consultative skills (Rothwell, Park, & Donahue, 2002).

Do you understand your own personal style of interacting with others? Many personality and interpersonal assessments are available in the marketplace that can help you analyze personality styles and types. In working with business clients, you must communicate in a way that matches the needs of the potential client, demonstrating genuine understanding of the situation and business environment. Traditional academic language is an obstacle that can turn off many busy people and hinder the establishment of a relationship with a higher education institution.

Do you understand the products and services your organization has to offer and the different ways they can add value for a client? Do you have an understanding of how business really works and how to size up a particular client organization's situation, performance gaps, and needs? Workforce development professionals at all levels need to assess realistically their own strengths and weaknesses and realize the impact they can have on helping others. Often, newer workforce professionals do not realize the positive impact they can have on clients, individuals, and the communities they serve. There are a number of quantitative and qualitative ways in which organizations measure impact:

- Increased revenue generation
- Cost avoidance
- Cost reduction
- Morale levels
- Quality of communication
- Work-related stress/climate
- Job satisfaction
- Contribution to furthering core values
- Employee retention
- Customer satisfaction

It is important to recognize that your organization may not be able to solve all of the challenges facing a client's organization. However, it is also important to recognize that you can play a significant role in providing access and linkages to other resources through a consultative problem-solving approach, as is illustrated in the critical situation "Real Impact Results."

Critical Situation: Real Impact Results

Management Situation and Needs

In response to a phone call, a visit was made to a small but growing plastic products manufacturing company in the heart of an urban area. Managers indicated that they faced a problem in attracting and retaining good people for the organization. They also indicated that it was often difficult to communicate with the workforce because it was a multicultural environment in which they thought there were at least five different languages spoken in addition to English. These factors contributed significantly to the company's poor operating results and several costly mistakes. Management expressed concerns that the workforce lacked basic literacy skills and heard that various grant monies might be available for training. A plant tour, listening to the client's needs, and further observation made it obvious that the owners of the company were very passionate people who cared deeply about their workforce. It was observed that several employees with special needs had been accommodated. Further probing indicated that the owners themselves had children or friends with special needs and were receptive to restructuring various job functions to give people a chance to perform jobs where otherwise they may not have that opportunity. A consultative approach in multiple workforce areas enabled the company to reduce operating costs, create a safer work environment, improve the quality of communication, and retain valuable talent.

Learning Needs and Interventions

Often workforce professionals underestimate the impact they have on the lives of people they help, organizations they assist, and communities they serve. In this case, a variety of learning needs and interventions were identified, resulting in the awarding of a sig-

nificant workforce development grant to help this company grow. The variety of learning needs and interventions included

- Basic literacy training in reading, writing, and math skills
- Instruction in English as a second language
- Occupational Safety and Health Administration (OSHA) training
- CPR and safety training
- Training in the fundamentals of plastics and processing
- Specialized technical skills training

Tips for Proposals

- As a starting point for this type of organization, propose a survey of the workforce's basic literacy skills. (It was interesting to find that, indeed, five different languages were present; however, one foreign language was common to 80% of the workforce.)
- Propose a multilevel literacy instruction initiative based on survey results and the awareness of the desire and commitment of individuals to learn.
- Communicate the variety of specialized technical training options that can be provided.
- Offer to provide linkage with local occupational vocational rehabilitation services. (This was done, and as a result, several special-needs clients were placed within the organization, creating a win–win situation.)
- Consider serving as the facilitator for obtaining grant services and as an independent advisor and extension to their organization.

Focus on Client Relationships in the Context of the Situation

Even after you indicate that you understand and begin to apply the services that your organization can provide, unforeseen situations will no doubt arise. Inevitably, discussions about a consultative approach to sales turn to the need for a high level of general business knowledge and knowledge of the products and services that can be offered to the client. Knowledge of the organization's products and services, as well as how businesses operate, is critical to the growth of consultative relationships. Clients must trust that you are a content expert who is

able to clarify the scope and depth of the educational products or services being proposed as a solution. Having knowledge of the product in a manufacturing organization is much different than it is in an institution of higher education. Training and education are intangibles, and they require a deeper understanding of program content and delivery methods.

Professional staff members must gain business knowledge and learn to prospect and appropriately interact with clients. Clients can be segmented in many traditional and nontraditional ways: manufacturing versus service, government versus health care, technology-based versus traditional bricks and mortar, retail versus wholesale or by dollar volume. Subsequently, organizations may be ranked in a traditional ABC framework, from highest potential to lowest. It is also important to note that a discussion of prospecting could be a chapter in itself. Potential sources of prospecting information include *Dunn & Bradstreet, Moody's Manuals, Value Line,* and *Harris Directory.* Professional association publications, newspapers, annual reports for publicly traded companies, and company Web sites are additional sources of information.

Of course, time and priority management for workforce professionals could be the subject of yet another chapter. Setting goals and priorities and implementing a process to stay focused are obviously critical. There are a number of contact or client management software packages available to manage sales activities and client data. Each has its own strengths and weaknesses, but one factor remains critical: If the package is not user-friendly and accessible, it will not be used. Client management systems are effective only if they are used and contain current, accurate information. In Appendix D you will find the following templates to help you develop a customized management system of your own: weekly call planner, monthly summary of prospecting activity, annual client visit planning calendar, program summary report, and record of client contact.

Identifying prospects is a key to success. However, you must still be able to get that face-to-face opportunity to talk with the client. This opportunity may come through persistence in making phone calls to set up an appointment, by networking when an opportunity comes through a referral, or by luck when you bump into the person you have been trying to meet at a business function or a social event. Regardless of how relationships are initiated, they rarely move forward unless they are cultivated in a face-to-face setting. (On the next page, we provide an example that emphasizes the importance of persistence in the consultative approach and the need to explore multiple contacts within an organization. Workforce development opportunities exist in small organizations as well as in large multinational corporations.)

Listen and Identify Performance Gaps, Needs, and Solutions

Are you able to listen to individuals in organizations and accurately assess the situation? Much of the consultative approach is centered on the ability to ask appropriate questions and actively listen to the client. For a few lucky individuals, active listening comes naturally, whereas for others it is a skill that must be developed and practiced. The active listening process requires a focus on content as well as the underlying meaning of the conversation. Opportunities to provide solutions that add value to the client's organization can surface in the listening process as problems and opportunities are shared.

Individuals inexperienced in sales can struggle with turning the focus of a meeting from themselves and their presentation of the organization's capabilities to one centered on listening to the clients and understanding their needs. One good rule of thumb frequently suggested as a guide for this type of interaction is the 80/20 rule: The client should be talking 80% of the time, and the professional making the sales call should limits his or her talking time to 20% of the meeting time. To accomplish the 80/20 ratio, you must plan your client calls and create a set of questions to guide interaction with the client. These questions can focus on several issues: understanding the organization's greatest challenges, identifying frequent training problems, understanding the strategy and future direction of the organization, and identifying issues that are preventing growth or development.

There are many strategies for maintaining clients' involvement in the consultative approach to sales. We have suggested that you can maintain a client focus by summarizing key points, using open-ended questions, and following up with appropriate probing questions that allow the client to go deeper into its explanations (Rothwell, Donahue, & Park, 2002). When you restate key points, you give the client the opportunity to validate that you understood the message presented. Finally, it is critical to send consistent verbal and nonverbal messages to the client affirming that you are focusing on the client and valuing what is being said.

Often there are clues all around that organizations may need help. An organization may simply call for specific program information, or perhaps news in a local paper reports the expansion or contraction of a particular organization. Or, friends or relatives who work within an organization may express the need for improvement and opportunities for training. (For an example of responding to such clues, see "Critical Situation: Compete Globally or Die," page 69.)

Implement Solutions for Success Collaboratively

It is critical in the early stages of a sales meeting that the potential client recognizes that you are not conducting an investigation but are working to understand the nuances of the organization and the challenges and opportunities it faces. Your focus at this point should be on creating an open, guided dialogue that encourages clients to voice

Critical Situation: Large Organizations Need Help, Too

Management Situation and Needs

Many large organizations, particularly multinational ones, need to have standard operating methods and procedures. When approaching a local facility of a large organization, it is important to recognize and expect resistance to new ideas.

XYZ Company was a large, foreign-owned company and a technical leader in its field. The company had an outstanding reputation and was a premier employer in its area. Gaining access to the decision makers of the local facility was no easy task. It took persistence and a lot of informal networking to be introduced to the right people and establish a rapport that eventually led to an opportunity to prepare a proposal. It was obvious from the initial plant tour that this was a well-run and lean organization. Employees were routinely sent to Europe for specialized training. However, like many large organizations, the local facility was held accountable for its own profit and loss. Obviously, a major cost to the local facility was travel for training, as well as the cost of time spent away from jobs. If training could be provided locally, significant cost savings could be achieved. Additionally, although international travel might be appealing to some, it can be a source of major anxiety for others. Increased time away from the workplace was affecting morale, organizational communication, and work climate. A consultative approach that would support the company's internal training efforts, reduce training costs, and improve job satisfaction and performance was certainly in everyone's best interests.

Learning Needs and Interventions

After conducting selected interviews and listening to management and floor workers alike, it was determined that some of the learning needs could be accomplished at the local level, if corporate buy-in could be achieved. These learning needs and interventions included

- Custom computer skills training
- Specialized technical training adhering to and using company manuals
- Customized supervisory-management program

Tips for Proposals

- Conducting individual and group interviews to gain firsthand information should be built into the proposal.
- Build into the program proposal the concept of establishing a steering committee that would meet periodically (in this case monthly) to review program design and contract execution.
- As part of the proposal, build in a final summary report prepared by the instructor. This can be packaged and presented at the conclusion as a program follow-up that includes recommended next steps.
- Ask local facilities management personnel to invite corporate training staff and visiting executives to attend various sessions.
- Suggest in the proposal that the highest available local company manage both open and close various programs and conduct recognition ceremonies at the end of each milestone segment where they can share their perspectives.

their perspectives on problems they encounter or perceived opportunities on which they are not capitalizing. You can accomplish this only if you have taken the time and patience to create a safe and trusting environment in which the potential client will feel comfortable sharing what could be very confidential information.

When using a consultative approach, you have an obligation to potential clients to maintain confidentiality. Client interactions must be planned and managed. You must do your homework to gain as much information and knowledge as possible prior to meeting with clients. However, in some situations, you may have more information available to you than a particular client does, and, if appropriate, you may be in a position to share the information across client groups for the benefit of all. An example may be in working with various government entities where one entity may not have the resources to properly address certain needs or situations, but combining with similar government entities may permit win–win solutions to be implemented (see the critical situation "Getting the Most from Taxes," page 70).

Provide Support and Follow–Up

Are you skilled in providing ongoing client support and obtaining repeat program opportunities? As clients share information, problems, and opportunities, you have the opportunity to gain the potential client's confidence in your ability to offer solutions aligned with the organization's broader strategy. This can be complex when you are

---

Critical Situation: Compete Globally or Die

Management Situation and Needs

ABC Company started as a small family-run business with a fine reputation for quality. Over the past several decades, it has grown steadily into a nationally known entity with more than 2,000 employees and multiple plants and retail outlets across the United States. However, as with many labor-intensive industries, competing on a global basis is a real challenge. Faced with the realization that it may eventually need to outsource much of its manufacturing capability to survive, the company had to rethink how it manufactured and distributed its products and services. The privately held company has enjoyed a steady, loyal workforce over the years, and the determination to grow and to retain as many domestic jobs as possible are at the forefront of management's minds. As with many organizations, cries for help come in many different forms, and the ability to recognize them is critical. In this case, one came in the form of an article in a local newspaper indicating that the company was trying new modular manufacturing techniques and piloting a new retail outlet concept. Following up and inquiring about what assistance might be needed resulted in a long-term consultative relationship that has helped this organization align and focus its human resources on the challenges it faces, improve its communication and work climate, and reduce product costs while improving quality.

Learning Needs and Interventions

This organization had some typical growing pains. First of all, it needed to implement a structured approach to developing and training its workforce at all levels. Also, with rapid growth, the company's traditional communi-

cation mechanisms were inadequate, and new systems were needed to ensure that its newly hired leaders had an opportunity to share ideas and communicate effectively. The company also needed to completely rethink its traditional manufacturing processes to be able to compete in a global marketplace. These needs translated into

- Change management
- Team development skills
- Process facilitation skills
- Basic communication and human relations skills
- Structured problem-solving techniques

Tips for Proposals

- Start small by proposing a formalized needs assessment to gain information and buy-in before initiating any training interventions.
- Build into the proposal mechanisms to mix talent from various areas of the organization, not only to enhance communication but also to get fresh new ideas.
- Promote the position of undertaking a series of pilot initiatives to explore new processes that meet client needs in lieu of implementing radical changes. Incorporate action-learning opportunities that include hands-on, organization-specific projects.
- Communicate the value of having outside facilitation to help streamline various processes.
- Suggest that the organization implement a formalized climate survey process to benchmark activities and obtain input from all employees.
- Recognize that multiple resources are needed beyond your capabilities.

---

not delivering the solutions but are part of a team that includes faculty members and, potentially, other administrative personnel. In this setting, it is critical that you recognize when the time is right to bring in the other members of the team. In the delivery of a standard technology program that requires little or no customization to the client's needs, you can offer the solution to the client as an opportunity to move the effort forward. If, however, the project requires faculty interaction and the creation of a new training curriculum, it becomes imperative that you bring in the faculty team early to allow the client to also gain trust in the team and get involved in the creation of the solutions.

Do you know how to design proposals that are clear and meet clients' needs? How you move forward the formal written proposal becomes a critical component in the finalization of the agreement to purchase the solution. Proposals must be accurate and easily read and understood, and must meet the specific information needs of the potential client. For example, potential clients who display "analytical attributes" will require in-depth outlines and administrative frameworks to make a decision. Potential clients who make decisions based on "the feel and look" of a proposal will want the proposal delivered face to face so they can talk about how the results of the program will look and feel.

Critical Situation: Getting the Most From Taxes

Management Situation and Needs

We all aspire to have our government entities operating in the most efficient manner. Although it is obvious that different areas of government have unique situations, they do have similarities at the local, state, and federal levels that should be considered. Senior leadership within government entities could be characterized as ever changing because of the political nature of the system. However, full-time employees could usually be characterized as dedicated loyal public servants, constrained by a typical annual budgeting-year system that makes funds carryover and long-term planning (often) difficult. This can affect cross-department collaboration efforts and deter entrepreneurial spirit for continuous improvement. And while there are many differences from a workforce development standpoint, many of the needs across the system are very similar. Workforce development professionals can serve a valuable role by providing programs and services that cut across departments and provide a structure that meets ongoing learning needs within the government sector, resulting in reduced costs from elimination of duplicated efforts, increased efficiencies from sharing and communication improvement, and improved morale.

Learning Needs and Interventions

Studies have identified various competencies and learning needs for various job functions within gov-ernment. Multiple learning needs and intervention opportunities exist, including

- Human relations and customer advocacy training
- Supervisory leadership skills
- Conflict resolution, influence, and negotiation skills
- Budgeting and planning skills
- Project management skills
- Specialized computer and technical training

Tips for Proposals

- Be proactive; do not wait for requests for proposals (RFPs).
- Develop offerings focused on government needs that can be budgeted and paid for at the department level without the need to generate a formalized contract.
- Propose and seek input on needs where offerings may be customized for multiple departments within government.
- Build into proposals a "consortium concept," where clusters of government departments with similar needs can share experiences as well as programmatic costs.

Do you understand the elements of a value-added approach to pricing? In a traditional approach to sales, clients look at salespeople as a conduit for product information and the focal point for negotiation on price and services. In a consultative approach, your goal is to establish yourself in the client's eyes as a resource who will help them to achieve their business objectives in an effective, profitable manner. You must consistently communicate to your clients the value you add to the interaction beyond providing the onsite or classroom delivery of educational activities. Examples of value-added factors include

- Linkage to other university resources
- Access to classroom space
- Access to technology and computer centers
- Access to student interns
- Advantageous payment terms
- State and federal grants

It can be eye-opening and enlightening to regularly convene workforce development professionals in your organization to brainstorm ways that they can add value for clients beyond this brief list. Having the ability to recognize and understand current client problems that can be solved by your services, as well as being able to help the client identify and plan for future problems and opportunities, can add value. However, sometimes the process takes considerable time and patience, as is illustrated in the critical situation "Proposal Patience."

CONCLUSION

The consultative approach can be learned. Skills in listening, asking questions, and formulating value-added solutions to clients' problems can be gained through training and honed through practice and coaching. However, individuals who are successful in sales-related activities over long periods of time must be goal-oriented and feel that their achievements are recognized and rewarded in a manner consistent with their efforts and level of success. Workforce development professionals taking a consultative approach to developing client relationships will be able to create long-term, win–win opportunities. It is important to consider that most organizations can essentially buy the same raw materials and equipment, but the organizations with the best-trained people will produce the best products and services. Workforce professionals who recognize their important role can provide solutions that have real impact for the constituents they serve. ❁

References

Donahue, W. E., & Park, J. E. (2003). *The 5-S consultative approach to sales.* Unpublished manuscript.

Rothwell, W. J., Donahue, W. E., & Park, J.E. (2002). *Creating in-house sales training and development programs.* Westport, CT: Greenwood.

Critical Situation: Proposal Patience

Management Situation and Needs

Over the years we have had folks from a company located quite a distance from our institution attend various courses we have offered. One of the participants from that organization said, "Wow, our management could sure use your help!" She explained that the company was located in a rural area, was the major employer in the area, and had some unique problems, one of which was almost no turnover of employees. For many organizations, this would be a good problem. However, the industry was undergoing tremendous change and in order to compete, whole new skill sets were required and many employees were set in their ways. To complicate matters, a large investment group had recently purchased the company, and rumors of consolidations and downsizing were being circulated.

Taking all of this as an invitation to learn more, our team made an appointment for a visit and followed up with a series of focus group discussions leading to a comprehensive proposal. According to the company's management, our proposal was right on target and addressed its needs. The proposal included suggestions for programming to better align and focus the company's human resources on the challenges it faced, improving communication and work climate, offering a series of specialized programs and services aimed at reducing product costs, and improving product quality. Months passed and we heard nothing about the status of the proposal except that we should be patient because the proposal needed to work its way through the corporate hierarchy. After nearly two years, they finally contacted us

and said they were ready. The relationship is now more than a decade old and growing stronger.

Learning Needs and Interventions

Multiple learning needs surfaced during the initial planning phases of this relationship. However, as work started, it became apparent that the company could benefit from an even broader consultative relationship and that one of the most important factors that eventually separated this local operation from others was the transformation they made to accept and embrace needed changes. The employees' training, flexibility, and willingness to change are probably major reasons that today this site continues to be one of the company's best facilities and a significant contributor to the local economy. Some of the specific learning needs and interventions included

- Change management
- Personal communication and writing skills
- Technical training
- Supervisory development skills
- Specialized computer and technical training
- Structured problem solving and quality enhancement

Tips for Proposals

- Think of proposals as marketing documents.
- Write proposals with multiple readers in mind.
- Use a systematic process for follow-up.
- Be supportive and patient.

Finance and Budgeting for Workforce Development Organizations

Leslie Roe

Managing the financial aspects of a workforce development center at a community college requires managers and leaders to relate differently than do their academic counterparts with the finances of the organization. Workforce development managers are responsible for making as well as spending money. They are obliged to understand both sides of the financial equation—revenue and expense—and the fundamental relationship between the two. These managers carry all the responsibilities of a small entrepreneurial business while existing within larger institutions. In this chapter, I examine how workforce development organizations can best manage their finances.

Financial management is more that just reconciling the budget report at the end of the month. Figure 9.1 outlines a workforce development center administrator's financial management responsibilities. Note the interdependence of the various elements.

In this chapter I apply traditional financial management theories and practices to the specialized environment of the workforce development center. I examine all aspects of financial management, from planning and controls to building and managing a budget designed to generate profits. I present examples and tips that are pulled from working, profitable workforce development centers, which, taken together, result in a comprehensive checklist of activities, actions, and tools for creating and managing all aspects of a workforce development center.

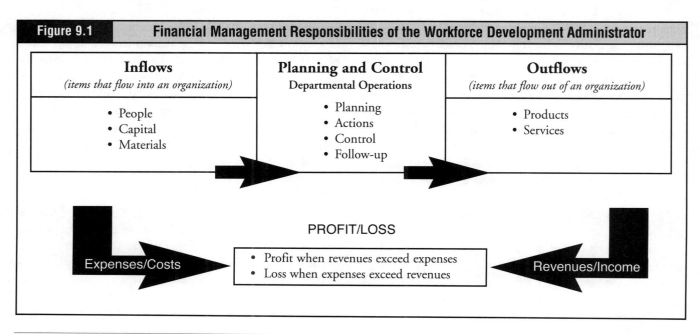

Figure 9.1 — **Financial Management Responsibilities of the Workforce Development Administrator**

Inflows *(items that flow into an organization)*	**Planning and Control** Departmental Operations	**Outflows** *(items that flow out of an organization)*
• People • Capital • Materials	• Planning • Actions • Control • Follow-up	• Products • Services

PROFIT/LOSS

Expenses/Costs

• Profit when revenues exceed expenses
• Loss when expenses exceed revenues

Revenues/Income

RESPONSIBILITIES OF THE WORKFORCE DEVELOPMENT CENTER MANAGER

Certo has maintained that "management is the process of reaching organizational goals by working with and through people and other organizational resources" (1997, p. 6). He clarified that "essentially, the role of managers is to guide organizations toward goal accomplishments" (1997, p. 4). The workforce development center manager takes on the responsibility for carrying out functions of planning, organizing, staffing, leading, and controlling the center's activities. I emphasize here those activities that are most directly supportive of profit planning and control.

Planning and Control

Planning is the process by which a center's primary goals and objectives are identified. A manager's relationship with key stakeholders is at the core of this plan. Key stakeholder groups consist of customers, employees, service providers (instructors, faculty, consultants), suppliers, institution management, and the community at large. The primary focus of a plan is the identification of a coherent and feasible way for the center to interact with its customers. Questions regarding what products and services the center will deliver and at what level it will compete need to be answered. Will the organization primarily be a training provider, competing by offering the lowest price? Or will the center offer a host of performance improvement services, competing by meeting the specialized requirements of its target audience? Answers to questions such as these serve to define an organization's primary objectives.

Strategies for addressing these questions must be realistic in terms of meeting the requirements of all stakeholders involved. Institutional management must be satisfied that the entity will meet their primary objectives. Employees need to be assured that they are being compensated fairly and that the work environment is adequate. Service providers must feel confident that the relationships they have established support their objectives as well as the center's. Suppliers of goods and services must be equally satisfied with their relationships with the center. Finally, the community must be assured that the entity will operate within existing laws, as well as provide some community leadership. Strategies employed to address these stakeholder groups create a plan's secondary objectives.

The expectations of these relationships are managed through the use of explicit or implied contracts. A contract defines what a stakeholder expects from an organization in return for what it provides. Examples of explicit contracts used in workforce development centers include employee contracts, customer agreements, and instructor agreements. Seldom does an explicit contract exist between a community and a workforce development center, but an implicit contract is often present. Execution of such a contract can be seen in a center's active participation in economic development and education forums and membership in local chambers of commerce and service clubs.

Control is the process that keeps a plan on track. When an organization's actions are moving it toward its objectives and stakeholders' expectations are being met, the entity is said to be in control. When this is not the case, the organization is considered to be out of control. Obviously, organizational control is the desired state for workforce development centers.

Maintaining organizational control begins with an entity's plan. The activities set forth in the plan are executed, while being continuously monitored and evaluated. This evaluation helps the manager determine whether activities are moving the organization toward its goals, and corrective action is taken if an activity is off course. To keep the organization in control, a manager must be knowledgeable about those situations identified as out of control and possess the ability to correct them. This process is often depicted as a cycle, as each step is dependent on the previous one, and all steps lead back to the beginning. Figure 9.2 illustrates the five-step process that links an organization's plan to control.

At the core of the control process is the organization's performance measurement system. This system measures how well an organization is performing against its primary and secondary objectives, providing a way of focusing the center's decision making. When used as an opportunity for organizational learning, this system also serves as a way of moving the organization toward higher levels of performance. Performance measurement systems for high-performing organizations are covered in chapter 3, and Appendix A provides an assessment tool to help measure performance. Such systems and tools are integral to an organization's ability to stay in control and are therefore critical to the financial management of a workforce development center.

Basic Financial Statements

The end products of the accounting process are financial statements that summarize all of an organization's financial transactions for a given period. Section 94806 (b) (3) of the California Education Code declares that educational institutions must prepare four primary financial statements annually: balance sheet, statement of operations, statement of retained earnings and capital, and statement

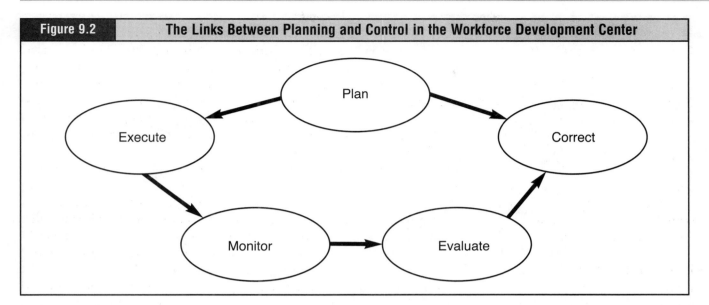

Figure 9.2 — **The Links Between Planning and Control in the Workforce Development Center**

of cash flow. This code further requires nonprofit institutions to provide this information in the manner generally accepted for nonprofit organizations. Fortunately for the workforce development center manager, the business office is normally responsible for the development of these annual financial statements. It is, however, important that managers understand what these reports are and how the center's financial activities affect them.

Balance sheet (statement of financial position). Whereas a statement of activities depicts the overall status of a center's profits (or deficits) by looking at income and expenses over a period of time, the balance sheet depicts the status of its finances at a fixed point in time. It totals assets and subtracts liabilities to compute overall net worth (or net loss). This statement is referenced particularly when applying for funding.

Assets are properties and resources the institution owns and can use to achieve its goals. Current assets include cash accounts, certificates of deposits and other investments, and items that will be converted to cash within one year, such as receivables. Fixed assets include land, buildings, and equipment. Liabilities are the debts of the organization. Current liabilities typically include accounts payable to vendors, short-term loans due, withheld payroll taxes due, and so on. Long-term liabilities include long-term debt, mortgages, and others.

Net assets (previously called fund balances) is the net of assets over liabilities. Three classes of net assets must be reported: unrestricted, temporarily restricted, and permanently restricted. Restrictions are determined by the source of funding. Figure 9.3 depicts a sample balance sheet for a community college district.

Income statement (statement of operations). The statement of operations adds money earned (revenue) and subtracts money spent (expenses), resulting in a total of unrestricted net assets. Basically, the statement includes total income minus total expenses. It presents the nature of overall profit and loss over a period of time, offering an indication of how well an institution is operating. A sample of a cumulative statement is shown in Figure 9.4. A center's plan and activity implementation will result in the creation of a departmental operations report that should be monitored on at least a monthly basis.

Statement of retained earnings and capital. This report shows the cumulative total of profits and losses reinvested in the institution over the period of its existence. It links the balance sheet to the income statement. Many educational institutions ask their auditors to prepare this statement.

Statement of cash flow. The statement of cash flow reports on how the organization's cash position changed during the year. Cash flow information is divided among receipts and disbursements from investing, financing, and operating activities. Many educational institutions ask their auditors to prepare this statement as well. Figure 9.5 provides a sample report.

Money comes into organizations and leaves organizations for a variety of reasons; the statement of cash flow explains the causes of changes in cash. Activities that affect the cash flow of a workforce development center are almost exclusively linked to the operation of the center. Activities such as investing and financing are not very common in a center environment. Operating activities that bring cash into a center (cash inflows) include collections from customers, grant monies, and other operating receipts. Operating activities that draw money out of an organization include cash payments to service providers, employees, and suppliers.

Figure 9.3	Sample Balance Sheet for a Community College District

XYZ Community College District
Statement of Financial Position (Balance Sheet)
Year Ending June 30, 2002

Assets	2002	2001
Cash and cash equivalents	$11,400	$6,300
Grants receivable	2,500	0
Prepaid expenses	950	1,300
Fixed assets at cost:		
Office equipment	15,496	
Less: Accumulated depreciation	<15,496>	
Net fixed assets	- 0 -	- 0 -
Total Assets	$14,850	$7,600
Liabilities		
Accounts payable	$1,500	$4,500
Net Assets (fund balance)	$13,350	$3,100

Figure 9.4	Sample Statement of Operations

Revenues

Government grants	$ 35,000
Other grants	50,000
Apportionment	25,000
Fees for service	45,000
Interest	2,000
Total income	$157,000

Expenses

Salaries and benefits	
Administration	$ 38,000
Faculty	50,000
Classified	27,000
Rent	12,000
Supplies	11,000
Telephone	3,300
Postage	2,500
Copying	2,950
Total expenses	$146,750

Increase/(Decrease) in Net Assets	$ 10,250

Figure 9.5	Sample Statement of Cash Flow

Change in net assets	$10,250
Adjustments to reconcile change in net assets to net cash <used by> operating activities:	
<Increase> in grants receivable	< 2,500>
Decrease in prepaid expenses	350
<Decrease> in accounts payable	< 3,000>
Net cash <used by> operating activities	< 5,150>
Net increase in cash and cash equivalents	5,100
Cash and cash equivalents —beginning of year	6,300
Cash and cash equivalents —end of year	$11,400

ACTIVITY-BASED COSTING

Fiscal managers of workforce development centers need to have an in-depth understanding of those things that pull cash out of their organizations: expenses or costs. Accurate and relevant cost information is critical for any organization that hopes to maintain or improve its competitive position. Workforce development centers have long operated under the assumption that their cost information reflected the costs of their products and services when in reality it did not. Overgeneralized cost systems were misleading decision makers, resulting in decisions that were inconsistent with organizations' needs and goals, principally because of misallocated costs.

Activity-based costing (ABC) is a model that can correct the shortcomings of the cost systems of the past. It is a system that ultimately directs an organization's costs to the products and services it needs. ABC provides an integrated, cross-functional view of a center, its activities, and its business processes.

As a result, ABC can be used for far more than developing accurate and relevant product, process, service, and activity costs. This process can be used to improve operations by managing the drivers of activities that incur costs. ABC can support major decisions on service offerings, market segments, and customer relationships. It is also useful in simulating the impact of process improvements. Both the financial and nonfinancial information of ABC can be used as part of a high-performance measurement system.

Traditional cost accounting techniques allocate costs to products based on attributes of a single unit. Attributes include the number of direct labor hours required to deliver a unit (e.g., an hour of training) or the purchase cost of merchandise resold. Allocations therefore vary directly with the volume of units delivered or the cost of merchandise sold. In contrast with this, ABC systems focus on the activities required to provide each service.

ABC traces overhead costs to products and services by identifying the costs and quantities of resources and activities. A unit or output (a driver) is used to calculate the cost of each activity during any given period of time. An ABC system can be viewed in two different ways. The *cost assignment view* provides information about resources, activities, and cost objects. The *process view* provides operational (often nonfinancial) information about cost drivers, activities, and performance. Both perspectives can provide valuable information about the financial performance of a center. (For more information about this system, visit Business.com and search on "activity-based costing" or "ABC.")

Table 9.1 outlines the commonly understood costs affiliated with the delivery of one unit of service: an hour of training. Taking the cost assignment view, we can clearly see that costs will vary depending on which instructor is used, which textbook is selected, and how many students will be in the class. An analysis of indirect costs has determined that the overhead rate per hour of instruction is 50%. In this case, if an instructor charged $75.00 per hour, the textbook cost $50.00, and the class was delivered to 20 students, the total cost of an hour of instruction would equal $116.25 [(75 + 50/20) + 50%(75 + 50/20)]. The process view shows that availability drivers can affect the ability of the center to deliver service on time. Procedures and processes designed to control this cost driver would therefore be necessary.

Obviously, the way in which a center manages its costs will have a direct effect on its ability to generate profits. This is the key determinant in how much customers will be charged for services. The relationship between costs and pricing is the key to running a profitable workforce development center. See Table 9.2 for examples of other common direct and indirect costs.

MANAGING REVENUE

In public institutions of higher learning, monies or revenues are provided via an apportionment process. The

Table 9.1	Costs Affiliated With Delivering One Hour of Training	
Direct Costs	**Drivers**	**Indirect Costs/Overhead**

Instructor	• Rate/hour
	• Availability
		• Marketing
		• Management oversight
		  • Center director
		  • Account manager
		• Accounting
		• Human resources
		• Other operating costs

Textbook	• Purchase price • Number of students • Availability	50%

Table 9.2	Examples of Direct and Indirect Costs of Training	
Cost Category	**Direct Costs**	**Indirect Costs**
People	• Instructors or faculty • Project coordinator • Curriculum developer • Consultant	• Department manager • Administrative assistant • Marketing consultant • Accountant
Materials	• Textbooks • Copies of a PowerPoint presentation • Notebooks to hold the copies • Solder for a welding class	• Office supplies • Conference expenses • Brochure printing

Note. Direct costs listed determine or manage cost drivers. Indirect costs listed are included in the overhead rate.

number of full-time (or full-time equivalent) students enrolled multiplied by the dollar amount allocated by their state agency equals the majority of the revenue the institution will receive. The organization's leaders determine how these monies are distributed throughout the organization.

Managers of individual departments receive an annual allocation and proceed to manage their spending, or expenses, within those limits. As such, many administrators are able to distance themselves from the "earning" of money, focusing their financial management efforts on controlling expenses. Administrators of workforce development organizations do not have that luxury; they are directly involved in the generation of their center's revenue.

Revenue is generated when something leaves an organization and money comes into it in exchange. As was shown in Figure 9.1, the primary sources of revenue for a workforce development center are product sales and service delivery. Exact sources of revenue are determined by an organization's financial plan (see Example).

Pricing strategy depends on an understanding of costs and sources of revenue. Figure 9.6 (see page 79) outlines the elements that determine how much to charge for a training session. Many of the cost drivers are captured in this cost analysis: rates, hours, number of students, and schedule. A workforce development center that is currently using this pricing model and the ABC model was operating at a deficit 3 years ago, but it has recently generated a profit of nearly $130,000.

DEVELOPING THE WORKFORCE DEVELOPMENT CENTER BUDGET

A budget can be defined as "a quantitative expression of the money inflows and outflows used to determine whether a financial plan will meet organizational goals" (Becker, Gonzales, Lupinacci, Pitts, & Sharghi, 1996, p.

Example: Sources of Revenue From Training

Product Sales

Books and materials
"Off-the-shelf" distance education programs
Skills assessment tests
Facility rental

Service Delivery

Performance consulting
Seminars
Workshops
Skills training classes
Needs assessment consulting
Grant management
Project coordination and management

---

322). A comparison of budgeted cash flows to actual deposits and expenditures, combined with an understanding of the nature of any variances, can strengthen a manager's ability to control the performance of a workforce development center.

The budget planning process can truly begin once you have (a) identified sources of revenue and the planning process to secure them, (b) know how to accurately cost the delivery of services and products so they can be priced with profitability in mind, and (c) understand the market served and how to compete in the marketplace. This information cumulatively allows the realistic setting of revenue targets for the year. These revenue targets are reflected in the first lines of the department budget.

People-related expenses. To develop the resource allocation or expense side of a budget, you must examine three primary categories of expense: people, capital, and

Figure 9.6	Sample Cost Analysis

COMPANY A — CULTURAL DIVERSITY   8/23/02

COST ANALYSIS for NOT-FOR-CREDIT COURSE

Format: 2-hour workshops in English; 4-hour workshops in Spanish; 4-hour workshops in Chinese

Instructor: Jose Feliciano (fluent in Spanish)

Must be scheduled between September 9-20. Anticipate 4 days for 9 groups, 4-6 hours
A separate 2 hr. executive staff session (English) has been added. Group size: 5.

Category	Cost/fees	Hours	# Students	Total $
Instructor curriculum development/client input	$100.00	2		$200.00
Instructor class lecture	$55.00	26		$1,430.00
Spanish translation instructor is fluent		0		
Chinese translation for one group of 7	$100.00	4		$400.00
Travel time		0		
Project management (program coordinator)	$24.50	4.5		$110.25
Subtotal — Direct Costs				$2,140.25
Overhead Contract Ed @ 50%	$2,140.25			$1,070.13
Subtotal — Indirect Costs				$3,210.38
Materials (copying/binders)	$5.00		225	$1,125.00
Subtotal				$4,335.38
Profit Margin (subtotal cost x 180%)				**$7,803.68**

materials. Begin with the most costly expense: human resources. Institutions pay many people to deliver products and services to the workforce: faculty, instructors, consultants, managers, classified staff, subject matter experts, project managers, program coordinators, graphic designers, temporary personnel, and others. It is imperative to possess an intimate understanding of this expense item.

Tip #1. Make a list of all the people associated with the delivery of your product and/or service. Understand how much you pay them: hourly rates and the number of hours they work, or salary schedules and benefit rate. Understand how and when they are paid: payroll, invoice, or special contract. Capture this information in a spreadsheet or database. Keep it updated with salary increases and cost of living increases. This will be an important tool when it comes to creating your department budget.

Capital expenses. Capital expenditures are purchased items that will have a multiyear life span in an organization. Items such as computers, furniture, special equipment, and buildings are all part of a capital expen-

diture plan. Most workforce development organizations are housed within an academic institution's buildings, and although they may pay rent, they do not usually purchase their own buildings. That large expense aside, it is important to know the answers to a number of questions about capital expenditures. Is there enough cash in the organization's accounts to purchase an item, or will it need to be financed? Does a purchase agreement already exist in the institution for particular types of items? Does an item meet the institution's definition of a fixed asset, thus making it subject to depreciation?

Tip #2. Work with your business services office to create your capital expenditure plan. They should know the parameters and procedures on how your organization handles capital expenditures, but of course you will still need to plan these purchases ahead of time. When developing a budget, it will need to reflect actual cash outflow for the year; this may or may not be the full cost of the item.

For example, you plan to purchase new computers for your staff. The total cost of the capital expenditure is $24,000. You lease them through your institution's existing leasing agreement with a local computer vendor. Lease payments are $2,000 a month, and the lease term is two years. Your budget for year one should reflect the total of the first 12 months of lease payments; the balance of the payments is reflected in year two's budget.

Materials expenses. Materials expenses are consumables, items that get used up. Common items in this category include office supplies, books for students, conference and travel expenses, subscriptions to publications, memberships to organizations, copying, printing, and rent. It is important to consider not only those items necessary for running an organization (indirect costs), but also those material-related expenses required for delivering products, training, and consulting services (direct costs).

Tip #3. Log your purchase requisitions for materials expenses by type or account code for a year. Separate those material expenses associated directly with the delivery of your services (books and classroom materials) from those that are required to run your center (telephone, rent, conferences, and travel). Note the ratio of your service delivery material expense to the revenue generated from the delivery of these services. You can use this ratio to project your service material expense for the new budget year.

For example, revenues for the center's training service delivery were $250,000. The materials expenses directly associated with the generation of this revenue were tracked at $5,000. That is a ratio of 50 to 1. If the center was projecting revenues for next year at $500,000, the projected service delivery materials expenses would be $10,000. Indirect expenses typically remain fairly static year to year. In the event of an unforeseen economic condition, such as a recession or dramatic cost of living increase, the factor associated with that condition is used to project expense totals for the new budget year.

Figure 9.7 (see page 81) depicts a workforce development center budget comparison report. It brings the entire financial picture together, showing revenue sources and expense items, both direct and indirect. This document indicates how resources are being expended, and how well an organization is performing year-to-date. It is a very powerful and informative management tool. ❋

References

Becker, T., Gonzales, L., Lupinacci, D., Pitts III, C., & Sharghi, G. C. (1998). *Finance: Profit, planning, & control for managers.* Needham Heights, MA: Simon & Schuster.

Certo, S. C. (1997). *Modern management* (7th ed.). Upper Saddle River, NJ: Prentice Hall.

Figure 9.7		Sample Budget Comparison Report		
Operating Budget for XYZ Contract Education Unit				
Acct	**Prog**	**Account title**	**Budget**	**YTD**
8893	701000	Contract services	300,000.00	230,000.00
8898	701000	Grant funds	250,000.00	250,000.00
		Revenue Totals	*550,000.00*	*480,000.00*
1301	701000	Teachers hourly	22,000.00	12,238.18
1480	701000	Other-non-teaching	0.00	0.00
		Teaching Salary Totals	*22,000.00*	*12,238.18*
2101	701000	Regular	48,587.00	32,913.49
2111	701000	Management	68,417.00	40,154.90
2115	701000	Management-vacation-payoff	0.00	273.71
2380	701000	Prof experts/prog leaders	30,000.00	33,198.55
		Salary Totals	*147,004.00*	*106,540.65*
3840	701000	Consolidated benefits	32,000.00	22,208.70
		Benefits Total	*32,000.00*	*22,208.70*
4301	680200	Office supplies	458.00	282.55
4301	701000	Office supplies	1,500.00	1,324.23
4302	701000	Materials production, CC media	120.00	50.55
4320	701000	Program/operating supplies	4,000.00	2,532.24
		Supplies and Materials Total	*6,078.00*	*4,189.57*
5110	701000	Professional services	52,000.00	44,892.78
5150	701000	Temporary employment service	0.00	0.00
5210	701000	Travel expense	115.00	157.59
5220	701000	Conference expense	50.00	50.00
5301	701000	Institutional membership	1,000.00	510.00
5540	701000	Telephone service	1,200.00	1,771.69
5611	701000	Rental of facilities	1,000.00	1,000.00
5810	701000	Communication & public information	1,000.00	526.50
5820	701000	Postal & delivery service	177.00	21.41
5821	701000	Courier services	23.00	22.88
5884	701000	Business expense	600.00	220.00
		Services and Misc Total	*57,165.00*	*49,172.85*
6401	701000	Other equipment	250.00	0.00
640101	701000	Other equipment - Inventory	0.00	0.00
6421	701000	Computers/software	1,972.00	1,972.21
642101	701000	Computers/software - Inventory	528.00	0.00
		Capital Outlay Total	*2,750.00*	*1,972.21*
Total Revenue			550,000.00	480,000.00
Total Salaries and Benefits			201,004.00	140,987.53
Total Operating Expenses			65,993.00	55,334.63
Total Expenses			266,997.00	196,322.16
Net profit/(Loss)			**283,003.00**	**283,677.84**

Establishing and Maintaining Effective Relations With Workforce Development Faculty, Staff, and Administrators

Dennis Bona

S everal myths are associated with successful customized training operations in the world of higher education. Perhaps the greatest of these is that customized training departments can function effectively only when they are organized as entities independent of the parent organization. This myth is often exaggerated further by the suggestion that total independence is the only way that customized training departments can be truly entrepreneurial; they cannot operate effectively within the confines of regular institutional processes. In this chapter I describe how a workforce development center can realize the benefits of full integration into regular college operations.

The integration of customized training into the larger institution depends on four major organizational components: leadership, organizational structure, institutional processes, and staffing. Obviously, these components are interdependent and necessitate excellent communication skills. I will analyze each component and how it relates to the success of customized training.

LEADERSHIP

The specific attributes of leadership vital to workforce development are commitment, support, and, above all, vision. A workforce development organization must be committed to making customized training a part of the larger institutional mission; this implies engagement with the rest of the institution, including involvement in institutional planning. Making and keeping promises to local businesses are also important. These organizations need to know that their needs are recognized, and that the college will endeavor to meet them in every way possible.

Support is not only about providing the financial resources to operate a customized training department, but it also requires a mindset that reflects an investment approach to funding. Investing in customized training not only sends a positive message to the staff and to the community, it also implies stability and sets high expectations. The other major application of support is associated with internal processes and procedures that will be detailed later. The primary point is that support must stem from the highest level of an institution. Vision implies direction; all of the truly successful customized training operations in the community college world have leadership that inspires a vision of something greater than a measured revenue source for the college.

ORGANIZATIONAL STRUCTURE

People become more creative, efficient, and effective when they work together, not in competition. It is simply contrary to contemporary management theories to create separate "silos" for customized training operations. Institutions can undeniably benefit from customized training staff's real-world experience with business and industry customers. Conversely, training staff can benefit greatly from an institution's valuable physical, financial, and staffing resources.

Customized training departments should be organized within the instructional division of the college. This can cause political stress within the organization, but perceived threats will eventually be replaced with a collective appreciation of the necessity of unifying traditional and nontraditional modes of instructional delivery. Figure 10.1 is an organizational chart that illustrates the model

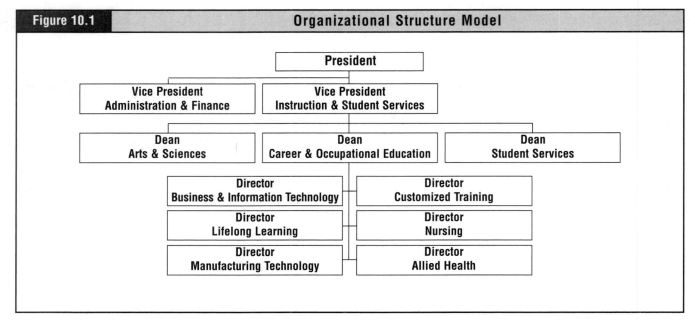

Figure 10.1 — **Organizational Structure Model**

currently employed at Kellogg Community College in Battle Creek, Michigan.

Customized training is embedded within the organization, specifically within the instructional division of the college. It can be very effective to have the director of business and the director of customized training reporting to the same person when a conflict arises over a turf issue such as facility, curriculum, or even staffing.

INSTITUTIONAL PROCESSES

One reason that institutions separate customized training from the rest of the college is that customized training is presumably unable to function within the constraints of institutional procedures and processes. Workforce development organizations want to accommodate the flexibility and speed demanded by their customers. Internal institutions such as academic cabinets, curriculum committees, and faculty senates are often considered applicable only to traditional students and conventional courses. The contention is that, in general, colleges are not sensitive to the needs of customized training customers, nor are they capable of reacting fast enough to help them effectively. Some may even believe that committee members will actually work to undermine an operation based on philosophical differences with the practice of customized training.

The reality is that legacy systems *can* accommodate the work that needs to be done, as long as people are willing to learn how to make it happen. Committees are about politics, and politics is fundamentally about leadership. If the people who make decisions share a vision and a commitment, the committees will eventually have to accept and endorse this significant culture shift. This can be achieved

by simply describing the benefits of integrating customized training into regular college operations. Benefits that relate to institutional processes can include the following:

- Increasing the flexibility of registration procedures, including nontraditional semesters, open registration, noncredit options, grading, and automation of archaic manual registration systems
- Streamlining course approval processes
- Developing advanced student tracking systems for purposes of quality assurance, accountability, increased customer service, and data from which improved student learning can occur
- Enhancing business office systems that deal efficiently with sponsor billing

In addition, customized training reaches much farther than a few corporate human resources people and line workers. Every student who has a quality experience with customized training has a quality experience with the institution that provides the training. Considering the sheer volume of students typical to this type of work, customized training can actually be considered a penetrating marketing effort for the institution. When presented in the right context, the benefits of embracing customized training into the regular operations of the college become difficult to dispute.

STAFFING

It is tempting for many customized training departments to outsource as many of their staffing needs as possible, including the coordination of training contracts, in particular those who deliver the training directly—that is, faculty, trainers, or facilitators. This staffing trend can have a negative impact on the institution that far outweighs the perceived financial efficiency provided by outsourcing.

The first drawback of outsourcing is the lack of commitment and understanding that outsourced people have regarding the parent organization. This is particularly true with short-term contracts that require narrowly focused training. The following questions need to be answered about outsourced employees:

- How invested are they in the long-term reputation of the college?
- How knowledgeable are they about the college, and how well can they represent the broad range of training options, opportunities, and services that the college may provide to the employer?
- Will their ultimate loyalty be to their personal best interests, with respect to potential conflicts of interest with the contracted employer—that is, employers hiring them directly to provide additional or ongoing training?
- How will they respond to supervision from within the organization, particularly when it involves demonstrating flexibility in meeting customers' needs?

There are additional questions that need to be asked regarding the maintenance of positive internal relations with the parent organization:

- How effective will outsourced employees be in developing and sustaining relationships with regular college personnel?

- Is the integration of college processes possible, or efficient, without consistent, positive relationships among departments?
- Is it easier for a nonproductive and competitive environment to develop when noninvested people work within the organization?
- Can a transfer of knowledge take place between contracted employees and regular employees about what happens in the contemporary workplace?

Simply stated, the outsourcing of staff is appropriate only under special circumstances, when no other viable options are present. Occasionally, an employer may request expertise that is not available within current staff, and scheduling issues alone can greatly constrain the use of regular staff. The point is that outsourcing brings with it both long- and short-term risk. The use of regular staffing facilitates the development of productive relationships, allowing enhanced institutional processes, transfer of knowledge from the workplace into the traditional college, long-term marketing opportunities, and, ultimately, the fulfillment of the broader institutional mission of the college.

CONCLUSION

The success of community colleges depends on their ability to develop and maintain effective relationships with customers, constituents, and employees. It is imperative that organizational structure promotes inclusion, integration, and support, allowing the development of effective internal relations. These factors are vital to the success of a workforce development organization in the long run. ✳

Assessing Needs for Training and Nontraining Projects

Elaine A. Gaertner and Cheryl A. Marshall

The transition to a knowledge economy has placed new demands on workforce educators. The need to assist workers as they become continuous learners, rapid problem solvers, and excellent performers is paramount to a strong economy. Workforce development professionals can serve as champions in this cause when they have the right set of tools for these new challenges. Over the past 15 years, *human performance technology* has emerged as a powerful means for analyzing the causes of performance problems and then designing the most suitable solutions for enhancing learning and productivity in the workplace. The first step in finding the right solution is to define the real problem. In this chapter we present methods for conducting a successful assessment, including which process to use and how to interact effectively with the client.

A PERFORMANCE ANALYSIS MODEL

The Importance of Using a Model

Models are important for two reasons: (a) they ensure a systematic and systemic look at the organization to identify the right problem, and (b) they help the workforce development professional to organize the data collected during an analysis and point to possible solutions (Gilbert, 1996; Mager & Pipe, 1997; Rosenberg, Coscarelli, & Hutchison, 1999; Rossett, 1999). As human beings, we bring our own biases into an analysis. Use of a good model is critical to ensuring a comprehensive and research-based analysis of the client organization. Otherwise, the consultant is prone to collect data in a haphazard, nondiagnostic way. When a model is used, data are collected in a variety of relevant categories and are transformed into information by using the model's parameters, which can then point to both training and nontraining solutions. When significant work environment issues are causing barriers to performance, the consultant knows to recommend nontraining solutions because a training solution will not produce the desired performance. In fact, it often makes matters worse.

In reality, the problem often includes both learning needs and work environment needs, which call for a variety of solutions. One of the advantages of using a performance approach is to ensure that training solutions are aligned with business needs and will be supported by factors back in the work environment (Robinson & Robinson, 1996). The term *transfer of training* is used to describe the ideal situation in which the knowledge and skills gained in a class are applied back on the job. One of the major purposes of conducting an analysis is to fully understand the business goals, the competencies needed to achieve those goals, and how the work environment can best support exemplary performance.

Training professionals have struggled for years to gain credibility and add value to their organizations. The difficulties often arose because the training solutions did not align with the organization's goals, nor could the skills be used in the work environment due to barriers. Participants became disillusioned and management viewed training as a nice reward, but not as a solution to performance problems. Countless examples of "failed" training sessions exist in areas as diverse as management, sales, interpersonal skills, computer skills, and many others. The root cause of these failures is that the true performance problems were never properly diagnosed and a training solution was applied like a Band-Aid to a bleeding ulcer. Just as a good doctor can diagnose the real ailment, a training professional using the performance approach can identify the underlying causes of performance problems and describe what exemplary performance looks like.

Information to Include in a Performance Analysis

When conducting an analysis, the consultant is interested in gathering information about the entire organizational system as it pertains to human performance. There are a number of questions a comprehensive analysis should answer (see Example). The goal is to identify the organization's business, performance, learning, and work environment needs.

WORKING WITH CLIENTS

Working with the right client team is critical to successful performance consulting projects (Block, 1981; Robinson & Robinson, 1996; Schwartz, 1994). The ideal client team

includes a project sponsor, managers and supervisors who own the problem, and an internal human resources manager. The project sponsor needs to have enough power in the organization to provide access to information and people, a large enough budget to pay for the analysis and implementation of interventions, and be credible with other managers in the organization. In short, the sponsor needs to have enough clout to help make the analysis and interventions happen.

Managers and supervisors on the client team should be people who are close enough to the problems and have a real need to resolve the issues and improve performance. They often provide critical information during the analysis and play an enormous role in tactical implementation of interventions. Because performance interventions often include training and nontraining solutions, it is very helpful to include high-level managers from the internal human resources and training departments. Outside consultants can be perceived as threatening to

---

Example: Questions to Ask in a Comprehensive Performance Analysis

Organization Systems and Alignments

1. Has the organization identified its purpose and goals? Has it considered customer input?
2. How rapidly is the business environment changing?
3. Is there a link between performer and organizational goals?
4. Are model (exemplary) performers present?
5. What is the current level of performance?
6. Is the organization designed appropriately?
7. Are the procedures and processes effective and efficient?
8. What is the organization's culture?
9. What is the management style like?

Performance Management

1. Is the job designed to achieve desired accomplishments?
2. Is there task interferenace?
3. Does the employee have the necessary tools and equipment?
4. Does performance matter? Are there any consequences?
5. Are the expectations and standards of performance clear?
6. Does the employee know the consequences of not meeting the performance standard?
7. Is feedback relevant, accurate, timely, specific, constructive, and easy to understand?
8. Is adequate pay provided in a timely manner?
9. Are there other rewards for valued accomplishments?
10. Is there an absence of punishment for performing well?
11. Are any hidden incentives present for poor performance?
12. Are there other methods for assessing quality?

Capability and Knowledge

1. Has the right person been matched to the job?
2. Is the person capable of learning the job?
3. How long does it typically take to learn the job?
4. Do employees have the skills and knowledge to do the job?
5. Is the person free from emotional limitations? What feelings are currently present?
6. Are job aids available?

Motivation

1. Does the employee have an interest in the job and expected achievements?
2. Does the employee have a desire to do the job well?
3. Does the employee have the big picture and under stand his/her role?
4. Do motives endure? Is there turnover?
5. Does a career development process exist?

internal human resource staff, particularly when they are using unfamiliar approaches and models. In the ideal situation, the external performance consultant partners work with internal human resources and training staff to gain buy-in and solicit support for systemic interventions related to training, reward and recognition, performance management, and selection. In reality, some performance improvement projects will not have the ideal client team. In these cases, the performance consultant must consider the implications before embarking on a frustrating and fruitless journey.

One of the reasons for working with the right client team is to gain access to as much information as possible during the analysis. The best performance analysis views the organization as an organic system and considers not only each of the individual elements within the system, but also how they interact with and influence one another (Brethower, 1995, 1999). The extensive data collection requires a level of intimacy with the organization that may not be comfortable for internal managers. Trust is a strong prerequisite; having the right client team to support the effort has a big impact on effectiveness and success.

Clients typically trust consultants who are honest and forthright, sensitive to the organization's culture, responsive to needs, and quickly follow through on their commitments (Block, 1981). A climate of trust can be established from the very first meeting by asking probing questions, carefully listening to responses, and educating the client on the process of performance analysis and its requirements. Clients often do not understand how performance analysis works and its level of invasiveness into the organization. When a client has a predetermined solution in mind, the consultant often needs to discuss why the solution will have limited impact or be totally ineffective. For example, when clients presuppose that training is the answer, the consultant must gently inform them that it may not fix the root cause of the problem and can only address learning needs.

Honesty at this phase of the project is essential. Failure to inform and educate will only reflect on the consultant, who can then be used as a scapegoat when the intervention goes awry. During this first meeting, the consultant asks a few probing questions to gain a clearer understanding of the situation. Some useful questions are

- What are the organization's goals?
- What is the organization's structure?
- Which work areas are involved in the performance problem?
- What kind of performance and behaviors are you seeing that you would like changed?

- What would it look like if everything were running perfectly? What would people be doing?
- Do you currently have anyone who you would consider a top performer?
- How have you tried to address the problem?
- Why did you call now?
- What significant changes are under way in the organization or are expected in the near future?
- What parameters or constraints will affect this project?

The client should do most of the talking during this first meeting. The consultant needs to listen and take notes to capture the key information. These questions not only serve as the beginning of the analysis, but also help the consultant determine if the person who made the call can serve as project sponsor and who the other members of the project team should be. The client appreciates hearing the initial interpretation of the situation, how the analysis would proceed, and its anticipated scope. The consultant should be sure to address the fact that the analysis will uncover a number of different issues, including some of the organization's vulnerabilities. Clients need to be prepared for the possibility of these kinds of findings and feel that they can do something about them.

If the client is interested in proceeding, the next step is usually the preparation of a proposal that includes activities, roles and responsibilities, timelines, and costs. Following through on the preparation of the proposal in a reasonable time frame gives the client further confidence in the performance consultant. Reviewing the proposal with other members of the organization who will serve as sponsors, supporters, or participants is usually the next step in the process. The consultant needs to be prepared to answer questions, deal with objections, and address concerns without becoming defensive or arrogant. Demonstrating professionalism and confidence secures further trust with client team members. If the team decides to move forward with the project, the consultant should delineate timelines and responsibilities as soon as possible. The consultant should be ready to offer dates for starting the analysis and identify the point person in the organization who will assist in setting up appointments for data collection.

THE ANALYSIS PROCESS

A valid analysis includes multiple data collection methods. Each method has advantages and disadvantages; using more than one method helps ensure the accuracy of the data and provides more than one view of the organizational system. Table 11.1 summarizes the major methods.

Table 11.1	Data Collection Methods for Assessing Clients' Needs	
Method	**Advantage**	**Disadvantages**
Observation	• Captures actual behavior, performance, and work environment factors	• Behavior is changed • Can be time consuming
Interviews	• Two-way communication • Depth of information	• Time consuming • Difficulty interpreting results • Interviewer bias
Focus groups	• Group synergy • Two-way communication • Saves time	• Groupthink • Domination by the few • Difficulty interpreting results
Meeting facilitation	• Group generates the data • Group dynamics can be observed	• Data may be skewed by participants' perceptions and group dynamics
Surveys	• Can be done quickly • Broad communication • Can be inexpensive • Provides overview of what questions to pursue in interviews or focus groups	• One-way communication • Low return rate
Historical data or written documents	• Provides a baseline for measurement of changes • Can offer objective data • Inexpensive and quick	• Author's bias may be unknown • Sometimes hard to get—may be confidential information
360-Degree Assessments	• Provides in-depth individual assessment of skill gaps • Aggregate data can identify training needs for an entire work group or job family	• Based on individual perceptions • Expensive • Does not reveal work environment issues
Assessment tests	• Objective measures of skill gaps • Provides a baseline measure	• Can be expensive and time consuming • Does not reveal work environment issues

Observing Exemplars

Observing people who are successfully performing in a position is one of the very best ways to discover how exemplars have adjusted to the work environment and how they achieve valued business goals. Because experts do not have to think about what they are doing and how they are doing it, observing their behaviors and performance is a better way to collect valid data than through an interview. During an interview the experts will describe how they think they do it but will often omit steps because the process has become automated in the brain. During observations, the consultant can actually watch performance, see how the exemplar deals with problems as they occur, and capture the critical aspects of performance. Valuable work environ-ment data are also collected while the consultant shadows the exemplar during the workday.

The major problem with observation is that the very presence of the observer will cause job incumbents to change their behavior. Therefore, the observer must be as inconspicuous as possible and must spend enough time for true behavior to be seen. Job incumbents can *act* for a limited amount of time, but once they forget the observer's presence or a crisis occurs, typical behavior returns. The challenge is to spend enough time to see real behavior without emptying the client's pocketbook.

Occasionally, a client will not have any exemplars to observe. Either no one is succeeding in the position, or the position is new and no one has become an expert. In this situation, ask if there are people who have mastered part of the expected performance or benchmark in other similar work environments to capture the desired performance.

Table 11.2 (see next page) shows desired performance for a new position and the related training classes for each level. It was based partially on observing job incumbents who were exemplars at one aspect of the desired performance. The rest was developed through a series of iterative discussions about business needs with the organization's middle and senior managers and about how performance at each level would help achieve those goals. For this particular client, pay increases would be granted as individuals achieved the desired level of performance and moved to the next higher level. Care was taken to ensure fairness in the expectations at each level and that each level was the appropriate precursor to the next level. The integration of classroom training to each level helped ensure transfer of training back to the job and that training would be reinforced through on-the-job coaches.

Conducting Interviews

Interviews have the advantage of two-way communication. Body language and voice tone are a fundamental part of the data collected and may help detect motivational problems such as resistance or overconfidence. Follow-up questions can also be asked when the client provides interesting information that will enhance the quality of the data collected. The typical interview will last between 30 and 90 minutes, so the questions need to be limited. Examples are provided of interview questions used in two separate analyses that address performance, learning, and work environment needs. Business needs were identified earlier through discussions with the client team.

Establishing rapport at the beginning of an interview sets a productive tone and puts the interviewee at ease. One technique is to ask interviewees what they know about the purpose and process of the analysis. This allows the analyst to explain the reason for the interviews, tell how the information will be used, define confidentiality and anonymity, and answer any questions. Interview participants will become more relaxed and open when they know that their names will not be attached to specific comments and that they will have the opportunity during the interview to delete anything they have said.

Unfortunately, despite the wealth of details provided during interviews, they are very time consuming and, therefore, costly. Most interviews are about one hour long and take another hour to process. For example, if 10 interviews are conducted, another 10 hours of analysis and writing will be required to create a meaningful report. Another challenge when conducting interviews is

dealing with prejudices and preconceptions about the problem. No consultant is immune from the infiltration of prior experiences, values, and beliefs. Once again, the use of a model forces one to collect a variety of data and to consider the organizational system from a number of different views.

Facilitating Focus Groups and Off-Site Planning Sessions

Focus groups offer another good way to collect data because they present the advantage of two-way communication but cost less than interviews. Participants can be grouped by job family or level in the organization or department, depending on the questions being asked. For example, if work environment barriers for a particular position need to be identified, it makes sense to include people working in that job from across the organization. A second focus group could include supervisors of those people to gain a different perspective of the same problem. When looking for barriers between departments, each group would include staff members from a single department to gain their perspective on the issues. So, who participates in a focus group will depend on the nature of the problem and the availability of people to attend.

The design of a focus group should include a brief introduction to the purpose of the session, ground rules describing how to behave, and enough questions to gather the needed data and fill up the time allotted. The typical focus group session runs between 60 and 90 minutes, so the questions will need to be carefully selected. Ideally, two consultants should run the session, with one scribing and the other facilitating. The scribe captures the group's comments, and the facilitator manages the discussion by keeping the group on track and making sure everyone participates.

Sometimes the consultant has the opportunity to facilitate an off-site planning session for a group. Although the off-site session will have its own purpose and goals, it is also a wonderful opportunity for gathering data. In fact, the session can be designed to gather information about a variety of needs as a by-product of working on the session's goals. For example, if the group is working on a strategic plan, the development of a vision and mission can include a description of the ideal business and work environment. This provides input on exemplary performance. When the group moves to action planning for achieving the vision, the gaps can be identified along with the group's perceived possible solutions. The consultant then has the opportunity to analyze the data and recommend further analysis or viable solutions not identified by the group. Because the consultant has

Table 11.2	Matching Desired Performance to Training Courses
Desired Performance	**Related Training**
Level 1 Able to perform all level A and B positions Accurately calculates raw material and packaging demands Calculates line capacity Knows product mix and mix percentages Knows product and packaging specifications by line Achieves minimum line standards Film waste no more than 10% Able to make group presentations Performs all housekeeping duties related to area of responsibility Accurately completes work orders Sets up and calibrates metal detectors Shows good attendance Works safely and monitors team's safety	English as a second language Business math How to read and interpret data Problem solving Customer focus Effective coaching and team leadership Communication skills How to implement continuous improvement Computer basics: keyboarding, basic functions, data entry Packaging workshop Good Manufacturing Practices training Chemical-handling training
Level 2 Able to perform all level C positions Demonstrates effective labor utilization practices (staffing and scheduling) Knows the productivity standards on the line Achieves production goals for single line by effectively scheduling line usage (balances the line) Begins departmental cross-training Member of the safety team	People skills (dealing with difficult people, conflict management, interpersonal relationships, etc.) Computer classes: Excel, WORD, 10-key, work order entry Food safety training Job-specific training
Level 3 Able to demonstrate every position in the department Trains technical positions D and E Writes schedules and plans for the day Reviews plans with area supervisor Maintains line housekeeping, GMP, and safety Film waste no more than 5% Cross-trains in another department	Business basics: first 30 modules (cost, service, quality, safety, and people) Preventative maintenance operations training: 2 days Phone skills and voice mail Computer classes: e-mail
Level 4 Trains all new associates Executes levels 1, 2, & 3 Schedules and runs the daily requirements Ultimately able to run multiple lines at once Consistently achieves pounds per associate hour and yield standards by line Balances line use to achieve all production goals Assists with line preventative maintenance Film waste no more than 3%	Business basics: second 30 modules Computer classes: proficient in all previous classes, cross-train in other support function areas

the benefit of using a performance model, it is often easy to see solutions unknown to the group.

The consultant also has the opportunity to observe group dynamics. It is very difficult for participants to "act" throughout the day at an off-site session. As they become more tired or as critical issues get raised, the true emotions and reactions of members become apparent. If the consultant is keen at watching body language, an enormous amount of data can be collected about group members' interactions with one another and their level of motivation regarding certain performance expectations. An off-site session is a more "normal" environment for the participants, and authentic reactions and thoughts are likely to occur in this setting, partially eliminating the disadvantages of observing in the work environment or facilitating a focus group.

Reviewing Written Documentation

When the client is willing to share written information, it creates an opportunity for using a nonverbal form of data. Written information can include monthly reports, production reports, customer satisfaction surveys, customer complaints, previous training materials, or any other form of prior documentation. The advantage of analyzing writ-

---

Example: Questions Used in a Performance Analysis Interview at an Information Technology Firm

These interview questions helped to identify exemplary customer service and project management:

1. Describe your job, including how you interact with customers.
2. Describe the most difficult customer you ever had to deal with and tell how you handled the situation.
3. Describe any projects you work on and how you manage them.
4. What do you like best about your job? What do you like least?
5. What gets in the way of getting your job done? What would you like to see changed?
6. How do you know you are doing a good job?
7. What are the rewards for doing a good job?
8. What are the consequences for not doing a good job?
9. Are there any training classes you have had that were helpful? Are there any additional training classes you would like to have?
10. Is there anything else you would like to add?

Example: Questions Used in a Performance Analysis Interview With Investigators

These interview questions helped to identify exemplary performance and barriers to performance:

1. Describe the most important parts of your job.
2. What parts of your job do you like the best? The least?
3. What are the hardest parts of the job?
4. How do you decide the level of complexity of a job? That is, what factors do you consider?
5. How long does it take to complete different investigations (based on the level of complexity)? How do these time frames compare to the standard?
6. What gets in the way of getting your job done? What would you like to see changed?
7. How do you know you are doing a good job?
8. How do the office charts play a part in providing information?
9. How about the feedback sheets on your cases?
10. What about the annual performance appraisal?
11. What are the rewards for good performance? What are the consequences for poor performance?
12. Describe how you were trained when you first started. What role did the mentor play? How would you recommend improving the orientation period?
13. Are there any training classes you've had that were helpful? Are there any additional classes or topics you would like to see?
14. How do you use the handbook? How useful is the handbook? Were the classes effective in helping you apply the information in the handbook? What changes would you recommend to make the handbook more useful?
15. Any other comments?

---

ten material is that it provides a source of objective data and can show baseline performance. However, the possibility of author bias still exists because individuals in the organization who had their own sets of perceptions and motives prepared it. The consultant will need to find out the purpose of the document, the author, and the meaning of its content. For example, a production report might be prepared by the manager whose performance is measured by its results. Customer surveys and feedback are often some of the most revealing sources of data because the performance gaps are usually clear. However, they may not show the source of the performance problem, so it is up to the analyst to uncover the root causes.

Previous training material is important to review, particularly if the client is asking for a new training program because the first one failed. One red flag signaling that a performance problem is not due to a learning need is when the client is asking for a second training program. The analysis then has to include findings on why the first program did not work and how a second training program will not necessarily fix performance problems. If the client insists on conducting a training program, prepare a blueprint for training based on the analysis results, show how it differs from the first training program, and present ways to "make training stick" back on the job. This allows the opportunity to implement nontraining interventions as part of an integrated solution to performance problems.

Using Surveys

When a broad overview of the problem is needed, surveys are the best option. This allows the opportunity for a large number of employees to give their opinions on the performance problem and its sources. In the past surveys had to be created, mailed out with a return envelope, and then processed by hand. Many online survey tools that are currently available make the entire process easier and more efficient. The software allows the survey to be developed and placed online so that employees can log onto a Web site and complete the survey, and then the results are automatically calculated. Using this new method helps mitigate the low return rate on hard-copy surveys. If respondents believe the survey will be quick and easy, they are much more likely to take it.

Two types of items are typically used on surveys. The first is a Likert-type scale that asks people to select a rating from 1 to 4 or 1 to 5. The scale labels can reflect attitudes (agree to disagree), frequency (never to often), or some other relevant metric (low to high). Likert-type questions allow for statistical calculations and can point to major problem areas or strengths in the organization. The second type of question is open-ended and allows respondents to write anything they think is important. This helps prevent missing a critical issue that the analyst or client team may have overlooked.

Survey construction is not as easy as it looks. Because the survey-taker will not be able to ask clarifying questions, take care to construct the survey and its scales so that it is clear and easy to understand. Several drafts will need to be prepared and reviewed by a number of fresh eyes before the survey reflects the intent of the analyst and client team.

Once survey results are compiled, the analyst has a better idea about follow-up questions to ask in interviews or focus groups. This is the major advantage to conducting a survey prior to using more extensive and costly data collec-

tion techniques. Broad issues are identified and will trigger a series of questions in the minds of the analyst and client team members. These questions can then be refined into good interview or focus group questions to gather a deeper level of data about the performance problem and its causes.

Using 360-Degree Assessments

A 360-degree assessment is a tool used to identify strengths and weaknesses in specific competencies, behaviors, or performance areas. It is a method whereby participants are rated by their bosses, their peers, their staff, and themselves—in effect, from every direction. Other groups can also be included, such as customers and clients, executives, and colleagues outside the immediate work group. A number of off-the-shelf assessments are available, or a customized profile can be created based on a performance analysis of the job.

Another option is to begin with a list of generic competencies and then modify each based on the performance required in the client organization. The Example on the next page shows a list of competencies that were developed by comparing the results of an analysis with a list of generic competencies. The process involved conducting interviews with exemplary performers, analyzing their behaviors and performance, and comparing the results against the list of generic competencies. Each competency area was rewritten to reflect actual exemplary performance.

Once the assessment instrument is selected or created, it can be used to identify developmental needs for participants. When managers within work groups have completed the assessment, the results can be aggregated and major developmental needs identified within the group. Common needs based on skill gaps can be addressed by training classes with discussion of how the skills will be reinforced within the specific work environment. Mentoring is another option within organizations; when a manager lacks a competency that is someone else's strength, partnering the two allows coaching and modeling to take place. The mentoring process allows for one-on-one coaching and feedback over time, a significant advantage over a one-day classroom session.

Setting the Scope of the Analysis Process

The very best analysis includes more than one method to compensate for the deficiencies of each. Depending on the needs of the client, the organization's culture, the timeline, and the budget, a number of methods should be used to collect the relevant data. The exact length of the analysis process is never known because things will change during the course of the project. However, the three major factors to consider when projecting the end

Example: Customized Competencies Developed From Analysis and a Generic List

Customer Service

- Identifies the customer's needs
- Understands the customer's work environment and priorities
- Responds to customer requests
- Resolves problems with the customer
- Achieves desired results

Composure

- Remains calm under pressure
- Is not rattled by the unexpected
- Does not show frustration when resistance is encountered

Interpersonal Skills

- Establishes rapport and trust with others
- Interacts effectively with others
- Observes body language to assess mood and affect
- Manages conflict well

Oral Communication

- Clearly and concisely expresses ideas
- Uses language the customer can understand
- Listens to others
- Asks questions to ensure understanding
- Adjusts to the customer's communication style

Problem Solving

- Quickly identifies problems
- Collects data needed to validate the source of the problem
- Generates multiple solutions
- Works as part of a team when necessary to solve the problem

Technical Knowledge

- Possesses specialized knowledge in the field that can be applied on the job
- Understands the organization and its customers
- Knows how the organization operates

Professionalism

- Demonstrates integrity by following through on commitments
- Strives to attain results
- Takes independent action when needed
- Willing to be held accountable for actions

Flexibility

- Adapts to changes in the work environment
- Changes approach or method to best fit the situation
- Accepts feedback and changes behavior accordingly

---

date of the analysis include the client's availability, the time needed to conduct the methods, and the consultant's availability. Clearly outline the client's responsibilities, including the assignment of a point person who can assist with logistics such as scheduling appointments and arranging rooms. Always, without exception, build in some cushion to account for shifting priorities, sickness, natural disasters, and so on. For the most part, data collection and analysis can and should take place in less than 60 days. A longer period of time will result in aging of the data and loss of interest by the client. Because the client has called with an immediate need (perceived or real), the analysis should address the causes of the problem and potential solutions within a reasonable time frame.

INTERPRETING AND COMPILING RESULTS

Once data gathering is complete, the next task is to transform the volume of details into information. This phase of the analysis involves writing a report that includes a description of business, performance, learning, and work environment needs; identifies gaps and their causes; and presents an integrated set of training and nontraining solutions. A report can be organized in a number of different ways depending on the methods used, the purpose of the analysis, and the client's needs. How it is organized and its exact contents will vary by project. At a minimum, the report should include an executive summary, methodology, significant findings, and recommended solutions.

Writing an Executive Summary

Virtually all executives prefer a short one- or two-page summary of the analysis methods and findings. Senior-level managers may or may not read the entire report, but the managers and supervisors who own the problem usually will. So, the executive summary serves two purposes: (a) it provides the busy executive with an overview of the key findings and recommendations, and (b) it provides a summary that the performance consultant can use as a debrief-

Example: Executive Summary

Background

In the spring of 2002 [consultants] met with [training manager] at [company name] to discuss partnering on a performance analysis project. As a result of the initial discussion, a performance analysis was conducted to assess the factors affecting human performance among supervisors at [company name]. The performance assessment would help [consultant] and [company name] determine whether [company name] human performance goals could in fact be affected by training solutions, or whether other performance development interventions [nontraining solutions] might be more appropriate.

Methodology

The analysis included three sessions of observations of the work environment and six interviews with supervisors who held positions throughout [company name]. The observations allow validation of verbal data collected during interviews. The general questions asked of participants included

1. Describe your job, including any communication that occurs with employees.
2. Describe what you think makes a good supervisor.
3. Describe your best employee.
4. Describe the problems you encounter on the job
5. What gets in the way of getting your job done? What would you like to see changed?
6. What do you like best about your job?
7. How do you know you are doing a good job?
8. What are the rewards for doing a good job?
9. What are the consequences for not doing a good job?
10. Are there any training classes you have had that were helpful? Are there any additional training classes you would like to have?
11. Is there anything else you would like to add?

Findings and Recommendations

- The supervisors are very excited about additional training and want to participate in the classes. Their primary areas of interest include English as a second language (ESL), computer skills, and supervisory training. They particularly look forward to improving their communication skills.
- When asked what they enjoy about their work, they reported achievement of results and solving problems.

- A few communication gaps were reported among managers, engineers, and supervisors.
- The majority of the supervisors reported that they enjoyed working at [company name] and would change very little about the work environment.
- Some of the supervisors are receiving anonymous feedback from their staff with the use of a new survey, and they appear to value this information. This feedback could be incorporated into a supervisory development program.
- Performance feedback is built into the process: Supervisors reported they know they are doing well when they meet the established production schedule deadlines and achieve the desired quality level. However, not all of the supervisors receive verbal recognition from their managers; increasing management feedback would further enhance performance.
- Consequences for poor performance are present. Employees know what is acceptable and unacceptable based on the consequences they see in the workplace.
- Appraisals and mini-reviews seem to be regularly completed and linked to raises. The analysis did not include a review of any appraisals, so whether they are accurate was not assessed.
- Several supervisors reported that the use of temporary workers is a challenge because of the continuous turnover and constant training. Consider developing job aids and instruction manuals that will assist supervisors and permanent employees in training temps. The examples seen on the "activity boards" would be a good place to start gleaning information.
- Supervisors did report some discomfort with the uncertainty of future work and the potential of some lines being transferred out of the country. We recommend keeping them informed about the future as much as possible and continuing to reward their efforts. There is some frustration with the current lack of promotional opportunities and raises.
- The need for ESL is critical based on the results of the analysis. The typical communication done during the day includes (a) morning meetings to discuss the production schedule, (b) quality meetings to resolve quality issues, (c) answering questions and guiding employee activities during the workday, (d) employee interaction to discuss work schedules or time-off needed, and (e) occasional performance improvement discussions.
- During job shadowing, the performance consultant

Example: Executive Summary (cont'd)

observed the difficulty of a Vietnamese-speaking supervisor trying to communicate with Spanish-speaking employees. The potential for miscommunication is great. ESL courses will assist supervisors in communicating with upper management, but a gap may still exist between supervisors and employees until team leads can participate in ESL training as well.

Training Solutions

- ESL for supervisors and team leaders
- Computer training, including Microsoft Office products and e-mail
- Supervisory training focused on performance management

Nontraining Solutions

- Educate middle managers to provide verbal recognition to supervisors and offer incentives or make the awards program easily accessible to them.
- Improve communication with supervisors during the current changes in the organization.
- Expand the use of 360-degree feedback instruments to all supervisors and managers.
- Create job and training aids for temporary workers.

ing tool in the review meeting. A useful format for creating an executive summary includes the following elements:

- *Project background*: Reasons for the analysis and any significant agreements made between the client and the consultant
- *Methodology:* The methods used during the analysis, including specific numbers of people dealt with in the organization
- *Major findings:* The major themes organized around the model used
- *Recommendations:* Overview of the solutions to performance problems
- *Next steps:* Activities needed to move the project forward

These descriptions can be accomplished in two pages or less. A longer executive summary defeats the purpose of having a succinct overview and will replicate too much of the body of the report. If one of the client team members has additional questions, the consultant can refer back to the pages in the body of the report that provide additional details.

Reporting Significant Findings

The body of the report should include significant findings from the analysis and can be organized based on the model used or by major themes. Once again, the project goals, the methodology used, and the client's needs dictate how to arrange the contents in a meaningful way. If, interviews or focus groups were conducted, the raw responses should be included and grouped by question or theme. An Example on page 98 shows the responses of seven different people to a question about feedback on performance. Including this type of raw data helps validate the summary of findings included in the executive summary and the subsequent recommendations.

Evaluating and Identifying Competencies

When the analysis includes a description of exemplary performance, it is helpful to incorporate the requisite competencies. Just as with the 360-degree assessment, a customized list can be created by integrating the analysis results with generic competencies. An Example on page 99 shows a description of exemplary project management for an information technology firm and the requisite competencies.

This example was developed on a project where training was one of the client's desired solutions. With that in mind, the analysis needed to identify ways to make a training solution authentic and representative of the work environment. The description of exemplary performance and its related competencies was used to define learning objectives and could later be used for the creation of course materials and activities.

For many work environments, classroom training is an inadequate solution when learning needs are involved. In manufacturing environments where learning needs are present, classroom training will play a minor role in the overall suite of solutions. On-the-job training is more appropriate and more likely to have impact on business needs. In these situations the analysis should address not only the requisite competencies, but also the actual problems encountered on the job and their impact on achieving business goals. An Example on page 100 outlines the results of an analysis in a commercial bakery that were used to create "developmental checklists" for on-the-job training and coaching.

Recommending Solutions

Consultants' true value comes from their expertise in (a) conducting the analysis and (b) making recommenda-

Example: Organizing Comments by Question and by Individual

Feedback: How do you know if you are doing a good job?

- Customers let her manager know if she is doing well and meeting their expectations.
- She gets compliments on her work.

- He doesn't really know if he is doing a good job. Some customers tell him.

- Hearing satisfaction from the customer and knowing they are happy.
- Solving the problem.
- She does not get feedback from her manager.

- The help desk uses metrics to track performance including number of tickets, time to resolve, average answering time, and number of calls received.

- The surveys provide official feedback. On the last survey they got dinged for not knowing one technical area. Sometimes the survey is inaccurate because the customer marks the wrong work group; roles and responsibilities overlap, so the customer gets confused.
- She talks to information technology management.
- One challenge is that one person may have the wrong perception and you then have to document everything to prove we are doing well. "Our court vs. their court."
- Keeping on schedule and things going well overall is a good sign.

- The surveys tend to be good. They don't reflect things we have control over.
- Uses survey results as a management tool: how well do they reply to open tickets.
- The results may not be intended for team members. His manager gets the results.

- He doesn't see the surveys.
- Interaction with customers and hearing through the grapevine
- Hears from manager: sends e-mail to recognize outstanding performance.
- Manager gives regular feedback. If someone is not happy or satisfied, he is told.

---

tions. Most projects will require both training and non-training solutions. The skill of the consultant comes in creating an integrated, elegant, and practical set of solutions (Spitzer, 1999). One of the first rules of intervention selection is to consider the level of intrusiveness into the organization. Solutions that require massive changes, huge budgets, and long time frames are the least likely to succeed. Look for the simplest ways to get the greatest performance improvement among the most staff. Be sure to position training solutions alongside their work environment counterparts. We have provided recommendations for improving performance among a work group of investigators (see page 101). The majority can be implemented quickly without significant costs or changes to the organization.

Writing Learning Objectives and Blueprints

Another benefit of using the performance approach is the opportunity to develop training solutions that mirror exemplary performance in the actual work environment. *Authentic* training addresses the critical competencies needed to perform well and uses exercises based on actual work environment factors. Examples on page 102 show two blueprints developed as a result of an analysis in an information technology firm to identify exemplary customer service and project management.

A Final Word on Compiling Results

The best analysis in the world will be useless if the client team does not understand the results and their implications. Careful consideration should be taken when preparing the report so that it is clear and concise, but also thorough. The exact contents and length will vary depending on the project goals, the findings, and the organization's culture. Be prepared to spend one hour of writing time for every hour of analysis, and be willing to make revisions based on the initial feedback from the project sponsor. The examples we provided are just some of the ways to present information. Being creative and sensitive to the client's potential reactions will help in writing a report that has its intended impact and will allow the project to move forward.

GAINING CLIENT BUY-IN AND SUPPORTING CHANGE MANAGEMENT

One of the frequent challenges in reviewing the contents of an analysis is dealing with the client team's reactions to the findings. It is helpful to review the report with the project sponsor before presenting its contents to the group. The sponsor will help you gauge the level of defen-

Example: Description of Exemplary Performance and Requisite Competencies

Brief Description of Exemplary Performance: Project Management

Exemplary project managers excel in three areas:

1. Project planning, including the use of Microsoft Project
2. Communicating with their customers
3. Communicating and managing staff to complete the project

The best project managers possess the ability to communicate effectively with their customers to identify project goals, negotiate scope of work, and define critical due dates. They provide regular progress reports in meetings and develop a sense of teamwork among their staff and their customers. Microsoft Project is a valuable tool for project managers because it allows them to track progress and revise project deadlines. The key is knowing how to use the software and spending the time needed to input changes. In terms of staff communication, exemplary project managers demonstrate the ability to delegate effectively and follow up on task completion.

Requisite Competencies for Exemplary Project Management

Project Management

- Communicates effectively with customer
- Develops project plans and uses software to track progress
- Communicates changes and progress to customers and staff
- Manages project team activity and coordinates efforts
- Delegates work to appropriate person and follows up
- Is able to identify and resolve problems

- Is able to handle multiple assignments and priorities
- Effectively manages meetings
- Demonstrates the ability to complete projects on time and within budget

Teamwork

- Encourages involvement of everyone on the team and fosters collaboration
- Shows commitment to the project objectives
- Contributes fair share of effort to the team's work

Oral Communication

- Clearly and concisely expresses ideas
- Uses language the customer can understand
- Listens to others
- Asks questions to ensure understanding
- Adjusts to the customer's communication style

Decision Making

- Collects adequate information
- Makes accurate decisions in a timely manner
- Is willing to accept the risk of a decision

Technical Knowledge

- Possesses specialized knowledge in their field that can be applied on the job
- Understands the organization and its customers
- Knows how the organization operates

Written Communication

- Clearly and concisely expresses concepts in writing
- Presents numerical data effectively
- Uses e-mail appropriately to communicate with others

sive reaction among other team members and can validate the report's findings. Discussion with the project sponsor will help develop a plan for presenting the findings. The goal is to diplomatically but honestly reveal the findings in a way that the client team will accept the results and recommendations.

For the most part, when the client team has been integral to selecting the analysis methods, it will ultimately accept the analysis findings. A short period of defensiveness may occur, particularly if team members discover that they are part of the problem. Managers do not like to hear how their styles negatively impact staff

performance, but they will accept the truth when it is tactfully stated. Telling the truth to a client is inherently powerful. Sometimes there is even a feeling of relief because the elephant on the table has finally been talked about and can now be dealt with. On occasion, an organization will not be ready to deal with honest feedback and will play "blame the consultant." These situations are never comfortable for either party, but the consultant can maintain integrity by doing what is right for the client and telling the truth, even if it means walking away from the job. In the long run, the consultant's credibility will be validated, and there may be a future opportunity to

---

Example: Analysis Results for a Bakery On-the-Job Training Program

Key Responsibilities

- Sets up machine for correct size and shape of loaf.
- Uses molder chart to adjust each knob or crank to proper setting.
- Makes sure sifter is filled.
- Places loaves seam side down in the center of the pan.
- Makes sure all pans are filled before loading onto rack.
- Works with pan man to load racks.
- Loads racks top to bottom.
- Keeps work area clean

Knowledge, Skills, and Abilities

- Reading numbers and accurately recording figures
- Reading molder chart
- Adjusting buttons and cranks on machine
- Communication with pan man, foreman, and supervisor
- Good judgment in following safety rules
- Moving quickly when a problem on machine occurs
- Eye-hand coordination
- Standing and walking for long periods of time
- Occasional squatting and lifting

- Occasional pushing and pulling
- Able to work in temperatures ranging from 65 to 100 degrees

Problems Encountered

- Too much or too little flour is applied to loaves
- Pans not filled
- Pans come too fast
- Pans come too slow
- Improper molding
- Pans not greased properly

Potential Impact on Quality

- Tracking is done by counting trays, not individual pans. If all pans are not filled, the count will be off.
- When pans are too fast, the tray is set aside to check later to make sure seam is down. Loaves baked with seam up are misshapen.
- When pans come too slowly, bread falls to the floor and is thrown away.
- Poor shape of finished loaves.
- Product sticks to pans after baking.

---

return and finish the project once the findings are proven to be true.

Once the client team is ready to move forward and implement some of the recommendations, the consultant's role can change from performance analyst to change management guide. Many clients will be tentative as they attempt to establish nontraining interventions, and the consultant can play an important role in helping them move forward. Regular meetings should be held to track progress, discuss barriers, provide advice, and develop workable solutions. The consultant may take on additional responsibilities and become part of the implementation team during the early stages. This can be a very exciting time as solutions begin to take effect and performance improves. The tangible results achieved from performance improvement projects leave everyone with a feeling of satisfaction.

CONCLUSION

The use of a performance improvement approach ensures that the right problem is identified and that the most effective, elegant solution is prescribed. Workforce devel-

opment professionals can avoid the pitfalls of implementing expensive programs that fail to impart knowledge and improve performance. Use of human performance technology will allow workforce development professionals to do the right things for the right reasons and gain further credibility in the process. ❊

References

Block, P. (1981). *Flawless consulting*. San Diego: University Associates.

Brethower, D. M. (1995). Specifying a human performance technology knowledgebase. *Performance Improvement Quarterly, 8*(2), 17–39.

Brethower, D. M. (1999). General systems theory and behavioral psychology. In H. D. Stolovitch & E. J. Keeps (Eds.), *Handbook of human performance technology: Improving individual organizational performance worldwide* (2nd ed., pp. 67–81). San Francisco: Jossey-Bass.

Gilbert, T. F. (1996). *Human competence: Engineering worthy performance*. Amherst, MA: HRD Press.

Mager, R. F., & Pipe, P. (1997). *Analyzing performance*

problems (3rd ed.). Atlanta: Center for Effective Performance.

Robinson, D. G, & Robinson, J. C. (1996). *Performance consulting: Moving beyond training*. San Francisco: Berrett-Koehler.

Rosenberg, M. J., Coscarelli, W. C., & Hutchison, C. S. (1999). The origins and evolution of the field. In H. D. Stolovitch & E. J. Keeps (Eds.), *Handbook of human performance technology: Improving individual organizational performance worldwide* (2nd ed., pp. 24–46). San Francisco: Jossey-Bass.

Rossett, A. (1999). Analysis for human performance technology. In H. D. Stolovitch & E. J. Keeps (Eds.), *Handbook of human performance technology:*

Improving individual organizational performance worldwide (2nd ed., pp. 139–162). San Francisco: Jossey-Bass.

Schwartz, R. M. (1994). *The skilled facilitator*. San Francisco: Jossey-Bass.

Spitzer, D. R. (1999). The design and development of high-impact interventions. In H. D. Stolovitch & E. J. Keeps (Eds.), *Handbook of human performance technology: Improving individual organizational performance worldwide* (2nd ed., pp. 163–184). San Francisco: Jossey-Bass.

Example: Recommendations for Investigators

1. More communication and discussion is needed regarding the shift to quantity and how to balance quantity and quality. The staff members perceive this shift as a major change and have not bought into it. In fact, some seem to resent the shift and feel it compromises their work.

2. Where possible, address some of the minor issues that impact efficiency, such as redundancy of data collected or the time to input data.

3. Take advantage of investigators' pride in their work and belief in the mission. Feedback and recognition should specifically address the quality of their work and how they were able to effectively implement a solution.

4. Reputation is a big deal. Pay attention to the negative aspects and attempt to minimize public humiliation. Monitor the validity of "reputation" and make sure it is based on actual performance and not just perceptions or rumor.

5. The annual bonus seems to be disconnected to performance results. If possible, use more spot bonuses and clarify to the group why someone received the award. This helps clarify expectations and reinforce positive behavior.

6. The loss of freedom and being placed on a performance improvement plan seem to be effective consequences to poor performance. Continue to use these techniques for dealing with poor performance.

7. Develop and implement processes for sharing expertise, especially around employer interactions and investigative techniques. The need to read body language and other things to look for/observe are such critical skills that they should be addressed through practical discussions in a group setting. Use specific, actual cases to develop capabilities among all investigators and improve performance for the entire office. Another area to address is giving results to the employer and dealing with potential confrontations. Those who have experience can share their ideas and techniques and help others prepare for potentially difficult situations. You will need to establish a learning environment where asking questions or seeking assistance is not "counted" as damage to one's reputation.

8. Consider extending the mentoring program to middle and senior investigators.

9. Charts and case review sheets are only effective if they relate to an individual's values and performance. Because the investigators are so highly intrinsically motivated, any external measures should be aligned with their personal measures of success.

Example: Blueprint for Customer Service Training

Module 1: Foundations of Customer Service: Learning Objectives

- Identify both internal and external customers.
- Define and describe customer service (treat every customer as #1).
- Understand the role of interpersonal skills in establishing a productive relationship with the customer.
- Deal with difficult customers.

Module 2: Communicating with the Customer: Learning Objectives

- Improve communication skills with the customer using active listening.
- Develop basic skills in reading body language.
- Understand and describe basic cultural differences and how they may impact communication.
- Identify terms the customer may not understand and select alternatives.
- Provide progress updates to customers.

Module 3: Solving Customer Problems: Learning Objectives

- Develop problem-solving skills to resolve different types of problems.
- Define the problem and identify possible causes.
- Prioritize multiple problems based on total impact.
- Identify possible solutions.
- Make decisions to implement the best solution.

Suggested Methods/Activities

- Conduct exercises to create lists of internal and external customers and their expectations that can be used back on the job.
- Practice resolving issues with difficult customers using case studies and role-plays.
- Prepare case studies of actual problems using small groups to identify the causes, determine priority, and develop alternative solutions.

How to Make Training Stick Back on the Job

- Use customer feedback to assess progress (surveys, informal follow-up calls, etc.).
- Use the problem-solving method in work group meetings when faced with problems.
- Assign coaches within the work group who can assist the trainee in applying the knowledge from training.

Example: Blueprint for Project Management Training

Learning Objectives

- Describe the role and responsibilities of the project manager.
- Develop the skills to accurately scope out project deliverables and due dates.
- Negotiate with customers to agree on deliverables and due dates.
- Use Microsoft Project software to track progress and identify critical pathways.
- Delegate tasks to team members and follow up accordingly to make sure assignments are accomplished.
- Manage meetings.

Suggested Methods/Activities

- Practice using Microsoft Project, applying it to an actual project.
- Spread the training over a 60-day period to reinforce skill application back on the job.
- Require participants to discuss real-life examples of success and the barriers they face in applying the skills.
- Have participants pair up and attend each other's meetings between sessions to coach and give feedback on meeting management skills.

How To Make Training Stick Back on the Job

- Managers should coach and give feedback on the project manager's success and/or skill improvement in managing projects.
- Track attainment of due dates and budget management and compare to previous projects.
- Seek customer feedback to inquire about satisfaction with the project.

CHAPTER 12

Integrating Complex Training and Nontraining Projects

Ethan S. Sanders

Planning, designing, developing, and implementing performance improvement projects can be a complex process. Although some projects involve only one intervention, most require multiple interventions, requiring the combination of both training and nontraining strategies. A systematic approach allows the project manager, who in many cases also serves as the performance improvement consultant, to implement each element of the intervention with accuracy. This approach helps the consultant budget money, time, and personnel to complete the project in a cost-effective and efficient manner. A project's design and implementation plan can be divided into five phases.

PHASE 1: ASSEMBLE AN INTERVENTION STEERING COMMITTEE

After the performance consultant and client have agreed on the intervention or interventions to implement, an intervention steering committee needs to be assembled to guide the intervention project. Members of this committee will vary from organization to organization. Minimally, the intervention steering committee should include stakeholders involved in the analysis of the problem, one or more people with expertise about the type of intervention being implemented, representatives from the population receiving the intervention (target population), and the performance consultant. When the intervention steering committee has been assembled, the group follows the same formation steps as any typical team. Time may be allocated for a "get acquainted" session, if such activity seems beneficial. The group needs to determine minimum meeting frequency and identify a meeting facilitator and record keeper.

The intervention steering committee must decide how decisions will be reached (e.g., majority rule or consensus) and ensure that each member obtains the information and knowledge necessary to contribute to the project. The committee also needs to be clear on what the group's role will be in the planning, design, development, and implementation of the intervention. Examples of the committee's responsibilities include the following:

- Clearly stating the project's objectives and scope
- Sequencing interventions
- Identifying the components of interventions
- Selecting members for the design team and the development team
- Approving the work of the project

To work successfully as a group, the committee needs to establish ground rules, which might include maintaining a commitment to the project (exhibited by attending meetings and coming prepared), respecting different opinions, and arriving promptly for meetings.

It is dangerous to assume that everyone involved understands a project's goals and scope. Time must be taken to clearly reiterate the performance problem, review the high points from the analysis, and explore the proposed intervention. The committee must also clearly delineate the objectives of the project. Objectives consist of three components: a description of desired performance, the conditions and environment in which employees will perform, and the criteria under which successful performance will be determined. When committee members have agreed on a project's objectives, they need to ensure that everyone understands the project scope, which sets borders around the entire project. Boundaries must be set regarding how large the project will be, how long it will take, how many people will be affected, how much money will be spent, and so forth.

Once the intervention steering committee is in place, understands its role, has set boundaries, and is committed to moving ahead with the intervention, establishing a written record of the intervention project—a discussion and decision record (DDR)—is advisable. The DDR can be simple, such as a compilation of committee meeting minutes, or it can be more sophisticated. The purpose of the record is twofold: Discussions leading up to decisions regarding the intervention, as well as the decisions themselves, need to be documented. Because the conversations leading up to an important decision are easy to forget, a written history can be an important resource during the intervention process, and even long afterward, if questions arise. Along with discussions and decisions made by the committee, the DDR should also include a problem description, project objectives, project scope, data analysis, and a written intervention proposal. The DDR will be passed on to the design and development teams as they begin their work; all team members should have easy access to the DDR.

Because correcting a performance problem with one intervention alone is rare, the intervention steering committee needs to agree on appropriate intervention sequencing. The performance consultant must be familiar enough with interventions to understand potential repercussions of improper sequencing. For example, launching an employee involvement intervention before determining and executing appropriate employee education would not be effective.

PHASE 2: ASSEMBLE A DESIGN TEAM

When the intervention steering committee has agreed on intervention goals, set project objectives, established a DDR, and sequenced the interventions, the committee is ready for Phase 2—selecting members for the design team. Depending on the size and makeup of the organization, members of the committee and the design team may overlap. The design team should include content experts, a representative from the target population, outside vendors (if applicable), and others. Designing interventions may require a variety of expertise, such as knowledge of employee selection, training, ergonomics, communication, compensation, information systems, evaluation and measurement, work design, safety, engineering, automation, and process improvement. Most clients do not expect the performance consultant to have

in-depth knowledge in all areas, but they do expect the consultant to be able to access individuals who do. The design team also needs to have a skilled facilitator and a record keeper.

There are various questions the intervention steering committee must ask when selecting a design team. For example, who can contribute the most to the team in terms of knowledge, experience, and interest level? Who is available to devote the necessary time and energy to the team? Do potential members have credibility within the organization? Will an individual work well in a team environment? Are there other projects on the horizon that will require this person's expertise? If the person is unavailable as a regular team member, can he or she contribute in an ad hoc manner? Are there potential team members who are off-site but could contribute virtually? Ideally, team members possess keen interpersonal skills, collaborative working styles, excellent technical skills, and in-depth content knowledge.

An interesting phenomenon often occurs when an intervention design team begins its work. People throughout the organization hear about the impending intervention, and rumors, fear, and anxiety begin to rise. Up to this point, probably only a few dozen people have been involved in the analysis of the problem and the planning of the solution. Designing the intervention, however, requires more participants, such as subject matter experts, representatives of the target population, vendors, managers, and others.

Effective communication is obviously important throughout the intervention project, but it requires particular emphasis during the design, development, and implementation phases. All stakeholders need to be kept informed about the intervention's progress. Communications should include

- Brief overview of the reason(s) for the intervention project
- Expected outcomes and benefits
- Names of intervention steering committee and design team members
- What employees can expect in the way of ongoing communication (including method, frequency, and feedback mechanisms)
- Who will be affected (target population)
- When to expect visible signs of the implementation
- How to request support and commitment

With the initial communications behind them, the design team can begin planning the intervention design by breaking interventions into components. A component is a piece of an intervention that results in some type of output. For example, components of a training intervention might include an outline, storyboard, facilitator's guide, participant's workbook, slides, or a video. Identifying the components of an intervention project is necessary to build a suitable design and subsequent development, effectively manage and oversee the project, hold people accountable, provide recognition, track progress, develop contingencies, establish milestones, communicate, revise plans, and celebrate success.

Once intervention components have been determined, the next step is to decide the sequence of the components, just as the steering committee determined the sequence of interventions earlier. The design team decides which components should be designed and developed first; in some cases, several components can be worked on simultaneously. For example, the course outline must come first, but facilitator and participant guides can be developed in tandem. The sequencing decision drives design, selection of development team members, schedule, budget, and further communications.

Once the design team is clear on the components of the intervention, it can begin to establish the primary tasks that must be accomplished to produce high-quality components. For example, to produce a course outline, the following tasks need to be accomplished:

1. Research available literature on course subject matter.
2. Sort information into course topics.
3. Identify a subject matter expert who will validate content.
4. Create a draft of the course outline.
5. Get stakeholder feedback.
6. Revise accordingly.

Knowledge of the components and tasks associated with an intervention allows the establishment of milestones for the project. A milestone marks the completion of one or more components. In some cases, a milestone may mark the completion of a critical task. Milestones highlight important points in the intervention project and facilitate the tracking of progress, accountability, contingencies, recognition, and celebration. When discussing potential milestones, it is important that the design team does not earmark too many of them or they will lose their importance. Nor should the team set milestones too close together or too far apart; milestones, by definition, should convey importance and progress. One thing to remember is that up to this point, none of the work is carved in stone. When the design team begins

developing actual intervention components, it may find that adjustments are necessary.

PHASE 3: DETERMINE THE NECESSARY RESOURCES

In Phase 3, the design team discusses the resources necessary for designing and developing the intervention, based on its components and identified tasks. Resources may include materials, information, technology, tools, equipment, and, of course, people. The time and money associated with the acquisition of these resources are considered during Phase 4. Although time and money are also resources, a clear picture of resource options should be attained prior to weighing the cost and speed of acquiring resources, thereby avoiding hasty decision making. Because the design team has not begun its work at this point, it may seem a bit premature to discuss resources, but, realistically, the sooner this discussion begins, the better. Waiting too long can cause implementation to be delayed if a resource is unavailable. Identifying resources to create a simple job aid is one matter; identifying resources for a new incentive system is quite another. The design team must have a solid sense of the broad resource categories, but it may not be possible to identify all necessary resources until the design is complete. The intervention steering committee needs to be kept in the loop as resources are identified.

There are a number of reasons to include vendors on the design team. The design team may need expertise that is unavailable from internal sources, and an external vendor may possess a degree of credibility or influence that internal personnel do not. Furthermore, top management may be committed to using external resources, or design and development needs may be met more rapidly and with more assurance using external resources. Stolovitch and Keeps have discussed vendor selection in terms of the idea of "resource brokering" (1998, p. 126). The resource broker acts as an intermediary between the client and intervention resources. The performance consultant often fills this role by identifying resources, verifying capabilities, maintaining a database of resources, and, in some cases, contracting for services. Some companies encourage insourcing, or "brokering in," because internal resources are more familiar with the organizational culture and are often less expensive than external vendors. Whether insourced or outsourced, the performance consultant must introduce "human" resources into the organization, pave the way for their integration, and facilitate communication. In *The Performance Consulting Toolbook*, Nilson (1999, pp. 19, 21) listed conditions and roles to be considered in deciding between internal and external resources (see box, next page).

Conditions and Roles for Internal and External Consultants	
Conditions for Internal Consultants • Present staff has the competencies and skills to handle the job. • Present staff has a wide network of colleagues. • Present staff is able to cross levels for information and service. • Present staff is trustworthy and engenders trust. • Present staff has its management's unconditional support (time, pay, project budget, ability to travel, resources, freedom of choice). • Present staff is not constrained by its present position or reputation. • Present staff wants to do the job. **Conditions for External Consultants** • Present staff does not have the competencies and skills to handle the job. • An outsider has a better chance of establishing rapport with key people. • Company culture is open enough to allow access to an outsider. • The outsider's reputation and references as a consultant are of high quality.	• Top management is committed to using external consultants and has whatever resources might be necessary. • Present staff is accustomed to working with outsiders. • Present staff does not want to do the job. **Roles for Internal and External Consultants** • Needs analyst • Negotiator • Diplomat • Interviewer • Feedback specialist • Facilitator • Interpreter • Evaluator • Extra pair of hands and feet • Project designer • Project manager • Communication channel • Collaborator with other leaders • Subject matter expert • Change agent

Note. From Nilson (1999). Adapted with permission.

PHASE 4: ESTIMATE THE PROJECT'S TIME AND COSTS

Phase 4 includes estimating both the time and costs of an intervention project. An estimate is a projection based on knowledge or understanding of similar situations or occurrences. Although the circumstances surrounding a performance project may be somewhat unpredictable, a performance consultant needs to minimize or compensate for as much unpredictability as possible. In estimating the time and cost of an intervention project, the consultant needs to be as close as possible to the actual requirements; this depends on having both accurate and pertinent information. Calling on memories of similar incidences, asking the appropriate people the right questions, and reviewing benchmarking data and historical information accesses this information.

The consultant must allow time for revisions, travel, illness, holidays, vacations, and more in the schedule and include costs for errors, price increases, external resources, and internal charge-backs in the cost projection. The client is paying the performance consultant to provide an accurate projection of how much the intervention project will cost. Knowing what to look for in advance helps the consultant avoid overages in lost time and money. Funding for contingencies should also be included in the budget. Because completing certain milestones may warrant some type of celebration, money for this should be included as well.

PHASE 5: TRACKING

There are several different ways in which project status can be tracked. A number of different tools are available for tracking an intervention project. Figure 12.1 displays a Gantt chart, which indicates deliverables and the time allocated to complete each task. Milestones, money, time, and overall progress are easily displayed with this tool. A number of software programs have versions of the Gantt chart (e.g., MS Project 2000, SmartDraw, ILOG, Visual Mining, Natara Project@Hand).

Figure 12.1	Sample Gantt Chart											
Activity	**Timeline (Weeks)**											
	1	2	3	4	5	6	7	8	9	10	11	12
1. Analyze task interference	●━●											
2. Create task elimination/ redeployment list	●━●											
3. Eliminate/redeploy tasks		●━━━━●										
4. Evaluate task elimination/ redeployment results				●━━━━●								
5. Analyze job	●━●											
6. Create new job description	●━●											
7. Implement new job description		●━●										
8. Evaluate impact of new job description			●━━━━━━●									

INTERVENTION DESIGN AND DEVELOPMENT

Differentiating between design and development is important. Intervention design identifies specific components for each intervention and the resources required for producing those components. The design steps are where components are actually specified. Component development subsequently uses these specifications to construct the intervention. Development includes the production of methods, instrumentation, and materials required to support the intervention.

The importance of a good intervention design cannot be overstated. Good design can be time consuming, but poor design and its consequences can be even more costly. Breaking design and development into steps makes this phase of the intervention more manageable. There are seven major steps in component design and development. The first three steps review some of the material regarding the design team covered in our discussion of planning. The last four steps cover development.

Step 1: Review the Analysis Data and Selection Criteria

Giving the design team the opportunity to review carefully all analysis data and selection criteria is the first step in designing an intervention. The team reexamines the problem and its root causes and revisits the constraints on—and limitations of—selected interventions. The design team's review includes reconsideration of the project's scope and goals, as well as the available resources

and support. The design team must establish a clear understanding of what stakeholders expect the project to deliver. They need as much feedback as possible from all relevant stakeholders, preferably early in the design process. The team also reviews any special requirements that the intervention must satisfy. For example, the intervention may need to appeal to both union and management, exceed federal requirements, or be written on a sixth-grade reading level. Requirements form the basis of the components.

Development and implementation requirements are particularly important during the design phase. The costs, complexity, and difficulty of implementing interventions typically pose the greatest challenge. Requirements for resources, time frames, and budget must be considered. Designers tend to focus on the technical requirements of an intervention rather than the human requirements, although both need to be included. There is a greater chance of developing successful interventions if requirements are delineated and refined.

Distinguishing between mandatory requirements (features the intervention must possess) and desirable requirements (features that stakeholders want) is particularly crucial. The design team must avoid situations in which requirements become nothing more than a wish list. Not only should requirements be identified, they should also be prioritized. The first pass of prioritization involves distinguishing the requirements that are "musts" from those that are "wants." "Must" requirements do not need to be prioritized, because they are all essential. The "want" requirements should be prioritized from most to least desired. Cost or time constraints can make it difficult to include all of the "want" requirements in an intervention.

Step 2: Identify Components and Objectives
The design team must identify components and their objectives using findings from the analysis data. The specification of objectives guides component design and development. The design team should ask questions such as, "What performance is desired?" and "How much improvement is needed?" In short, ends, not means, should drive the components. For each component, the design team determines specifications and drafts and makes detailed plans for goals, work steps, responsibilities, and resources.

Step 3: Create a Detailed Design Plan
The design plan describes and outlines a proposed intervention and all its components. At first, the plan is described by the design team in generalities, not details. The team then uses previously acquired information to "color in" the design plan. Specific events, activities, tasks, schedules, and resource requirements necessary to developing and implementing the component are identified. Contingency design and development plans are formed here as well. The design team, in concert with an evaluation specialist, begins designing evaluation methods for collecting formative evaluation data on the development and implementation of the intervention. Evaluation is actually a subprocess in the overall process of intervention design, development, and implementation, but it is essential nonetheless.

Rothwell's Job Aid
Rothwell created a comprehensive eight-step job aid to help in the design and development of interventions (see box, next page). Rothwell's first three steps represent our model's first step: reviewing the analysis data and selection criteria. It is important to consider the target population's thoughts and feelings about the performance problem and the proposed intervention. For an intervention to be effective, the target population must believe that a problem really exists, and it must be motivated to participate in the intervention. The physical, mental, and emotional demands of the intervention on the target population can be extensive. It must possess the knowledge, skills, attitudes, time, and resources to participate in the intervention. If it does not have the necessary competencies, the organization must first take steps to build such competencies. An intervention cannot be successful if the target population is not able to participate fully. The environment in which the intervention will be implemented is of

particular concern; therefore, environmental conditions that will support or inhibit an intervention must be considered.

Rothwell's Step 4 (formulate performance objectives) mirrors our model's Step 2 (identifying the components' objectives). Performance objectives should be drafted to guide the intervention's design. Rothwell's Step 5 (formulate specific measurement methods) helps the design team plan the evaluation of performance objectives. Means of measuring the outcomes of performance objectives must be devised.

Development
As stated earlier, the component development phase is where the design is actually constructed into tangible products that can be implemented. Some interventions require extensive development, whereas others require very little. An intervention might be as simple as clarifying a policy or offering an existing training course, or as complex as creating new processes or updating a technology system. Even with a simple intervention, it is important to consider thoroughly all development and implementation issues.

Step 4: Assemble a Development Team
The first step in getting the development phase moving is to assemble an intervention development team. Development team members are often different from design team members, although some overlap may occur. The performance consultant is a member of both teams, providing expertise, guidance, and facilitation for the development team and serving as a link to the design team. The development team is composed of people who have the requisite production skills. The team may be assembled based on suggestions made by the intervention steering committee, the design team, or the performance consultant. Other staff members may volunteer their services on a limited basis, and involving representatives of the target population is often appropriate. If production demands are great, outsourcing the work is often considered.

After the development team has been assembled, it prepares a comprehensive plan that details each component's prototype. A prototype is a model or draft of a component. The plan identifies the development tasks and resources required to develop each prototype, includes a timeline that proposes a start and finish for each task, and identifies the team member responsible for the task. A Gantt chart (see Figure 12.1) and a RACI (responsible, accountable, consulted, keep informed) matrix (Figure 12.2) are often used to guide the development process. It is essential that the client and other stakeholders approve the plan.

William Rothwell's Design and Development Job Aid

Step 1: Examine the characteristics of the participants in the intervention.

- Who (specifically) will participate?
- To whom do the participants report?
- What (specifically) are the participants expected to do during the intervention?
- What do the participants think and feel about the performance problem and the intervention intended to address it? Do they believe that the problem is a problem? Do they support the intervention? Are they motivated to participate in it?
- How will the participants be involved in designing and developing the intervention? The materials and media needed to implement it?
- What disabilities, if any, might affect the intervention, and how can reasonable accommodation be made for them?
- What physical, mental, and emotional demands will the intervention put on of participants?
- How much time and effort will the intervention require, and are participants able to devote that time and effort to the intervention? Do their immediate organizational superiors support it? Do their superiors support it?

Step 2: Examine the competencies (knowledge, skills, attitudes, and other requirements) necessary for successful achievement of performance in the context of the intervention.

- What competencies do participants already possess that are relevant to addressing the performance problem and designing and developing the intervention?
- What competencies do participants need to possess that are relevant to addressing the performance problem and designing and developing the intervention?
- How can the organization build the competencies required of participants to be successful in the intervention?
- How can the organization build the competencies required of the participants' immediate organizational superiors in the intervention?
- What experience, if any, have the participants had in the past with a similar intervention, and how do they feel that experience went? Was the intervention successful or unsuccessful? Why?

Step 3: Examine the characteristics of the work environment in which the intervention will be implemented.

- What conditions in the work environment will influence the preparation and planning of the intervention? Its implementation? Its success in changing attitudes, behaviors, or results?
- What conditions in the work environment are most likely to support the intervention?
- What conditions in the work environment are most likely to pose barriers to the intervention?
- How can the conditions supporting the intervention be intensified, and how can barriers to the intervention be surmounted?

Step 4: Formulate performance objectives to guide the intervention.

- What specific performance problems are to be addressed by the intervention?
- What is the performance gap that is to be closed by the intervention?
- What final results or outcomes, taken together, will fully describe the final outcomes desired upon completion of the intervention? (When these results are achieved, the performance gap will be closed or its effects at least minimized).

William Rothwell's Design and Development Job Aid (cont'd)

- What interim results or outcomes are desired at various milestones (points in time) during the implementation of the intervention?
- What results or outcomes will performers be achieving upon intervention completion?
- What conditions or resources will be necessary for the performers if they are to demonstrate the desired results or outcomes?
- How can the conditions or resources be measured?

Step 5: Formulate specific measurement methods by which to measure performance objectives.

- What should be happening (and what should be the final measurable performance levels) upon completion of the intervention?
- How should results be measured?
- When should results be measured? When are the milestones, and what results should have been achieved by each milestone?
- Who will conduct the measurements of the intervention?
- Where will results be measured? Will comparison groups (such as pretest and posttest groups or experimental and control groups) be established? If so, where? How?

Step 6: Create a detailed project plan to guide implementation of the intervention.

- Who will take action during each part of the intervention?
- What tasks should they carry out, and what measurable results are they expected to achieve?
- What are the deadlines for achievement?
- What is the budget, and what are the other resources available, for the intervention?

Step 7: Create a detailed communication and marketing plan to clarify what is happening, what has happened, and what will happen in the intervention.

- What are the phases, steps, tasks, or events of the intervention?
- Who has a need to know about each step?
- What do they need to know at each step, and when do they need to know it?
- What are the most effective ways to communicate to participants and other stakeholders for introducing each phase, step, task, or event of the intervention?
- How should the communication plan be prepared, approved, tested, and evaluated?
- How many details should be provided about the intervention?
- What should be communicated about what is happening in the intervention, what has happened (progress to date) in the intervention, and what is expected or planned to happen in the intervention in the future?

Step 8: Make, buy, or buy and modify materials and media to support the implementation of the intervention.

- What materials are necessary for use in the intervention to help meet the performance objectives?
- Where can the materials be obtained? Should they be made, bought, or bought and modified? If so, from where or from whom?
- How should the materials be most cost-effectively delivered to participants and other groups to support achievement of the performance objectives?
- Where can media support, if required, be obtained?

Note. From Rothwell (2000, pp. 121–127). Adapted with permission.

Step 5: Develop a Prototype

The development team would be wise to produce a prototype of each intervention component before investing extensive time, money, and effort in developing the finished product. A prototype for classroom training might be a rough draft of the facilitator's guide, whereas prototypes for a wellness program might include an information session outline and a script for an informational video. One of the most important development decisions is whether to build or buy the intervention prototype. Buying off-the-shelf products can be more cost-effective if they are appropriate and can be easily and sensibly customized for the client's use. Ways of customizing off-the-shelf materials include

- Adapting materials to the capabilities of the target audience and the organization (e.g., with computer software and hardware)
- Changing examples and case studies to represent the organization's industry
- Changing or eliminating industry jargon and terminology
- Omitting or adding content
- Altering exercises to fit the target population's needs

Off-the-shelf products and services have numerous advantages. They have been tested, revised, and validated among a large target population, so the development team knows whether they accomplish what they are purported to achieve. They can also be implemented more quickly. They can be less expensive, because their costs are distributed to many rather than to just a few, and these products and services may add new dimensions to the team's skill set.

The development team, however, should be wary of abusing off-the-shelf products by forcing them to fit into situations in which they are not appropriate. But it should not be reluctant to use them, either. Of course, the team can produce materials from the ground up, provided it has the time and resources necessary. Steps 6, 7, and 8 of Rothwell's job aid will help participants assemble a development team and develop a prototype.

Step 6: Evaluate the Prototype

Evaluation of the prototype is necessary, as the purpose of prototype development and testing is to obtain preliminary feedback so improvements and revisions can be made prior to final production. This formative evaluation can identify weaknesses in the intervention. The client, managers, stakeholders, subject matter experts, and potential users evaluate the prototype through a pilot program. Having some members of the target population try out the intervention and make recommendations for improvement is also advisable.

Step 7: Revise the Prototype

Based on feedback from the reviewers and target population participants, the development team revises and improves the prototype. It is the development team's

Figure 12.2	Sample RACI Matrix Using a Nautical Example

R = responsible
A = accountable
C = consulted
I = keep informed

	Milestone/Task	Captain	Navigator	1/2 Officer	Chief Engineer	Purser	Stores Provisions	Port Authority
1	Chart route	C	R/A	I			I	
2	Order provisions	C				C	R/A	
3	Order fuel	C			A		R	
4	Gain approval to leave	A			R	R	R	
5	Set sail	A	C	R	I			
6	Take control from pilot	R/A				I		I

responsibility to make judgments as to what changes will be incorporated into the final version. Reviewers must be informed that the development team will not be capable of incorporating all suggested changes. Revision is the last step before the prototype enters final production, where the final component elements are produced, packaged, and prepared for implementation.

INTERVENTION IMPLEMENTATION

Logistics and Timing

The first considerations in implementing interventions are logistics and timing. The term *logistics* can mean different things to different people, but *The American Heritage Dictionary* defines it as "the procurement, distribution, maintenance, and replacement of material and personnel." Examples of materials that need to be procured for an intervention implementation are as follows: job aids, software, newsletters, handouts, audiovisuals, machinery, computers, ergonomically correct chairs and workstations, safety equipment, tools, phone systems, educational materials, recognition symbols, celebration symbols, forms, and handbooks.

As stated in the definition, logistics also encompasses the procurement of people. This can be a long list of players such as facilitators, engineers, counselors, clerks, and other intervention experts. Distribution also plays a role in logistics, getting supplies and materials where they are needed at the correct time without loss or damage. Paying attention to the logical sequencing of events is important during distribution. In some cases, materials can be distributed simultaneously, but in other cases the order in which materials are distributed is vital. For example, it would not be efficient to receive new office furniture at the workplace if the target population is set to move to a different location within a week.

It is important to consider how often an intervention will require maintenance, and how long it can be expected to last. For example, most technology-based interventions will require software upgrades, and it is rare that hardware lasts more than five to seven years. With a list of logistical items in mind, it is useful to create a chart like the one in Table 12.1 to ensure that the necessary information is in place to effectively monitor and manage implementation logistics.

Handling the logistics of intervention implementation can be a daunting task, but knowing the right questions to ask and consistently monitoring and managing progress can alleviate much of the anxiety. Timing is key. At the brink of implementation, the organization needs to be examined to make sure nothing is occurring that could potentially interfere with the intervention. As actual intervention implementation becomes imminent, the organization needs to be scrutinized more and more frequently. For example, if implementation of a new software program for payroll falls at the same time as quarterly bonuses are scheduled to go out, briefly delaying implementation may make sense. If the organization has just landed a large account, implementing a job redesign for customer service representatives may interfere with customer relations. The timing of an intervention must be considered right up to the moment of implementation. Even the best contingency planning may not be able to anticipate all potential interference.

Communication

Effective communication is necessary throughout all phases of a performance improvement project. How well communication is handled influences the overall effectiveness of an intervention. An appropriate starting point for communication is a forum or meeting, gathering together representatives from key stakeholder groups. These individuals will have had varying degrees of involvement in the intervention process to date, and they can be useful in providing updated information on the organizational climate or status of logistics. They can also play a key role in communicating with the target population.

Table 12.1	Sample Logistics Chart		
Procurement	**Distribution**	**Maintenance**	**Replacement**
• Are bids required for item? • Can we get these items from internal resources?	• Is storage of the procurement item an issue due to space, security, etc.? • Which performers need the intervention first?	• Who will maintain the procurement item? For example, an employee suggestion process? • Are parts available?	• What are the costs for replacement? • How long can we expect components to last?

The makeup of this group will vary from organization to organization. In communicating with target populations, it is important to identify who and how many will be affected by the intervention. Various factors must be examined, such as the education level of the group, the hours and days that they work, the sites where they are located, and the demographics of the group. Others in the organization, outside of the target population, may need to be included in communications as well.

The information gathered on the target population will drive the vocabulary and terminology of communication. Several basic guidelines should be followed for any communication on implementation. Messages should be clear and as brief as possible, and if unclear terminology must be used, it needs to be defined. Any intervention invokes a degree of change; this must be addressed by scripting messages that include

- Succinct description of the performance gap
- Who will be affected by the intervention
- When they will be affected by the intervention
- How matters will be different after the intervention is implemented
- Anticipated benefits of the intervention
- Honest depiction of potential challenges
- Kind of support for the intervention that can be expected
- Scheduled implementation date

Shifts that the intervention will cause in the overall organizational culture should be addressed, along with an explanation of why these shifts are necessary. If the intervention is aligned with the organizational culture, this should be highlighted.

People respond differently to various communications media, just as learners respond differently to various educational techniques. The key to an effective communications plan is repeating communications in a variety of media, including small meetings, e-mail/voicemail announcements, posters, paycheck stuffers, videos, or newsletters. Initial communication may need to be coordinated with other sites, and alternate work shifts may need to be addressed. Determining the timing of communications is key.

It is important to know who will play a part in orally communicating information about an intervention; some organizations have the highest-level stakeholder kick-off announcements concerning interventions. If other stakeholders will play a role in the delivery, this must be known ahead of time. An interpreter may be needed for individuals whose first language is not English. Unions, as well as members of the target population, may play a role in message delivery. Some interventions even lend themselves well to the participation of local business leaders or politicians.

The individuals who participated in the stakeholder meeting continue their roles by funneling information on the status of implementation back to the performance consultant. These stakeholders are in positions that allow them to provide some level of input on how the intervention is received by the target population. Feedback helps the performance consultant determine if contingencies need to be activated. Wise performance consultants, however, do not rely too heavily on the feedback of others. At some point, they must view and judge the intervention's progress firsthand. As in the intervention proposal meeting, the key to effective communication is familiarity with the audience, and the ability to provide them with the information they need. Communication must be two-way to monitor intervention progress and to know when to activate contingencies.

Managing Vendors

If outside vendors are being used for all or part of intervention implementation, this part of the process needs to be managed. Vendors should attend the stakeholder meeting. If this is not possible, a vendor can participate via a conference call or teleconferencing. During this meeting, the vendor should exhibit the final intervention product (if applicable). For example, if the intervention involves performance management, the vendor might show and explain the 360-degree feedback form. Building this piece into the meeting allows stakeholders to review the item, check to see that it meets specifications, and ask questions. Bringing these people together ensures that everyone is on the same page.

If vendors are not providing a product, but a service (e.g., counseling), they should explain the service and any processes involved. Again, this provides stakeholders with an opportunity to ask questions and fully understand the final product. The vendors are also given the opportunity to ask pertinent questions of stakeholders about their roles during implementation. Of course, the need to ask questions will vary according to what kind of intervention the vendors are providing. Vendors should also provide feedback to the performance consultant on the status of their part in intervention implementation. Managing vendors is predicated on establishing a strong and positive relationship early on. Setting very clear requirements and expectations at the beginning of this relationship minimizes the chances of misunderstandings occurring at the time of implementation.

Celebrating Milestones

If logistics are ironed out, the facility is abuzz with perfectly crafted communications, and vendors are working diligently, a celebration is in order. A celebration serves to call attention to a completed milestone, communicate progress, and provide group and individual recognition. Milestones serve as completion beacons, signifying the successful culmination of major elements in an intervention plan. Celebrations can be as simple as boxed lunches at a stakeholders' meeting, or as involved as a facility-wide celebration with prizes, refreshments, and so on. These celebrations can be orchestrated spontaneously or planned ahead during the planning or design phases. It can be useful to have a special "celebrations committee," or it may suffice to use one or two people who have served in some capacity on the project to plan the celebrations. However celebrations are organized, highlighting successes is important.

Conclusion

As Henry Ford once said, "Before everything else, getting ready is the key to success." Although planning, monitoring, and managing the details of an intervention might not be as exciting as analyzing performance problems, it is the line of demarcation between critics and solvers of performance problems. In an era in which consultants are viewed as organizational leeches, we simply cannot afford for anyone calling themselves a performance consultant to recommend an intervention and then disappear when it comes time to carry out the solution. ✳

References

Fuller, J. (1997). *Managing performance improvement projects.* San Francisco: Jossey-Bass.

Nilson, C. (1999). *The performance consulting toolbook.* New York: McGraw-Hill.

Rothwell, W. J. (2000). *Workplace learning and performance roles: The intervention selector, designer, and implementer.* Alexandria, VA: American Society for Training & Development.

Stolovitch, H., & Keeps, E. (1998). Implementation phase: Performance improvement interventions. In D. G. Robinson & J. C. Robinson (Eds.), *Moving from training to performance* (pp. 95–133). San Francisco: Berrett-Koehler.

CHAPTER 3

Evaluating Workforce Development Efforts

William J. Rothwell

E valuation is a perennial hot topic in the field of workforce development. There are good reasons for that. One reason is that all institutions are increasingly accountable to the groups they serve. Another reason is that customers have become more demanding, wanting to know that they will get a favorable return on any investments they make.

To help you understand the issue of evaluation, I will first provide a definition of evaluation and describe some reasons why evaluation has become a focus of attention in recent years. I then explore the question, What key issues should be considered when conducting the evaluation of workforce development efforts? I conclude the chapter with a summary of trends.

Evaluation is perhaps best understood to mean the process of placing value on a person, thing, or process. Workforce development evaluation, then, is the process of determining the value of workforce development efforts. Although too often associated with the most common form of evaluation—that is, evaluations handed out to participants at the end of training, or student-rating sheets handed out at the end of a credit course—workforce development evaluation has a broader meaning. Much has been written about evaluation in recent years. (For a sample of such analyses, see Bersin 2002; Chapnick, 2001; Heum, Lee, & Pershing, 2000; Korth, 2001; Phillips & Burkett, 2001; Rossen & Hartley, 2001; Rothwell, 1999, Swanson, 2001; Van Brakel, 2002; Welber, 2002.)

There are four good reasons why evaluation has become the focus of attention in recent years. One is that business clients want to know what returns they receive on their financial investments. A second reason is that

college administrators want to know what results workforce developers have achieved and—more specifically—what measurable impact a workforce development program has had on community development, economic development, and workforce development so as to justify the existence of their units, demonstrate benefits provided to others inside the institution, and collect information about results that can then be used in subsequent marketing to prompt repeat business. Third, state policymakers want to know what results were realized in return for taxpayer dollars expended. They are sometimes more keenly interested in job retention, job creation, job development, or even how many people were moved off the welfare rolls and onto the taxpayer rolls. And finally, program participants sometimes want to know what happened to others who successfully completed training or educational programs offered by a community college: Did they get better paying jobs? Promotions? How did they benefit?

KEY ISSUES TO CONSIDER IN EVALUATING WORKFORCE DEVELOPMENT EFFORTS

Several key issues, organized around the famous journalistic questions to be answered by any news story, must be considered when evaluating workforce development efforts:

- *Who* wants the evaluation information?
- *What* information do they want?
- *When* do they want it?
- *Where* do they want it?
- *Why* do they want it, and what decisions will they make based on it?

- *How* should evaluation be conducted to gather the information desired by the stakeholders?
- *How much* are stakeholders willing to spend on evaluation?

Different stakeholders may require different answers to these questions, of course. The challenge, then, is to give stakeholders just what they need. It is worthwhile to examine each question in turn. You can make a worksheet, which you can use to organize your thinking around a workforce development evaluation, by listing these questions and leaving space below them to jot down your thoughts. You can use a separate sheet for each specific situation (e.g., a training program delivered to a client).

Who Wants the Evaluation Information?

Evaluation is a service. As with any service, a key place to start is to clarify who wants it. After all, not everybody wants to know exactly the same things about a workforce development effort. Clients may wish to know what people learned or what financial results were achieved from the effort. Instructors may wish to know how well they delivered material. The managers of participants may want to know what they learned—and how much of it they can actually apply on their jobs.

Too often, however, nobody wants the evaluation information. Managers may not want to take time to read participants' end-of-course rating summaries. Instructors may disregard the opinions of participants, feeling that they know best about what people should learn and how they should be trained. Participants may not want the results of their examination scores because they worry about who might see them or how those results might be used in making future employment decisions that affect them. One real challenge facing workforce developers is to convince stakeholders to remain informed of workforce development efforts.

What Information Do Stakeholders Want?

It must be clear who wants evaluation information before the next step can be taken to clarify exactly what stakeholders want to know. There is no point gathering useless information. Therefore, workforce developers should clarify exactly what the stakeholders want to know.

It is sometimes helpful to think about the classic Kirkpatrick (1996) evaluation pyramid, which distributes the key issues of reactions, learning, behavior, and results within a pyramidal hierarchy. Questions can then be designed to help guide workforce developers to vector in on what they want (and need) to know through an evaluation. For example, if stakeholders want to know about

participants' reactions, workforce developers can ask, How much did participants like the program in which they participated? If about participants' learning, How much did participants learn in the program? If about participants' behavior change, How much did participants take back to their jobs and actually apply? If they want to know about results, they can ask, How much productivity improvement did the organization achieve as a direct consequence of the workforce development experience? On occasion, a fifth issue level is added to the pyramid that focuses on return on investment, which can be explored with the question, How much net gain resulted to the organization as a result of an investment made in a workforce development effort?

When Do Stakeholders Want the Evaluation Results?

One unfortunate consequence of focusing attention on participants' end-of-course ratings is that it tends to build the expectation that evaluation should be conducted only at the end of a workforce development effort. My own research, conducted in 1995, revealed that most corporate-trained participants are not asked to provide evaluative information until after a training program is delivered (Rothwell & Cookson, 1997). The result is that it is difficult for trainers to target evaluation efforts. You must know what results you want before you can measure them. The reality, however, is that evaluation can be conducted before, during, and after program delivery. Kirkpatrick's pyramidal hierarchy of evaluation can be transformed into a grid, with each level examined at different points in time (see Figure 13.1).

Evaluation that occurs before program delivery is called forecasting. Reaction forecasting measures what participants expect of a program and what attitudes they have about it. Learning forecasting has to do with screening criteria and pretests. Participants' behavior change forecasting has to do with planning conditions back in the work setting that will support individuals in applying what they have learned in off-the-job workforce development experiences. Perhaps most important of all is forecasting the financial benefits of training, because it places a cost on the problem that training is designed to solve and provides a basis for making sound investment decisions.

It seems that many corporate trainers are looking for a silver bullet to use when they are challenged on the results achieved by a training experience. They think it is a simple accounting problem. If only a formula could be found, they reason, they could convince skeptics of how valuable their offerings are. What they do not realize is that evaluating workforce development efforts is more akin to a legal prob-

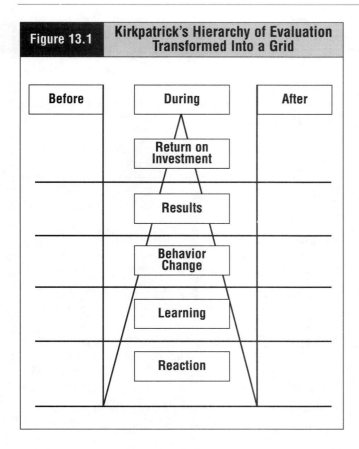

Figure 13.1 | **Kirkpatrick's Hierarchy of Evaluation Transformed Into a Grid**

feedback. Methods of communicating results might include group meetings, written reports, bulletin board postings, and Web sites.

Do the stakeholders have a special reason for wanting evaluation results? If so, their reasons should be clarified so that workforce developers can identify the most appropriate means of collecting that information. Additionally, if it is clear what decisions are to be made based on evaluation results, workforce developers can focus on gathering the essential information.

Although some people confuse the method of evaluation—such as a questionnaire or interviews—with the evaluation process itself, it is important to clarify how the evaluation should be conducted. Here the issue centers on what evaluative information is being sought, because various data gathering methods may be better suited to evaluating some issues than others.

How much are stakeholders willing to spend on evaluation? Evaluation is not free. Someone must spend time to plan it, collect the information, analyze that information, feed it back, and use it to plan improvements. Have the costs of evaluation efforts been appropriately communicated to and approved by decision makers before those efforts begin?

EVALUATION TRENDS

Five important trends are evident in evaluation. First, growing recognition exists that there is a direct relationship between needs assessment and evaluation (Korth, 2001). Needs assessment focuses attention on the root causes of performance problems and selects from a broad array of potential solutions or interventions (Rothwell, Hohne, & King, 2000), and evaluation tracks the outcomes. Many problems stem directly from inadequate root cause analysis of performance problems or needs assessment (see Example, next page).

Second, growing interest exists in all forms of evaluation. Although many workforce developers associate evaluation with end-of-course rating sheets, they are now also paying more attention to knowledge testing, performance testing, employee certification for job suitability, and even portfolio (work sample) assessments.

Third, growing interest exists in the documentation of evaluation. Some organizations use end-of-course rating sheets, but they never compile or distribute the results as feedback to others. Consequently, senior decision makers never get any feedback about the impact of workforce development efforts—and it is no wonder that training is cut back when times are tough.

Fourth, growing awareness exists that evaluation can

lem than an accounting one. Any good trial lawyer knows that a jury can be given evidence, but the issue is not proven until the jury believes it. Even compelling DNA evidence may not convince a skeptical jury. There is thus an important difference between supplying evidence and proving the case. Gathering evidence is the role of the trainer, but proof rests in the minds of the managers and clients.

A better approach is to seize an advantage that workforce developers enjoy over trial lawyers: Workforce developers can involve their jury—that is, managers and clients—in discovering, before an effort is delivered, how its success will be measured and ultimately judged. That can be done during the needs assessment process to ensure that the root causes of problems are uncovered and that the best ways to solve the problems are identified. After all, training may not be the most appropriate—or even the most cost-effective—strategy to solve a problem, because training merely equips individuals with new knowledge, skills, and attitudes.

Where, Why, How, and How Much?

The remaining questions can be answered succinctly. The question, Where do stakeholders want evaluation information? focuses on the best format for providing feedback on workforce development results. Each stakeholder group should be asked about its preferred method of

---

Example: Inadequate Root Cause Analysis

Suppose a manager is trying to solve the problem of an employee who shows up late to work every day, always with an excellent excuse. One approach is, of course, for the manager to confront the individual. But some managers do not want to be cast as villains; others honestly worry about confrontations with their workers; and some even worry that confrontation could lead to workplace violence. Clearly, some managers would rather avoid confrontations and so turn the matter over to the training department or to a local community college, making a request for help similar to this: "We need you to conduct a training course for all our people on the importance of timely arrival at work."

If workforce developers do that, they are engaged in *order-taking behavior*—just like a waitress who takes an order from a restaurant menu but ignores the customer's real needs. Although taking orders may be a waitress's job, it is not enough for workforce developers. To effectively solve their customer's problems, they must dig deeper to uncover the root causes of the problems.

If a training program is designed and delivered without analyzing the company's real needs, the workers will wonder why they are being given this kind of training. The many employees who do not have a tardiness problem may be offended. And the one person who was the target for the actual change effort may think it is directed at others—certainly not at him or her. The result? The program is a waste of time and money, which is reflected in poor evaluation results. At some point a senior manager may demand proof that the program resulted in a return on investment, when, in point of fact, training could never have solved the problem, which was actually an issue of individual supervision. In this case, if a proper performance analysis or needs assessment had been conducted, an alternative solution would have been identified, and training would not have been used.

---

serve several purposes. Many people are familiar with how valuable evaluation results can be in improving programs. But results can also be turned into testimonials that can convince potential clients of how valuable an improvement effort can be. Evaluation results have program improvement uses, but they may also have uses in marketing and in finance.

Fifth, growing recognition exists that one-size-fits-all evaluation approaches rarely work. Evaluation must be tailored to the needs of the organization, institution, stakeholders, and program. What evaluation information should be gathered and how it should be gathered hinges on *who wants to know* and *what they want to do with it*. For that reason, using one approach is rarely practical or useful (Rothwell, 1998). ❊

References

Bersin, J. (2002). Measuring e-learning's effectiveness. *e-learning, 3*(3), 36–41.

Chapnick, S. (2001). Kirk-Chapnick's level 5? *Training and Development, 55*(8), 79–80.

Heum L. S., & Pershing, J. A. (2000). Evaluation of corporate training programs: Perspectives and issues for further research. Performance *Improvement Quarterly, 13*(3), 244–260.

Kirkpatrick, D. (1996). *Evaluating training programs: The four levels.* San Francisco: Berrett-Koehler.

Korth, S. (2001). Consolidating needs assessment and evaluation. *Performance Improvement, 40*(1), 38–43.

Phillips, P. P., & Burkett, H. (2001). *Managing evaluation shortcuts* (Info-line No. 250111). Alexandria, VA: American Society for Training and Development.

Rossen, E., & Hartley, D. (2001). *Basics of e-learning.* (Info-line No. 250109). Alexandria, VA: American Society for Training and Development.

Rothwell, W. J. (1998). *Creating, measuring and documenting service impact: A capacity building resource: Rationales, models, activities, methods, techniques, instruments.* Columbus, OH: EnterpriseOhio Network.

Rothwell, W. J. (1999). *The evaluator.* Alexandria, VA: American Society for Training and Development.

Rothwell, W. J., & Cookson, P. (1997). *Beyond instruction.* San Francisco: Jossey-Bass.

Rothwell, W. J., Hohne, C., & King, S. (2000). *Human performance improvement: Building practitioner competence.* Houston, TX: Gulf.

Swanson, R. (2001). *Assessing the financial benefits of human resource development.* San Francisco: Berrett-Koehler.

Van Brakel, R. (2002). Why ROI isn't enough. *Training and Development, 56*(6), 72–74.

Welber, M. (2002). Final analysis. *e-learning, 3*(6), 22–25.

CHAPTER 14

Outsourcing Training

Karen A. Flannery

Today, most workforce development/continuing education departments in community colleges are considered to be revenue-generating for the institution. Being one of the few departments expected to generate enough revenue to cover its costs and turn a profit for the institution, the workforce development department is under pressure to develop new markets and create a consistent stream of revenue. One way to do that is through developing partnerships with clients, becoming the source they regularly turn to with their training needs.

Understanding why companies look to outside vendors—specifically, training providers—will help lay a foundation of lasting, more effective relationships between providers and clients. In this chapter I examine the reasons why companies choose to outsource training and the criteria they use to select training providers. I also briefly discuss marketing as it relates to training partnerships. The chapter is designed to assist training providers in becoming more competitive and better able to develop solid strategic partnerships with clients.

REASONS TO OUTSOURCE TRAINING

With the move to a global economy, the development of e-business, and the shift in the economy, companies are refocusing their business operations and the core purpose of operations. Such reexamination has led companies to consider many in-house functions for possible outsourcing because they are not essential to the core purpose of operations. Training is one of those functions.

Recognizing that development of human capital will give them the competitive advantage needed in today's global economy, companies are increasing their training budgets to new levels. American companies with 100 or more employees budgeted $54.2 billion for training in 2002 (Galvin, 2002). Of that amount, over $6 billion was spent on seminars and conferences and $15.1 billion on training provider services and products. As for the delivery of training, 28% of traditional and 37% of technology-based training programs were outsourced (Galvin, 2002). This is a substantial market—but why are training providers not getting a bigger part of it? To begin to answer that question, we must first examine why companies outsource their training.

The main reason for outsourcing is that it allows a company to concentrate on the function for which it is in business in the first place—that is, producing goods and services, not training (Kaeter, 1995; Quinn & Hilmer, 1994). Companies are looking to outsource training in areas other than core competencies, particularly if a provider can do it more effectively and efficiently, if the company itself lacks the resources needed to support internal training, or if the company needs to redirect the resources presently used for training in nonstrategic operations to more strategic ones (Makson, 1995). Other reasons for outsourcing are as follows.

Company downsizing or mergers. After a reorganization, the training department has usually been reduced to a small staff and cannot handle the volume of training necessary to prepare remaining employees to handle their additional responsibilities. Outsourcing some or all of the training can help employees meet their new demands (Allshouse, 1993; Gruebele, 1995; Kaeter, 1995; McDonald, 1993).

Managing costs. Operating a training function can

be expensive. Often there is a need to train one or a small number of employees or to develop a detailed and expensive program. Maintaining dedicated space (classrooms, labs) and resources (audiovisual equipment) for training is very costly. By outsourcing training, the company can shift the responsibility for development, location, and equipment to the provider. In many cases, the provider may have an open enrollment program that can accommodate a single employee, which would lower the cost to the client because the training provider is spreading the expenses (development, equipment, and overhead) among several clients (DeRose & McLaughlin, 1995; Harkins, Brown, & Sullivan, 1995; Kaufman, 1995; Robinson, 1991).

Government and industry regulations. Regulations can change every day. It takes a lot of time for someone to research rules and regulations, develop a training program to keep employees up-to-date, and then teach the program. If a company does not have a dedicated staff person for this task, then someone will need to take on this additional responsibility, which takes time away from what that individual was hired to do. It may be less expensive for the company to have an outside training provider partner to update or certify company personnel to meet the requirements. Training providers can deliver the necessary training where and when the company wants it. They can help the company's employees maintain their certification—a great opportunity for training providers to show return on investment (ROI). The cost to the company is only the cost for services and attendees' time.

The need for specialists. Changing technology makes it difficult for companies to employ the various trainers needed to upgrade and maintain employee skill levels. And, as mentioned earlier, if the training is occasional or for just a few employees, the cost may not justify employing a full-time trainer in-house. Outsourcing this function can be a cost-effective option because the company can hire a specialist to conduct the training only as needed.

Competitiveness. To stay competitive, a company needs to keep up with technology and the demands of customers. Outsourcing helps train employees in an efficient way and provides a quick response time to meet the company's changing needs. It allows the company to decrease its investment in training personnel or enable its training staff to redirect their talents to more strategic areas. For example, many company trainers have presented leadership training or sexual harassment training dozens of times and have begun to feel they are losing their effectiveness because of constant repetition.

Bringing in outside trainers for repetitive training allows in-house trainers to focus on a variety of other training and guards against burnout.

CRITERIA USED IN SELECTING TRAINING PROVIDERS

Because companies are deciding to outsource some or all of their training functions, their in-house training departments are increasingly becoming brokers who select outside providers that most closely match the needs of the company (Bassi, Benson, & Cheney, 1996). But what influences a company's decision to partner with a particular training provider? As a workforce development professional who has worked in contract training for a community college, I have witnessed the difficulty companies experience in making the decision to outsource training. To explore this further, I conducted a survey of a broad range of companies of varying sizes to find out what criteria they use in selecting a training provider (Flannery, 1998). The study identified seven key criteria in the selection process.

1. **Experience.** Companies look for a solid record of experience when choosing a training provider. Training providers should provide references listing clients who have purchased similar types of training or with whom the provider has a formal partnership. Evaluations or comments on the training or letters of recommendation are also key in helping clients to evaluate the quality and relevance of a provider's experience.

2. **Appropriate training materials.** By understanding the company culture prior to the final development of the training program or formation of the partnership, training providers can save themselves from missteps and embarrassment. Understanding the company's philosophy and goals is key in determining whether a particular training provider is a good match for a particular company.

3. **Attentiveness.** The ability to listen to the customer is a critical skill for effective training providers. To accurately develop a training program or formalize a partnership, training providers must prove to clients that they understand and are attentive to their needs.

4. **Expertise.** Although expertise relates to the provider's record of experience, it is more than that. If providers come up short on *experience* in a particular area, they can emphasize their *expertise*. Providers must be prepared and do their homework,

researching the company and its possible training needs prior to meeting the client. Providers should include subject matter experts to answer technical questions, prepare a checklist of questions to ask during the meeting, and anticipate outcomes that a company might expect at the completion of the training. Providers must show that they know themselves and that they know their clients as well.

5. **Resources.** All things being equal, can a provider supply the volume of training needed by the company? Does it have enough trainers available to conduct the number of sessions needed at the times desired by the company? Many companies need training provided on all three shifts at multiple locations. Good providers examine their resources before making commitments. Unfulfilled promises can be devastating to business relationships—both current and potential.

6. **Ability to customize.** Companies are looking for a training provider who can customize training to meet their specific needs. If a provider understands a company's culture, philosophy, and goals, it can tailor existing training programs or design new ones to address a company's unique challenges and environment.

7. **Quality.** Saving money is an important criterion in selecting a training provider, but it is not the sole criterion used. The responding companies in the study did identify budgetary constraints as a significant barrier in outsourcing training. The financial impact of outsourcing is in the forefront of this decision-making process. However, these same companies felt that a decrease in the training budget was not a perceived benefit of outsourcing. It appears that companies, when examining outsourcing, consider costs and budgets important but may not be looking to save money—or at least it is not their top priority. Their responses indicate that they perceive the benefits of outsourcing to be that training providers can deliver quality training that has a greater impact on employees and the operation as a whole than they can provide themselves.

MARKETING

Marketing requires time and effort to identify the most effective ways to let companies know that providers have what it takes to meet their training needs. How do training providers make those important contacts to begin forging a relationship that will turn into a long-term partnership? As part of the survey just discussed, companies were asked to indicate the importance of sources of information when selecting an outside training provider. The results are surprising. Companies indicated that some of the most familiar sources of marketing were not the most effective: Chamber of commerce services, direct calls from providers soliciting work, and mailings from providers made the least impact on the companies.

Because these traditional ways of soliciting business may not be as effective as once thought, training providers need to rethink how they will market their services to prospective clients. Training providers will need to concentrate more on informal networks, word-of-mouth, and responding to RFPs (requests for proposals). Training providers may themselves need training in ways to effectively market their services. They need to learn how to identify information networks that will be beneficial in securing new clients, to develop networking skills, to develop writing skills to respond to RFPs, and to send more personalized correspondence to prospective clients. Membership in associations that cater to prospective clients can also help training providers reach their audience in new and fresh ways.

CONCLUSION

Human capital is the most important asset a company has. If a company cannot continually develop this asset, it cannot remain competitive. However, for most companies, the focus of the organization is not training. Outsourcing allows them to focus on producing goods or providing services, while still developing human capital and adding value to the operation.

To create an effective long-term training partnership with a company, training providers must understand the business needs of their client. Unlike when a company hires a training provider for a single project here or there, the long-term partnership continues over many projects, and finding the right training partner becomes even more critical to a successful relationship.

Drawing on the survey results of what companies indicated was important to them, I have formulated a checklist for training providers to follow in developing training partnerships with their clients. The checklist not only provides guidance on what training providers should do to prepare for developing partnerships but also shows clients of those services what they should expect from their training providers. If training providers can develop strategic partnerships with their various clients, they will be well on their way to developing new markets and creating a more consistent stream of revenue for themselves and their sponsoring institutions. ❋

Developing Training Partnerships: A Checklist for Providers

- Understand client companies' core competencies.

- Find out how much training the company outsources. Does it outsource one area of training or the entire training function?

- Provide reasons why it would be more cost-effective for the company to outsource training rather than do it itself or not at all. Show ROI.

- Know your strengths and weakness as a training provider. Know what you are capable of and do not overpromise. The goal of training should be to strengthen the workforce and make it more competitive.

- Use a variety of methods to contact prospective clients. One is to respond to RFPs. To stand out from other providers, ask to meet with the prospective client to ask clarifying questions before responding to the RFP. Another method would be to have a current client refer you to similar clients.

- Consider the client's philosophy and goals. Make sure that you have the expertise to design and provide the training that meets the company's goals and expectations.

- Provide references. Show that you have designed and provided programs for similar organizations. Demonstrate through reference letters and evaluations how your programs successfully met the needs of those organizations.

- Make sure that you have the resources to fulfill the company's needs.

- Design a budget that is reasonable and all-inclusive and identifies any hidden or additional costs.

- Design your training content to meet the company's needs and be flexible in both content and delivery.

- Develop an effective method for follow-up and evaluation.

- Ask yourself whether you feel comfortable with this client. Consider whether or not this will be a good working relationship.

References

Allshouse, T. (1993). The role of vendor training. *Manufacturing Systems, 11*(8), 34.

Bassi, L. J., Benson, G., & Cheney, S. (1996). The top ten trends. *Training and Development, 50*(11), 28–42.

DeRose, G., & McLaughlin, J. (1995). Outsourcing through partnerships. *Training and Development, 49*(10), 51–55.

Flannery, K. (1998). *Outsourcing training: A survey of decision makers regarding the influence of selected organizational factors and their effect on decisions to outsource training.* Unpublished doctoral dissertation, Pennsylvania State University, University Park.

Galvin, T. (Ed.). (2002). 2002 industry report. *Training, 39*(10), 24–73.

Gruebele, D. (1995). Working together to go it alone. *Training and Development, 49*(3), 9–10.

Harkins, P. J., Brown, S. M., & Sullivan, R. (1995). Shining new light on a growing trend. *HR Magazine, 40*(12), 75–79.

Kaeter, M. (1995). An outsourcing primer. *Training and Development, 49*(11), 20–25.

Kaufman, M. (1995). Outsourcing—Once a curiosity, now a necessity. *Legal Management, 14*(1), 49–54.

Makson, S. (1995). Three questions are key to outsourcing decision. *National Underwriter, 99*(23), 28.

McDonald, K. (1993). Buying IT training services. *Purchasing and Supply Management, 23*(12), 28–29.

Quinn, J. B., & Hilmer, F. (1994, Spring). Strategic outsourcing. *Sloan Management Review, 2*, 43–55.

Robinson, R. (1991). Outsourcing's potential in higher education. *Cause/Effect, 14*(2), 3, 39.

Lessons Learned and Emerging Issues

Patrick E. Gerity

As my fellow editors and I finalized this volume, we thought that a fitting conclusion would be to pose some key questions to contributors Elaine A. Gaertner, Mary Gershwin, James Jacobs, and Laurance J. Warford, and to our colleague Michael Taggart. As facilitator of this process, I have included my comments here as well. Three deceptively simple, but ultimately difficult, questions were posed.

What Is the Most Important Lesson You Have Learned in Your Career?

Laurance J. Warford: The most important lesson I have learned in my career is the importance of developing good personal working relationships. In the business of workforce development we, as educators, are catalysts in getting our important work done. Being a good collaborator ensures that "what goes around, comes around" is positive and that your efforts are multiplied by those of others.

James Jacobs: The most important lesson I have learned is that good policies need to be accompanied by good detailed work. Indeed, for most of the workforce development issues, the questions are execution of designs. You must be good at not just talking about things but actually doing them. Institutions need to be more than a few talented individuals. The devil is in the details.

Michael Taggart: My experience with the operation of community college–based business and industry training operations has shown that their success is determined largely by the extent to which parent organization polices and practices support entrepreneurial success. Too many community colleges issue directives setting cost-recovery goals for their business and industry training operations but neglect their responsibility to create crucial, supportive policies, practices, and shared organizational understandings of what is required to support the speed, flexibility, and responsiveness that a business and industry services operation must have to be successful. Those colleges that create and maintain supportive environments are the ones that enjoy high levels of success.

Elaine A. Gaertner: I want to echo Michael Taggart's comments about a supportive institutional environment. Even stellar performers cannot build successful business and industry service organizations when colleges do not regard serving business as yet another important way of serving their communities. Sponsorship from state and local leadership is crucial to success and must be present for colleges to be a partner in building economic growth through workforce preparation.

Patrick E. Gerity: The most important lesson I have learned involves the mission of the community college and the role that I fulfill in accomplishing this mission. I started my career in business and industry training during one of the most severe economic recessions in southwestern Pennsylvania history. I had always focused on how our college could best serve the community, and it was my role to be a good steward of community resources. The most satisfying lesson I have learned is that the community college can make a big difference in our community, and my role allows me to assist in building a stronger community.

Mary Gershwin: The work is never done, so keep your "bait on the water" to increase your odds of reeling in the big victories for your students and college! Creating partnerships is a game of numbers, so do not get too tied up in working just one or two opportunities. Remember also to keep your bait on the water within your college by becoming a resource that creates opportunities for fulfilling your college's strategic vision through specific workforce development activities.

WHAT DO YOU BELIEVE IS THE MOST IMPORTANT TREND AFFECTING WORKFORCE DEVELOPERS IN COMMUNITY COLLEGES?

Laurance J. Warford: The most important trend affecting community college workforce development over the next five years is that the working pattern of people has changed. Today it is estimated that average American workers will make five to seven career changes in their lifetimes. This means that workers could easily have that many different employers over their lifetimes, contrasted to workers in the past who did not change employers and retired in a "gold watch" mentality. Specifically, this trend will affect workforce training in the following ways:

- *Comprehensive workforce training will be required.* Attention will need to be placed with all of the workforce segments: emerging, transitional, entrepreneurial, and incumbent workers.
- *Learning will be required throughout life.* Every time a career change is made, training will be required.
- *Employees will be increasingly responsible for their continuing training.* Employers will hesitate to spend money to train employees due to anticipated shorter on-the-job longevity.
- *More people will be in transition more often.* For example, more older workers than ever before will retrain for jobs following retirement.

James Jacobs: The most important trend in the next five years will be the growing combination of credit and noncredit instruction. More of what is now called noncredit instruction will have some forms of credit given, plus there will be more utilization of industry-specific credentials and certifications. The workforce development mission will also be extended into a general community development mission, and colleges will play roles in both of these matters.

Elaine A. Gaertner: By adding front-end assessment services and other nontraining offerings, colleges have the potential to substantially increase their market share of corporate training. Billions are spent every year on outsourced training in the United States, yet community colleges' collective share of that training continues to be very

small in comparison to what is possible. If colleges are to achieve their full potential, they will need to move beyond taking orders for training and use a performance-based approach to partnering with their customers on improving performance. Adopting a performance-based approach as a way of doing business with employers will distinguish community colleges from the vendors and consultants who represent their competition.

Michael Taggart: Three trends should be reinforced and continued. First, the number of community colleges providing assessment services should increase, to help employers better understand performance improvement issues. The transition from the traditional "order-taker" model to the performance consulting approach to service delivery will be a key factor in determining the future viability of community colleges in the customized training business. Without increased coupling of worker skill assessments with training delivery, companies that purchase training without a full understanding of the performance situation may find that training alone does not solve their performance problems, which may lead them to incorrectly conclude that the training does not work.

Second, there should be an increase in efforts to help human resource administrators measure return on company training investment. Currently, many more companies profess the importance of training than the number of companies making needed investments in employee training. Community colleges are working increasingly with human resource and training professionals to measure and report the return on training investments. To convince more employers that continuous employee development is the key to their future business success, community colleges must better document return on investment successes that result from their assessment and training work.

Third, there should be increased collaboration among community colleges as a deliberate strategy to build service capability, grow market share, and increase revenues. Diverse employer training needs often require resources and expertise not available from one single community college. However, a community college that has a mechanism in place to tap the resources and expertise at other community colleges increases its value to its community and demonstrates the value of collaborative service arrangements among colleges. In Ohio, the EnterpriseOhio Network is such a mechanism that has enhanced individual community college service capabilities and has drawn state funds to support this statewide delivery system, which is recognized as an Ohio economic development asset.

Patrick E. Gerity: The first trend will be in the increase of professional development for the community college workforce, community, and economic development professionals. Over 50% of current community college workforce professionals will retire in the next 10 years (Gerity, 1999). The second trend will be in the development of regional learning networks focusing on collaboration of community colleges, career schools, and colleges and universities to address regional workforce and economic development issues. The third trend will be an increase in community college workforce development organizations (WDOs) becoming self-sustaining profit centers due to decreases in state and federal funding. The most successful and profitable community colleges fund their WDOs, recover their expenses, and make significant profit while staying within their mission.

Of course, the results of a recent survey also provide valuable clues about some major trends and issues with which workforce developers are grappling (see Table 15.1). Although some issues are more important today than they might turn out to be in the future, the survey results are worth pondering for what they might bode for the future.

WHAT ADVICE WOULD YOU GIVE TO A NEWCOMER TO THE WORKFORCE DEVELOPMENT FIELD BASED ON YOUR EXPERIENCE?

Laurance J. Warford: I would advise a new workforce developer to develop strong working relationships with employers and organizations both inside and outside the institution. The successful workforce developer is a broker of resources to business and industry from the community college as well as from employers to the college.

James Jacobs: Always ask three questions in doing your work: Who are the customers and what are their needs? What is the importance of any particular project or program? How do you measure and communicate your success to others?

Table 15.1	Current Policy Issues in Community College Workforce Development		
Policy issue		# of states debating issues	# of states enacting legislation or board policy
Implementation of Workforce Investment Act		16	27
Level of funding for workforce development		17	18
State role in customized training for industry		17	18
Worker shortages		22	17
Welfare to Work		19	15
Coordination of workforce funding		25	14
Retraining displaced workers		17	13
School to Work		21	12
Funding of technology for workforce development		20	12
Distance learning for workforce training		22	10
Workplace or vocational literacy for adults		19	9
Transfer of AAS credits toward bachelor's degrees		16	9
Digital divide		22	4

Note. From Jenkins and Boswell (2002, p. 5). Reprinted with permission.

Michael Taggart: I would share two thoughts. First, collaborative relationships are critical to success. Building a loyal customer base in today's competitive marketplace requires speed and flexibility that can test even the best delivery system. Often the strength of interpersonal business relationship can mobilize support essential in an environment of limited resources and competing institutional priorities. Second, vigorous networking with counterparts at other community colleges can be enormously productive in sharing best practices, testing ideas, avoiding pitfalls, and accessing needed resources. If your state has not organized such a network, perhaps your advocacy for doing so will spark others to pursue this direction with you.

Patrick E. Gerity: Follow these three steps: (a) learn as much as you can about your community college's resources; (b) listen to what your customer says and ask questions—that is, learn as much as you can about each customer; and (c) look for new opportunities every day with both current and new customers. If you commit to continuous learning and improvement of your performance, you will become a great asset to your community and a future leader in workforce development.

Elaine A. Gaertner: The job of helping the institution understand what you do, what you need from them, and why is it important to you and the college will be an ongoing part of your job. Although many of your measurable results will come from successful relationships with your business clients, people internal to your organization—board members, faculty leadership, senior administrators, and the business services office staff—are also critical to your success with those external clients. Make sure to take time to let them know how important they are, especially when they have done something tangible that has helped you or your organization's performance.

Linking Training to Performance: A Guide for Workforce Development Professionals provides the basic information necessary for the many workforce developers who work in community colleges. This final chapter, "Lessons Learned and Emerging Issues," is written to provide community college workforce developers with a description of what they will most likely face in their jobs. The major issues that emerged from the answers to the key questions asked are building strong relationships, forming alliances and networks, and providing workplace assessment and performance consulting services.

The first major issue that emerged was developing strong working relationships internally and externally.

Within the internal community college organization, it is critical for workforce developers to develop collaborative relationships and acknowledge how important they are in providing these services. It is also important to focus on external customers and how you develop your relationships with them. The focus should be on results and how the community college can respond rapidly.

The second emerging issue is increased collaboration among community colleges to better serve customers, grow market share, and provide coordinated efforts to improve regional and state economic development. These collaborative initiatives may take the form of alliances and networks that focus on providing shared services and resources to address large workforce development situations, such as industry clusters. This trend of collaborative alliances and networks is growing consistently across the United States and is usually led by the local community college. A few examples are EnterpriseOhio Network, Workforce and Economic Development Network for Pennsylvania (WEDnetPA), MASS*NET (MA), and Economic and Workforce Development Program (CA).

The third issue is the growth in the number of community college workforce development providers offering front-end assessment services, performance consulting services, and other nontraining services. In terms of economic development, being a full-service provider means expanding service offerings to a variety of human performance improvement services designed to help a company improve its own performance in the marketplace. These expanded services enhance the value that community colleges can provide to their customers and will also allow them to assess a company's real business needs and evaluate the need for training versus other kinds of services.

Community college workforce development is here to stay and remains the first choice for U.S. business and industry workforce training. The future is bright, but steps need to be taken to stay the "number one" choice. The first step is to develop a succession plan to address the large number of community college workforce development retirements in the next eight years. The second step would be for the American Association of Community Colleges and its councils that focus on workforce development to make preparations for the professional development of the next generation of workforce developers and to continuously improve and update the skills of the existing practitioners. Third, community college leadership programs need to emphasize the importance and value of supporting colleges' workforce development initiatives. By being prepared for the future and by investing in continuous improvement strategies, community colleges will continue to lead the nation in providing the best workforce development services and growing their local economies. ❋

References

Gerity, P. E. (1999). *A study to identify community college workforce training and developmental professionals' perceived competencies and their perceived professional development needs.* Unpublished doctoral dissertation, Pennsylvania State University, University Park.

Jenkins, D., & Boswell, K. (2002). *State policies on community college workforce development: Findings from a national survey.* Chicago: Center for Community College Policy Education Commission for the States.

The seven appendixes that follow contain a wealth of useful information, resources, and tools. They are printed in the book so that you can read their contents. They are printed on a companion CD (inside the back cover) so that you can use their contents. We wanted to make it easy for you to reprint or adapt these resources, which you may do without permission, unless otherwise indicated. Appendix G is hot-linked on the CD so that you can go directly to Web sites from the disk.

APPENDIX CONTENTS

A: Developing a High-Performing Organization: Self-Assessment Instrument for Workforce Development Professionals in Higher Education

B: Competency Model for Community College Workforce Developers

C: Competency Assessment Instrument for Community College Workforce Developers

D: Templates for Conducting 5-S Consultative Sales
   1. Weekly Call Planner
   2. Monthly Summary of Prospecting Activity
   3. Annual Client Visit Planning Calendar
   4. Program Summary Report
   5. Record of Client Contact

E: Coaching Checksheet for Community College Workforce Developers

F: Templates for Community College Workforce Developers
   1. Strategic Planning Checklist
   2. Strategic Plan for a Community College Workforce Development Effort
   3. Job Profile of a Workforce Development Dean or Director
   4. Job Profile of a Workforce Development Coordinator
   5. Job Description for a Contract Education Sales/Account Manager
   6. Interview Guide for an Initial Meeting With a Client
   7. Worksheet for Drafting Proposals to Clients
   8. Contract Training Business Plan
   9. Action Planning Worksheet
   10. Interview Guide for Mandated Training Program Planning
   11. Training Agreement

Developing a High-Performing Organization: Self-Assessment Instrument for Workforce Development Professionals in Higher Education

Pamela Tate and Rebecca Klein-Collins

This instrument is a checklist that enables workforce development professionals to identify potential performance improvement areas (based on the performance model presented in chapter 3). The instrument was originally developed by the Council for Adult and Experiential Learning (CAEL) for the Ohio Board of Regents, to assist in the development of Ohio's network of college-based business and industry centers. In this research, CAEL identified best practices of high-performing, college-based, workforce development organizations from both secondary sources and site visits conducted at five high-performing centers.

This strategic planning instrument is organized according to the performance outcome categories outlined in chapter 3. Under each performance outcome is a list of questions to determine whether a workforce development organization (WDO) operates according to identified best practices. As a planning tool, it identifies specific actions that will lead to the achievement of best practices. By individually addressing each desired performance outcome and assessing areas of strength ("yes" responses) and areas for improvement ("sometimes" and "no" responses), higher education professionals can identify those practices that are most likely to lead to high performance.

More information about CAEL's research for the Ohio Board of Regents can be found in "Best Practices of College Business and Industry Centers: A Self-Improvement Guide" by Ruth Barber and Rebecca Klein-Collins (1998), which can be ordered from CAEL online at www.cael.org or by phone at 312-499-2600.

HOW TO USE THIS INSTRUMENT

In using this instrument, the first step is to read each question and respond "yes," "sometimes," or "no." After completion of the entire survey, WDO staff can systematically examine each area of operation and assess the responses to identify areas for improvement and areas of strength.

There is no formal scoring mechanism for this instrument because it is not meant to be evaluative or comparative, but rather strategic. Its purpose is to

- Identify areas in which workforce development professionals can target resources and
- Provide specific, incremental suggestions for how to implement best practices.

Once the checklist has been completed, the information gathered can be applied in various ways:

- **For internal use by workforce development professionals as a tool for continuous improvement and strategic planning.** This instrument allows staff and leadership of workforce development organizations to determine where they are performing well and where they need improvement. The instrument also offers specific tactics aimed at improving performance.
- **For collaboration between higher education institutions and workforce development operations.** This instrument provides an objective manner in which to facilitate ongoing communication between the WDO and the college. In addition, it can serve as a springboard for discussions regarding the coordination of marketing, business office, and other procedures.

- **For use by networks of workforce development professionals and community college organizations.** Multi-campus or multi-college educational systems can use the instrument to facilitate discussions within their system. After all workforce development organizations involved have completed the self-assessment instrument, they can use the collective information in planning topics for annual conferences, organizing group discussions, developing online study groups, and hiring consultants to assist in continuous improvement efforts.

Self-Assessment Instrument for Workforce Development Professionals			
PART I: SERVICE DELIVERY			
	Yes	Sometimes	No
1. _DEVELOP and maintain a full-range of high impact services for customers_			
1. Does the WDO define the objectives of training programs in terms of the identified business and individual performance needs of the customer?			
2. Does the WDO use examples and materials directly related to customer performance requirements in the content of training programs and evaluations?			
3. Does the WDO offer nontraining services to customers?			
4. Does the WDO regularly recommend nontraining solutions?			
5. Does the WDO partner with other providers to offer services that are not available at the college or WDO?			
6. Does the WDO offer credit and degree options?			
7. Does the WDO develop plans for specific actions to encourage workplace application of skills?			
8. Does the WDO employ computer-based and distance learning technology?			
9. Does the WDO use technology to increase the cost-effectiveness and availability of services for customers?			
2. _SYSTEMATICALLY approach the sales and marketing process_			
1. Does the WDO have a dedicated sales staff member?			
2. Does the WDO have a dedicated marketing staff member?			
3. Does the WDO collect data on win/loss ratio, type of business customer, project data (such as estimated dollar value versus gross profit/loss), and an ideal customer profile?			
4. Does the WDO have a documented sales plan?			
5. Does the WDO identify and track sales leads using a sales database and a prospect list?			
6. Does the WDO use a consultative selling approach?			

	Yes	Sometimes	No
2. SYSTEMATICALLY *approach the sales and marketing process (cont'd)*			
7. Does the WDO have team and/or individual incentives for sales results?			
8. Is the business volume of the WDO increasing?			
9. Does the WDO have an annual written marketing plan?			
10. Does the WDO use advanced marketing methods?			
11. Does the WDO maintain a Web site?			
12. Does the WDO research which marketing methods are most effective?			
3. DIAGNOSE *customer needs*			
1. Does the WDO contract for performance assessments when appropriate?			
2. Do WDO staff redefine service requests in performance terms?			
3. Does the WDO use multiple data collection methods to gather information on business and performance needs?			
4. Does the WDO conduct formal or informal analysis of performance and causes for nonperformance?			
5. Do WDO proposals for service identify the business and individual employee needs to be addressed?			
6. Do WDO proposals for service identify the expected business performance outcomes to be achieved by the service?			
7. Does the WDO conduct customer team briefings to report on findings, and to educate customers on performance improvement?			
8. Does the WDO distribute materials and offer presentations on performance improvement to customers?			
4. PROMOTE *a customer orientation*			
1. Do the services of the WDO reflect the requirements, expectations, and preferences of customers?			
2. Does the WDO monitor technological, competitive, economic, and environmental factors that influence customers?			
3. Do WDO staff use strategies to understand service issues from the customer's perspective?			
4. Does the WDO use evaluation information to improve survey design and increase or decrease the importance of service features to customers?			
5. Does the WDO have a contact person or electronic network so that customers can comment, complain, and seek information and assistance?			

	Yes	Sometimes	No
4. PROMOTE a customer orientation (cont'd)			
6. Does the WDO have a process for following up on inquiries and on contracts that are either in-process or have been completed?			
7. Does the WDO train customer-contact employees in key knowledge of services, listening, solicitation of comments, and anticipating and handling problems?			
8. Does the WDO have a documented service history for every customer?			
9. Does the WDO utilize a system to measure satisfaction that includes participant evaluations, post-workshop surveys, sales calls, or informal conversations with customers?			
10. Does the WDO use feedback to change training midcourse?			
11. Does the WDO reply to customer requests, proposals, and contracts in a timely manner?			
5. MEASURE the impact of programs and services			
1. Does the WDO use and document participant evaluations and conversations with customers?			
2. Does the WDO measure the impact of services provided on the identified performance needs of the customer?			
3. Does the WDO offer ways for the company to measure its return on investment?			
4. Do trainees/students complete evaluations at the end of training?			
5. Do WDO staff administer pre- and post-tests or performance demonstrations to determine what was learned?			
6. Do instructors receive impact data and make appropriate changes to training content and delivery?			
7. Does the WDO have a large incidence of repeat customers or referrals?			
6. DEVELOP strong partnerships and alliances			
1. Does the WDO have partners that offer capabilities or competencies that the WDO itself is unable to provide to its customers?			
2. Does the WDO solicit and receive training grants from the state?			
3. Does the WDO advise state and regional agencies on the design of industry training and assistance policies to the competitiveness of local companies?			

PART II: MANAGEMENT AND OPERATIONS	Yes	Sometimes	No
7. OPTIMIZE WDO financial performance			
1. Does the WDO have a financial analysis and projection for the year?			
2. Does the WDO have long-term repeat customers?			
3. Does the WDO have its own budget?			
4. Does the WDO have an identified section of the budget for which heavy sales and marketing is not necessary?			
5. Does the WDO track costs and determine price based on comprehensive cost of delivery?			
6. Does the WDO continually expand its methods for raising funds, charging fees, paying staff, and using consultants?			
7. Is the WDO able to reinvest a portion of its revenue into the development of new products and services?			
8. Does the WDO have control over any portion of its budget surplus?			
9. Does the WDO pursue opportunities to acquire flexibility and control over its budget?			
10. Does the WDO have a computerized accounting system?			
8. MANAGE human resources			
1. Does the WDO have human resource plans, including performance goals in staff preparation and development, staff recruitment, compensation, promotion, and benefits?			
2. Does the WDO have access to a pool of part-time consultants to meet fluctuating customer needs?			
3. Does the WDO have its own pay scale based on market value?			
4. Does the WDO director create opportunities and initiative for self-directed responsibility?			
5. Does the WDO have a compensation, promotion, and recognition system that reinforces high performance?			
6. Do WDO staff participate in training and workshops that help to meet WDO and personal objectives?			
7. Does the WDO offer professional development opportunities to all staff?			
8. Does the WDO director ensure that the work environment is safe and healthful?			
9. Does the WDO director monitor staff-related and WDO performance data to adjust work flows and staffing patterns?			

	Yes	Sometimes	No
8. MANAGE human resources (cont'd)			
10. Is the WDO able to locate and hire qualified individuals for service delivery?			
9. APPLY strong strategic and organizational planning			
1. Does the WDO conduct extensive research on trends and events in the external environment?			
2. Does the WDO conduct internal performance audits using institutional research data and program information?			
3. Does the WDO have a planning committee of faculty, staff, board members, students, and community residents?			
4. Does the WDO use listening sessions for community members, business, government, and other providers?			
5. Does the WDO have a written strategic plan?			
6. Does the WDO update the strategic plan yearly?			
7. Does the WDO monitor its financial progress monthly?			
8. Is the WDO director on the planning committee for the college?			
9. Are members of the college faculty on the planning committee for the WDO?			
10. MAINTAIN responsive operational processes			
1. Does the WDO have documentation for all processes from sales call to termination of contract?			
2. Does the WDO have designated staff assigned to each step of the process?			
3. Does the WDO conduct periodic reviews of process flow documentation?			
4. Does the WDO continually upgrade its systems?			
5. Does the WDO director provide training on system and other procedural changes within the WDO to affected staff?			
6. Does the WDO director communicate any changes and the reason for these changes directly to staff?			
7. Does the WDO director hold staff meetings at least once per month?			
8. Does the WDO use appropriate technology for the information, planning, and service delivery needs of the WDO?			

	Yes	Sometimes	No
11. ESTABLISH and maintain a productive relationship with the college			
1. Do the WDO director, vice-CEO, and CEO of the college participate in verbal and written summary reports on at least a quarterly basis?			
2. Does the WDO director submit summary reports to the board agenda or have scheduled reports to the board?			
3. Do the CEO and vice-CEO of the college publicize the activities of the WDO?			
4. Do the WDO and college share facilities, instructors, curriculum, grant leads, and other resources?			
5. Does the WDO provide professional development for the college faculty?			
6. Does the CEO or campus dean of the college market the services of the WDO?			
12. DEMONSTRATE strong WDO leadership			
1. Does the director provide WDO staff with a clear sense of direction and a vision of the WDO's role in the college and the larger community?			
2. Does the WDO director establish and communicate high performance expectations?			
3. Does the WDO director regularly provide information to staff on overall organizational performance?			
4. Does the WDO have priorities for improvement actions?			

APPENDIX *B*

Competency Model for Community College Workforce Developers

William J. Rothwell and Patrick E. Gerity

Competency Model for Community College Workforce Developers	
Competencies	**Activities**
Basic Level	
1. **Office Management**	a. Manage time and priorities and meet deadlines b. Schedule and prepare for meetings c. Establish and maintain basic files, recordkeeping, and follow-up systems d. Use appropriate office technologies and software
2. **Communication**	a. Write/dictate letters, reports, and memos b. Give presentations c. Facilitate meetings, seminars, and ceremonies d. Actively listen to others e. Use e-mail
3. **Internal Relations**	a. Develop knowledge about the workforce development professionals in the college b. Participate in campus meetings c. Develop knowledge about the campus culture and values d. Identify and establish working relationships with appropriate campus units e. Develop familiarity with and linkages to academic departments f. Market continuing education internally to the college community g. Participate on college committees
4. **Program Support**	a. Pick up and deliver supplies and materials b. Schedule and maintain facilities c. Handle arrangements with food services and caterers d. Handle arrangements with hotel and conference facilities e. Order instructional materials

Competency Model for Community College Workforce Developers (cont'd)	
Competencies	**Activities**
Basic Level	
4. **Program Support (cont'd)**	f. Arrange for and coordinate audiovisual assistance and support g. Provide logistical support h. Coordinate travel arrangements with faculty i. Arrange for and coordinate registration of students and collection of fees j. Confirm registration and logistics to participants k. Arrange for and coordinate selling textbooks and supplies l. Maintain program records and statistics m. Assess participants' reaction to programs
Intermediate Level	
5. **Financial Management and Budgeting**	a. Monitor existing individual program budgets b. Analyze and adjust existing program budgets c. Prepare new individual program budgets d. Evaluate profitability of individual programs e. Initiate and approve purchases for program materials and support f. Identify potential funding sources g. Cultivate relationships with potential funding sources h. Spell out components of memoranda of agreement i. Work with faculty and contracts and grants offices to write grants j. Administer contracts and grants k. Secure scholarships l. Identify and negotiate with vendors m. Make purchasing decisions for office-wide equipment, services, etc. n. Use MIS for financial decision making o. Develop and monitor budget for the workforce development office p. Evaluate workforce development office profitability
6. **Student Relations and Services**	a. Understand and communicate college requirements to students b. Recruit students c. Facilitate adult reentry to higher education d. Arrange for and coordinate registration of students e. Arrange for and coordinate counseling for students f. Develop system to track students' progress g. Recognize students' achievements h. Mediate conflicts among students and faculty i. Provide access and referrals to student services (e.g., financial aid, career development, etc.) j. Conduct student surveys
7. **Faculty Relations**	a. Recruit and hire adjunct faculty, working with the DAA as is appropriate b. Orient part-time faculty c. Give directions and information to faculty members d. Assist faculty with curriculum development e. Monitor faculty and follow up with faculty evaluations f. Work to foster positive relationships with faculty

Competencies	Activities
Competency Model for Community College Workforce Developers (cont'd)	
Intermediate Level (cont'd)	
8. **Client Management**	a. Identify prospective clients b. Gather information about clients c. Understand competitors d. Respond to clients' requests e. Build relationships with clients f. Assess clients' needs g. Make initial calls on prospective clients h. Source best ways to meet clients' needs i. Maintain contact with clients j. Build project teams with clients k. Negotiate contracts and agreements with clients
9. **Training and Organizational Development**	a. Choose appropriate methods to assess training needs b. Separate training and nontraining (management) needs c. Identify gaps that can be corrected by training d. Prioritize training needs to align with organizational goals e. Develop training strategies f. Establish instructional goals g. Deliver and evaluate training
10. **External and Community Relations**	a. Articulate the goals and mission of the workforce development unit to the community and community organizations b. Join and participate in community organizations, professional associations, community meetings and boards, including those that present opportunities to work with alumni c. Identify and meet with prospective partners in the community d. Consult with community resource people about community needs and programs e. Develop alliances and articulation agreements with other colleges f. Communicate with local, state, and federal politicians g. Communicate with international organizations as opportunities arise
11. **Marketing and Promotion**	a. Read newspapers and other publications in the service area to identify prospective clients b. Develop an understanding of marketing and demographic resources for the service area c. Acquire in-depth familiarity with competitors' products and services d. Identify, purchase, organize, and supervise mailing lists e. Form partnerships with market programs f. Assess current market needs formally (e.g., via survey) and informally (e.g., via discussion) g. Develop newsletters, program brochures, and catalogs h. Write press releases i. Conduct open houses j. Conduct telemarketing campaigns k. Write proposals for training programs

Competency Model for Community College Workforce Developers (cont'd)	
Competencies	**Activities**
Intermediate Level (cont'd)	
11. Marketing and Promotion (cont'd)	l. Develop program pricing strategies to accomplish marketing goals m. Position the college properly as a supplier of education and training
12. Programming	a. Identify and analyze needs b. Understand the workforce development requirements of professional and other groups c. Identify program topics and outcomes based on need d. Select appropriate media for program delivery e. Set program objectives f. Obtain the necessary college approvals g. Work with faculty to develop curriculum and materials h. Negotiate program locations and schedules i. Learn and meet the accreditation requirements of accrediting agencies j. Implement programs k. Monitor programs l. Establish and use program evaluation procedures m. Use evaluation results to improve programs n. Use MIS program management screens o. Understand the program approval process for workforce development requirements p. Conduct environmental scanning to identify future program needs q. Understand the workforce development requirements of various groups as they affect marketing impact
Advanced Level	
13. Recruitment, Hiring, and Orientation	a. Identify staffing requirements b. Recruit prospective staff c. Select staff members from among multiple possibilities d. Orient and train staff
14. Supervision	a. Supervise staff daily b. Mentor staff c. Establish accountability guidelines and communicate them to staff d. Delegate work as necessary e. Support staff members in achieving their goals f. Provide performance feedback and counseling to staff continually g. Evaluate staff performance h. Provide staff members with professional development and growth opportunities i. Promote staff j. Lay off or terminate staff as necessary
15. Management	a. Manage office workflow b. Make decisions promptly and effectively c. Identify and manage priorities daily d. Juggle multiple and conflicting priorities e. Use database management systems

Competency Model for Community College Workforce Developers (cont'd)	
Competencies	**Activities**
Advanced Level (cont'd)	
16. Leadership	a. Serve as an exemplary role model b. Motivate and encourage staff c. Remain aware of public issues d. Tolerate ambiguity in the organization and community e. Appreciate and actively support diversity in thought and deed f. Lead strategic planning efforts g. Develop and articulate a vision for the workforce development effort h. Articulate values and guiding principles for the workforce development effort i. Build enthusiasm for the workforce development mission j. Set policy k. Arbitrate disputes and conflicts l. Form coalitions with others in the college and community m. Lead continuous quality improvement efforts n. Develop and maintain "content expert" status
Ongoing at all Levels	
17. Personal and Professional Development	a. Establish personal and professional goals b. Read broadly and remain aware of events affecting goals c. Attend conferences and training programs relevant to goals d. Participate in professional organizations relevant to goals e. Pursue advanced degrees and professional certification or licensure f. Conduct research on issues relevant to goals g. Make presentations relevant to goals h. Publish on issues relevant to goals i. Mentor others whose personal and professional goals coincide

Note: Adapted from *Hierarchy of Competencies for Continuing Education Professionals,* unpublished manuscript (Rothwell, 1997). For more information, contact William J. Rothwell, PhD, Pennsylvania State University, College of Education, Department of Learning and Performance Systems, Workforce Education and Development, 305C Keller Building, University Park, PA 16802, Phone: 814-863-2581.

APPENDIX C

Competency Assessment Instrument for Community College Workforce Developers

Patrick E. Gerity and Marsha King

Directions: Use this assessment instrument to identify how important various competencies associated with success in community college workforce development are to your job in your institution and how much need you have for professional development. For each competency listed in the left column below, *circle an appropriate response code in the middle column to indicate how important you consider it to be for success in your work.* Use the following scale for the middle column: **1 = No importance**; **2 = Some importance**; **3 = Importance**;

4 = Much importance; **5 = Very great importance.** Then *circle an appropriate response code in the right column to indicate how much need for professional development you feel you need in this work activity area.* Use the following scale for the right column: **1 = No need**; **2 = Some need**; **3 = Need**; **4 = Much need**; **5 = Very great need.** When you finish the rating, use it as a discussion tool with your immediate supervisor or other relevant stakeholders to identify areas for your professional development and as a foundation for establishing a professional developmental plan.

Competency		How Important?					How Much Need for Professional Development?				
		No Importance			Very Great Importance		No Need			Very Great Need	
		1	2	3	4	5	1	2	3	4	5
1. Office Management											
a	Manage time and priorities and meet deadlines	1	2	3	4	5	1	2	3	4	5
b	Schedule and prepare for meetings	1	2	3	4	5	1	2	3	4	5
c	Establish and maintain basic files, recordkeeping, and follow-up systems	1	2	3	4	5	1	2	3	4	5
d	Use appropriate office technologies and software	1	2	3	4	5	1	2	3	4	5
2. Communication											
a	Write/dictate letters, reports, and memos	1	2	3	4	5	1	2	3	4	5
b	Give presentations	1	2	3	4	5	1	2	3	4	5
c	Facilitate meetings, seminars, and ceremonies	1	2	3	4	5	1	2	3	4	5

Competency		How Important?					How Much Need for Professional Development?				
		No Importance			Very Great Importance		No Need			Very Great Need	
		1	2	3	4	5	1	2	3	4	5
2. Communication (cont'd)											
d	Actively listen to others	1	2	3	4	5	1	2	3	4	5
e	Use e-mail	1	2	3	4	5	1	2	3	4	5
3. Internal Relations											
a	Develop knowledge about the workforce development professionals in the college	1	2	3	4	5	1	2	3	4	5
b	Participate in campus meetings	1	2	3	4	5	1	2	3	4	5
c	Develop knowledge about the campus culture and values	1	2	3	4	5	1	2	3	4	5
d	Identify and establish working relationships with appropriate campus units	1	2	3	4	5	1	2	3	4	5
e	Develop familiarity with and linkages to academic departments	1	2	3	4	5	1	2	3	4	5
f	Market continuing education internally to the college community	1	2	3	4	5	1	2	3	4	5
g	Participate on college committees	1	2	3	4	5	1	2	3	4	5
4. Program Support											
a	Pick up and deliver supplies and materials	1	2	3	4	5	1	2	3	4	5
b	Schedule and maintain facilities	1	2	3	4	5	1	2	3	4	5
c	Handle arrangements with food services and caterers	1	2	3	4	5	1	2	3	4	5
d	Handle arrangements with hotel and conference facilities	1	2	3	4	5	1	2	3	4	5
e	Order instructional materials	1	2	3	4	5	1	2	3	4	5
f	Arrange for and coordinate audiovisual assistance and support	1	2	3	4	5	1	2	3	4	5
g	Provide logistical support	1	2	3	4	5	1	2	3	4	5
h	Coordinate travel arrangements with faculty	1	2	3	4	5	1	2	3	4	5
i	Arrange for and coordinate registration of students and collection of fees	1	2	3	4	5	1	2	3	4	5
j	Confirm registration and logistics to participants	1	2	3	4	5	1	2	3	4	5
k	Arrange for and coordinate selling textbooks and supplies	1	2	3	4	5	1	2	3	4	5
l	Maintain program records and statistics	1	2	3	4	5	1	2	3	4	5
m	Assess participants' reaction to programs	1	2	3	4	5	1	2	3	4	5

Competency		How Important?					How Much Need for Professional Development?				
		No Importance				Very Great Importance	No Need				Very Great Need
		1	2	3	4	5	1	2	3	4	5
5. Financial Management and Budgeting											
a	Monitor existing individual program budgets	1	2	3	4	5	1	2	3	4	5
b	Analyze and adjust existing program budgets	1	2	3	4	5	1	2	3	4	5
c	Prepare new individual program budgets	1	2	3	4	5	1	2	3	4	5
d	Evaluate profitability of individual programs	1	2	3	4	5	1	2	3	4	5
e	Initiate and approve purchases for program materials and support	1	2	3	4	5	1	2	3	4	5
f	Identify potential funding sources	1	2	3	4	5	1	2	3	4	5
g	Cultivate relationships with potential funding sources	1	2	3	4	5	1	2	3	4	5
h	Spell out components of memoranda of agreement	1	2	3	4	5	1	2	3	4	5
i	Work with faculty and contracts and grants offices to write grants	1	2	3	4	5	1	2	3	4	5
j	Administer contracts and grants	1	2	3	4	5	1	2	3	4	5
k	Secure scholarships	1	2	3	4	5	1	2	3	4	5
l	Identify and negotiate with vendors	1	2	3	4	5	1	2	3	4	5
m	Make purchasing decisions for office-wide equipment, services, etc.	1	2	3	4	5	1	2	3	4	5
n	Use MIS for financial decision making	1	2	3	4	5	1	2	3	4	5
o	Develop and monitor budget for the workforce development office	1	2	3	4	5	1	2	3	4	5
p	Evaluate workforce development office profitability	1	2	3	4	5	1	2	3	4	5
6. Student Relations and Services											
a	Understand and communicate college requirements to students	1	2	3	4	5	1	2	3	4	5
b	Recruit students	1	2	3	4	5	1	2	3	4	5
c	Facilitate adult reentry to higher education	1	2	3	4	5	1	2	3	4	5
d	Arrange for and coordinate registration of students	1	2	3	4	5	1	2	3	4	5
e	Arrange for and coordinate counseling for students	1	2	3	4	5	1	2	3	4	5

Competency		How Important?					How Much Need for Professional Development?				
		No Importance				Very Great Importance	No Need				Very Great Need
		1	2	3	4	5	1	2	3	4	5
6. Student Relations and Services (cont'd)											
f	Develop system to track students' progress	1	2	3	4	5	1	2	3	4	5
g	Recognize students' achievements	1	2	3	4	5	1	2	3	4	5
h	Mediate conflicts among students and faculty	1	2	3	4	5	1	2	3	4	5
i	Provide access and referrals to student services (e.g., financial aid, career development, etc.	1	2	3	4	5	1	2	3	4	5
j	Conduct student surveys	1	2	3	4	5	1	2	3	4	5
7. Faculty Relations											
a	Recruit and hire adjunct faculty, working with the DAA as is appropriate	1	2	3	4	5	1	2	3	4	5
b	Orient part-time faculty	1	2	3	4	5	1	2	3	4	5
c	Give directions and information to faculty members	1	2	3	4	5	1	2	3	4	5
d	Assist faculty with curriculum development	1	2	3	4	5	1	2	3	4	5
e	Monitor faculty and follow up with faculty evaluations	1	2	3	4	5	1	2	3	4	5
f	Work to foster positive relationships with faculty	1	2	3	4	5	1	2	3	4	5
8. Client Management											
a	Identify prospective clients	1	2	3	4	5	1	2	3	4	5
b	Gather information about clients	1	2	3	4	5	1	2	3	4	5
c	Understand competitors	1	2	3	4	5	1	2	3	4	5
d	Respond to clients' requests	1	2	3	4	5	1	2	3	4	5
e	Build relationships with clients	1	2	3	4	5	1	2	3	4	5
f	Assess clients' needs	1	2	3	4	5	1	2	3	4	5
g	Make initial calls on prospective clients	1	2	3	4	5	1	2	3	4	5
h	Source best ways to meet clients' needs	1	2	3	4	5	1	2	3	4	5
i	Maintain contact with clients	1	2	3	4	5	1	2	3	4	5
j	Build project teams with clients	1	2	3	4	5	1	2	3	4	5
k	Negotiate contracts and agreements with clients	1	2	3	4	5	1	2	3	4	5
9. Training and Organizational Development											
a	Choose appropriate methods to assess training needs	1	2	3	4	5	1	2	3	4	5

Competency		How Important?					How Much Need for Professional Development?				
		No Importance				Very Great Importance	No Need				Very Great Need
		1	2	3	4	5	1	2	3	4	5
9. Training and Organizational Development (cont'd)											
b	Separate training and nontraining (management) needs	1	2	3	4	5	1	2	3	4	5
c	Identify gaps that can be corrected by training	1	2	3	4	5	1	2	3	4	5
d	Prioritize training needs to align with organizational goals	1	2	3	4	5	1	2	3	4	5
e	Develop training strategies	1	2	3	4	5	1	2	3	4	5
f	Establish instructional goals	1	2	3	4	5	1	2	3	4	5
g	Deliver and evaluate training	1	2	3	4	5	1	2	3	4	5
10. External and Community Relations											
a	Articulate the goals and mission of the workforce development unit to the community and community organizations	1	2	3	4	5	1	2	3	4	5
b	Join and participate in community organizations, professional associations, community meetings and boards, including those that present opportunities to work with alumni	1	2	3	4	5	1	2	3	4	5
c	Identify and meet with prospective partners in the community	1	2	3	4	5	1	2	3	4	5
d	Consult with community resource people about community needs and programs	1	2	3	4	5	1	2	3	4	5
e	Develop alliances and articulation agreements with other colleges	1	2	3	4	5	1	2	3	4	5
f	Communicate with local, state, and federal politicians	1	2	3	4	5	1	2	3	4	5
g	Communicate with international organizations as opportunities arise	1	2	3	4	5	1	2	3	4	5
11. Marketing and Promotion											
a	Read newspapers and other publications in the service area to identify prospective clients	1	2	3	4	5	1	2	3	4	5
b	Develop an understanding of marketing and demographic resources for the service area	1	2	3	4	5	1	2	3	4	5
c	Acquire in-depth familiarity with competitors' products and services	1	2	3	4	5	1	2	3	4	5
d	Identify, purchase, organize, and supervise mailing lists	1	2	3	4	5	1	2	3	4	5
e	Form partnerships with market programs	1	2	3	4	5	1	2	3	4	5

Competency		How Important?					How Much Need for Professional Development?				
		No Importance			Very Great Importance		No Need			Very Great Need	
		1	2	3	4	5	1	2	3	4	5
11. Marketing and Promotion (cont'd)											
f	Assess current market needs formally (e.g., via survey) and informally (e.g., via discussion)	1	2	3	4	5	1	2	3	4	5
g	Develop newsletters, program brochures, and catalogs	1	2	3	4	5	1	2	3	4	5
h	Write press releases	1	2	3	4	5	1	2	3	4	5
i	Conduct open houses	1	2	3	4	5	1	2	3	4	5
j	Conduct telemarketing campaigns	1	2	3	4	5	1	2	3	4	5
k	Write proposals for training programs	1	2	3	4	5	1	2	3	4	5
l	Develop program pricing strategies to accomplish marketing goals	1	2	3	4	5	1	2	3	4	5
m	Position the college properly as a supplier of education and training	1	2	3	4	5	1	2	3	4	5
12. Programming											
a	Identify and analyze needs	1	2	3	4	5	1	2	3	4	5
b	Understand the workforce development requirements of professional and other groups	1	2	3	4	5	1	2	3	4	5
c	Identify program topics and outcomes based on need	1	2	3	4	5	1	2	3	4	5
d	Select appropriate media for program delivery	1	2	3	4	5	1	2	3	4	5
e	Set program objectives	1	2	3	4	5	1	2	3	4	5
f	Obtain the necessary college approvals	1	2	3	4	5	1	2	3	4	5
g	Work with faculty to develop curriculum and materials	1	2	3	4	5	1	2	3	4	5
h	Negotiate program locations and schedules	1	2	3	4	5	1	2	3	4	5
i	Learn and meet the accreditation requirements of accrediting agencies	1	2	3	4	5	1	2	3	4	5
j	Implement programs	1	2	3	4	5	1	2	3	4	5
k	Monitor programs	1	2	3	4	5	1	2	3	4	5
l	Establish and use program evaluation procedures	1	2	3	4	5	1	2	3	4	5
m	Use evaluation results to improve programs	1	2	3	4	5	1	2	3	4	5
n	Use MIS program management screens	1	2	3	4	5	1	2	3	4	5

Competency		How Important?					How Much Need for Professional Development?				
		No Importance				Very Great Importance	No Need				Very Great Need
		1	2	3	4	5	1	2	3	4	5
12. Programming (cont'd)											
o	Understand the program approval process for workforce development requirements	1	2	3	4	5	1	2	3	4	5
p	Conduct environmental scanning to identify future program needs	1	2	3	4	5	1	2	3	4	5
q	Understand the workforce development requirements of various groups as they affect marketing impact	1	2	3	4	5	1	2	3	4	5
13. Recruitment, Hiring, and Orientation											
a	Identify staffing requirements	1	2	3	4	5	1	2	3	4	5
b	Recruit prospective staff	1	2	3	4	5	1	2	3	4	5
c	Select staff members from among multiple possibilities	1	2	3	4	5	1	2	3	4	5
d	Orient and train staff	1	2	3	4	5	1	2	3	4	5
14. Supervision											
a	Supervise staff daily	1	2	3	4	5	1	2	3	4	5
b	Mentor staff	1	2	3	4	5	1	2	3	4	5
c	Establish accountability guidelines and communicate them to staff	1	2	3	4	5	1	2	3	4	5
d	Delegate work as necessary	1	2	3	4	5	1	2	3	4	5
e	Support staff members in achieving their goals	1	2	3	4	5	1	2	3	4	5
f	Provide performance feedback and counseling to staff continually	1	2	3	4	5	1	2	3	4	5
g	Evaluate staff performance	1	2	3	4	5	1	2	3	4	5
h	Provide staff members with professional development and growth opportunities	1	2	3	4	5	1	2	3	4	5
i	Promote staff	1	2	3	4	5	1	2	3	4	5
j	Lay off or terminate staff as necessary	1	2	3	4	5	1	2	3	4	5
15. Management											
a	Manage office workflow	1	2	3	4	5	1	2	3	4	5
b	Make decisions promptly and effectively	1	2	3	4	5	1	2	3	4	5
c	Identify and manage priorities daily	1	2	3	4	5	1	2	3	4	5
d	Juggle multiple and conflicting priorities	1	2	3	4	5	1	2	3	4	5
e	Use database management systems	1	2	3	4	5	1	2	3	4	5

Competency		How Important?					How Much Need for Professional Development?				
		No Importance			Very Great Importance		No Need			Very Great Need	
		1	2	3	4	5	1	2	3	4	5
16. Leadership											
a	Serve as an exemplary role model	1	2	3	4	5	1	2	3	4	5
b	Motivate and encourage staff	1	2	3	4	5	1	2	3	4	5
c	Remain aware of public issues	1	2	3	4	5	1	2	3	4	5
d	Tolerate ambiguity in the organization and community	1	2	3	4	5	1	2	3	4	5
e	Appreciate and actively support diversity in thought and deed	1	2	3	4	5	1	2	3	4	5
f	Lead strategic planning efforts	1	2	3	4	5	1	2	3	4	5
g	Develop and articulate a vision for the workforce development effort	1	2	3	4	5	1	2	3	4	5
h	Articulate values and guiding principles for the workforce development effort	1	2	3	4	5	1	2	3	4	5
i	Build enthusiasm for the workforce development mission	1	2	3	4	5	1	2	3	4	5
j	Set policy	1	2	3	4	5	1	2	3	4	5
k	Arbitrate disputes and conflicts	1	2	3	4	5	1	2	3	4	5
l	Form coalitions with others in the college and community	1	2	3	4	5	1	2	3	4	5
m	Lead continuous quality improvement efforts	1	2	3	4	5	1	2	3	4	5
n	Develop and maintain "content expert" status	1	2	3	4	5	1	2	3	4	5
17. Personal and Professional Development											
a	Establish personal and professional goals	1	2	3	4	5	1	2	3	4	5
b	Read broadly and remain aware of events affecting goals	1	2	3	4	5	1	2	3	4	5
c	Attend conferences and training programs relevant to goals	1	2	3	4	5	1	2	3	4	5
d	Participate in professional organizations relevant to goals	1	2	3	4	5	1	2	3	4	5
e	Pursue advanced degrees and professional certification or licensure	1	2	3	4	5	1	2	3	4	5
f	Conduct research on issues relevant to goals	1	2	3	4	5	1	2	3	4	5
g	Make presentations relevant to goals	1	2	3	4	5	1	2	3	4	5
h	Publish on issues relevant to goals	1	2	3	4	5	1	2	3	4	5

Competency		How Important?					How Much Need for Professional Development?				
		No Importance			Very Great Importance		No Need			Very Great Need	
		1	2	3	4	5	1	2	3	4	5
17. Personal and Professional Development (cont'd)											
i	Mentor others whose personal and professional goals coincide	1	2	3	4	5	1	2	3	4	5

Note: Adapted from *Hierarchy of Competencies for Continuing Education Professionals*, unpublished manuscript (Rothwell, 1997). For more information, contact William J. Rothwell, PhD, Pennsylvania State University, College of Education, Department of Learning and Performance Systems, Workforce Education and Development, 305C Keller Building, University Park, PA 16802, Phone: 814-863-2581.

In what other areas do you feel a need for professional development? Please list them in order of priority below, with 1 = Greatest Area of Need.

Importance	Area
1	
2	
3	

APPENDIX *D*

Templates for Conducting 5-S Consultative Sales

Wesley E. Donahue and John E. Park

TEMPLATE 1: WEEKLY CALL PLANNER

Weekly Call Planner				
Client Representative: _____ **Week of:** _____				

Day	Call Type*	Client or Prospect	Location	Purpose of Contact
Mon.				
Tues.				
Wed.				
Thur.				
Fri.				

Central Support Needed:

* P = personal visit; T = telephone call; E = e-mail

TEMPLATE 2: MONTHLY SUMMARY OF PROSPECTING ACTIVITY

Monthly Summary of Prospecting Activity					
Client Representative: _____ **Month Ending:** _____					
Best Prospects	Priority*	Product Service Requested	Potential Annual $ Volume	Possible Closing Date	Action Needed (By Whom & When)
Current Clients Additional Activity					

* Priority = A (highest), B, or C

Template 3: Annual Client Visit Planning Calendar

Annual Client Visit Planning Calendar												
Client Representative: _____ **Year:** _____												
Client (Location)	J	F	M	A	M	J	J	A	S	O	N	D

Template 4: Program Summary Report

Program Summary Report

Client Representative: _____ **Date:** _____

Program Title: _____

Organization Name and Address: _____
_____

Point of Contact (POC): _____
POC Phone Number: _____
POC E-mail: _____
Period of Performance: _____
Program Cost: _____

Organization Profile- Industry (SIC): _____
Number of Employees: _____
Products/Services: _____
Revenue: _____

Employees Involved: _____

The Challenge: (What were the performance gaps or needs?) _____
_____
_____
_____
_____

The Solution: (What actions, education, or training interventions were conducted?) _____
_____
_____
_____
_____

The Results, Benefits, or Impact: (How was performance improved?) _____
_____
_____
_____
_____

Acknowledgments and Follow-Up: _____
_____
_____
_____
_____

TEMPLATE 5: RECORD OF CLIENT CONTACT

Record of Client Contact			
Client Representative: _____			

Name of Organization	Phone:	Call-back Dates:	
	Fax:		
	E-mail:		
Location/Address			

Contact People	Phone	Fax	E-mail

Products and Services of This Organization

Record of Products/Services Furnished to This Organization (By Whom)

Date		Date	

Record of Contacts

Date	Contact	Purpose/Goal	Actions Taken or Required

Coaching Checksheet for Community College Workforce Developers

William J. Rothwell

irections: Use this checksheet to plan for mentoring and coaching newcomers to workforce development. For each activity listed in column 1, indicate in column 2 whether you (as mentor) have coached the mentee on how to conduct the activity.

(Be sure to explain what to do, why it is worth doing, and how it is done.) Then, both you and the mentee should initial column 2. Mentors and mentees should use column 3 to make any comments about the quality of the mentoring given or received.

Coaching Checksheet for Community College Workforce Developers						
Name of Mentor:		**Name of Mentee:**			**Period Covering:**	
Column 1	Column 2					Column 3
Have you, the mentor, coached the mentee on:	Yes ☒	No ☒	N/A ☒	Mentor's Initial	Mentee's Initial	Comments
1. Office Management						
a Manage time and priorities and meet deadlines	❏	❏	❏			
b Schedule and prepare for meetings	❏	❏	❏			
c Establish and maintain basic files, recordkeeping, and follow-up systems	❏	❏	❏			
d Use appropriate office technologies and software	❏	❏	❏			
2. Communication						
a Write/dictate letters, reports, and memos	❏	❏	❏			
b Give presentations	❏	❏	❏			
c Facilitate meetings, seminars, and ceremonies	❏	❏	❏			
d Actively listen to others	❏	❏	❏			
e Use e-mail	❏	❏	❏			

Coaching Checksheet for Community College Workforce Developers (cont'd)

Column 1	Column 2					Column 3
Have you, the mentor, coached the mentee on:	Yes ☒	No ☒	N/A ☒	Mentor's Initial	Mentee's Initial	Comments
3. Internal Relations						
a	Develop knowledge about the workforce development professionals in the college	❑	❑	❑			
b	Participate in campus meetings	❑	❑	❑			
c	Develop knowledge about the campus culture and values	❑	❑	❑			
d	Identify and establish working relationships with appropriate campus units	❑	❑	❑			
e	Develop familiarity with and linkages to academic departments	❑	❑	❑			
f	Market continuing education internally to the college community	❑	❑	❑			
g	Participate on college committees	❑	❑	❑			
4. Program Support						
a	Pick up and deliver supplies and materials	❑	❑	❑			
b	Schedule and maintain facilities	❑	❑	❑			
c	Handle arrangements with food services and caterers	❑	❑	❑			
d	Handle arrangements with hotel and conference facilities	❑	❑	❑			
e	Order instructional materials	❑	❑	❑			
f	Arrange for and coordinate audiovisual assistance and support	❑	❑	❑			
g	Provide logistical support	❑	❑	❑			
h	Coordinate travel arrangements with faculty	❑	❑	❑			
i	Arrange for and coordinate registration of students and collection of fees	❑	❑	❑			
j	Confirm registration and logistics to participants	❑	❑	❑			
k	Arrange for and coordinate selling textbooks and supplies	❑	❑	❑			
l	Maintain program records and statistics	❑	❑	❑			
m	Assess participants' reaction to programs	❑	❑	❑			

Coaching Checksheet for Community College Workforce Developers (cont'd)

		Column 1		Column 2				Column 3
	Have you, the mentor, coached the mentee on:		Yes ☒	No ☒	N/A ☒	Mentor's Initial	Mentee's Initial	Comments
5. Financial Management and Budgeting								
a	Monitor existing individual program budgets		❑	❑	❑			
b	Analyze and adjust existing program budgets		❑	❑	❑			
c	Prepare new individual program budgets		❑	❑	❑			
d	Evaluate profitability of individual programs		❑	❑	❑			
e	Initiate and approve purchases for program materials and support		❑	❑	❑			
f	Identify potential funding sources		❑	❑	❑			
g	Cultivate relationships with potential funding sources		❑	❑	❑			
h	Spell out components of memoranda of agreement		❑	❑	❑			
i	Work with faculty and contracts and grants offices to write grants		❑	❑	❑			
j	Administer contracts and grants		❑	❑	❑			
k	Secure scholarships		❑	❑	❑			
l	Identify and negotiate with vendors		❑	❑	❑			
m	Make purchasing decisions for office-wide equipment, services, etc.		❑	❑	❑			
n	Use MIS for financial decision making		❑	❑	❑			
o	Develop and monitor budget for the workforce development office		❑	❑	❑			
p	Evaluate workforce development office profitability		❑	❑	❑			
6. Student Relations and Services								
a	Understand and communicate college requirements to students		❑	❑	❑			.
b	Recruit students		❑	❑	❑			
c	Facilitate adult reentry to higher education		❑	❑	❑			
d	Arrange for and coordinate registration of students		❑	❑	❑			
e	Arrange for and coordinate counseling for students		❑	❑	❑			
f	Develop system to track students' progress		❑	❑	❑			
g	Recognize students' achievements		❑	❑	❑			

Coaching Checksheet for Community College Workforce Developers (cont'd)						
Column 1	**Column 2**					**Column 3**
Have you, the mentor, coached the mentee on:	Yes ☒	No ☒	N/A ☒	Mentor's Initial	Mentee's Initial	Comments
6. Student Relations and Services (cont'd)						
h	Mediate conflicts among students and faculty	❏	❏	❏			
i	Provide access and referrals to student services (e.g., financial aid, career development, etc.	❏	❏	❏			
j	Conduct student surveys	❏	❏	❏			
7. Faculty Relations						
a	Recruit and hire adjunct faculty, working with the DAA as is appropriate	❏	❏	❏			
b	Orient part-time faculty	❏	❏	❏			
c	Give directions and information to faculty members	❏	❏	❏			
d	Assist faculty with curriculum development	❏	❏	❏			
e	Monitor faculty and follow up with faculty evaluations	❏	❏	❏			
f	Work to foster positive relationships with faculty	❏	❏	❏			
8. Client Management						
a	Identify prospective clients	❏	❏	❏			
b	Gather information about clients	❏	❏	❏			
c	Understand competitors	❏	❏	❏			
d	Respond to clients' requests	❏	❏	❏			
e	Build relationships with clients	❏	❏	❏			
f	Assess clients' needs	❏	❏	❏			
g	Make initial calls on prospective clients	❏	❏	❏			
h	Source best ways to meet clients' needs	❏	❏	❏			
i	Maintain contact with clients	❏	❏	❏			
j	Build project teams with clients	❏	❏	❏			
k	Negotiate contracts and agreements with clients	❏	❏	❏			
9. Training and Organizational Development						
a	Choose appropriate methods to assess training needs	❏	❏	❏			
b	Separate training and nontraining (management) needs	❏	❏	❏			
c	Identify gaps that can be corrected by training	❏	❏	❏			

Coaching Checksheet for Community College Workforce Developers (cont'd)						
Column 1	**Column 2**					**Column 3**
Have you, the mentor, coached the mentee on:	Yes ☒	No ☒	N/A ☒	Mentor's Initial	Mentee's Initial	Comments
9. Training and Organizational Development (cont'd)						
d	Prioritize training needs to align with organizational goals	❏	❏	❏			
e	Develop training strategies	❏	❏	❏			
f	Establish instructional goals	❏	❏	❏			
g	Deliver and evaluate training	❏	❏	❏			
10. External and Community Relations						
a	Articulate the goals and mission of the workforce development unit to the community and community organizations	❏	❏	❏			
b	Join and participate in community organizations, professional associations, community meetings and boards, including those that present opportunities to work with alumni	❏	❏	❏			
c	Identify and meet with prospective partners in the community	❏	❏	❏			
d	Consult with community resource people about community needs and programs	❏	❏	❏			
e	Develop alliances and articulation agreements with other colleges	❏	❏	❏			
f	Communicate with local, state, and federal politicians	❏	❏	❏			
g	Communicate with international organizations as opportunities arise	❏ '	❏	❏			
11. Marketing and Promotion						
a	Read newspapers and other publications in the service area to identify prospective clients	❏	❏	❏			
b	Develop an understanding of marketing and demographic resources for the service area	❏	❏	❏			
c	Acquire in-depth familiarity with competitors' products and services	❏	❏	❏			
d	Identify, purchase, organize, and supervise mailing lists	❏	❏	❏			
e	Form partnerships with market programs	❏	❏	❏			
f	Assess current market needs formally (e.g., via survey) and informally (e.g., via discussion)	❏	❏	❏			
g	Develop newsletters, program brochures, and catalogs	❏	❏	❏			

Coaching Checksheet for Community College Workforce Developers (cont'd)

Column 1		Column 2					Column 3
Have you, the mentor, coached the mentee on:		Yes ☒	No ☒	N/A ☒	Mentor's Initial	Mentee's Initial	Comments
11. Marketing and Promotion (cont'd)							
h	Write press releases	❑	❑	❑			
i	Conduct open houses	❑	❑	❑			
j	Conduct telemarketing campaigns	❑	❑	❑			
k	Write proposals for training programs	❑	❑	❑			
l	Develop program pricing strategies to accomplish marketing goals	❑	❑	❑			
m	Position the college properly as a supplier of education and training	❑	❑	❑			
12. Programming							
a	Identify and analyze needs	❑	❑	❑			
b	Understand the workforce development requirements of professional and other groups	❑	❑	❑			
c	Identify program topics and outcomes based on need	❑	❑	❑			
d	Select appropriate media for program delivery	❑	❑	❑			
e	Set program objectives	❑	❑	❑			
f	Obtain the necessary college approvals	❑	❑	❑			
g	Work with faculty to develop curriculum and materials	❑	❑	❑			
h	Negotiate program locations and schedules	❑	❑	❑			
i	Learn and meet the accreditation requirements of accrediting agencies	❑	❑	❑			
j	Implement programs	❑	❑	❑			
k	Monitor programs	❑	❑	❑			
l	Establish and use program evaluation procedures	❑	❑	❑			
m	Use evaluation results to improve programs	❑	❑	❑			
n	Use MIS program management screens	❑	❑	❑			
o	Understand the program approval process for workforce development requirements	❑	❑	❑			

Coaching Checksheet for Community College Workforce Developers (cont'd)					
Column 1	**Column 2**				**Column 3**
Have you, the mentor, coached the mentee on:	Yes ☒	No ☒	N/A ☒	Mentor's Initial	Mentee's Initial	Comments

12. Programming (cont'd)

p	Conduct environmental scanning to identify future program needs	❑	❑	❑			
q	Understand the workforce development requirements of various groups as they affect marketing impact	❑	❑	❑			

13. Recruitment, Hiring, and Orientation

a	Identify staffing requirements	❑	❑	❑			
b	Recruit prospective staff	❑	❑	❑			
c	Select staff members from among multiple possibilities	❑	❑	❑			
d	Orient and train staff	❑	❑	❑			

14. Supervision

a	Supervise staff daily	❑	❑	❑			
b	Mentor staff	❑	❑	❑			
c	Establish accountability guidelines and communicate them to staff	❑	❑	❑			
d	Delegate work as necessary	❑	❑	❑			
e	Support staff members in achieving their goals	❑	❑	❑			
f	Provide performance feedback and counseling to staff continually	❑	❑	❑			
g	Evaluate staff performance	❑	❑	❑			
h	Provide staff members with professional development and growth opportunities	❑	❑	❑			
i	Promote staff	❑	❑	❑			
j	Lay off or terminate staff as necessary	❑	❑	❑			

15. Management

a	Manage office workflow	❑	❑	❑			
b	Make decisions promptly and effectively	❑	❑	❑			
c	Identify and manage priorities daily	❑	❑	❑			
d	Juggle multiple and conflicting priorities	❑	❑	❑			
e	Use database management systems	❑	❑	❑			

Coaching Checksheet for Community College Workforce Developers (cont'd)							
Column 1			Column 2				Column 3
Have you, the mentor, coached the mentee on:		Yes ☒	No ☒	N/A ☒	Mentor's Initial	Mentee's Initial	Comments
16. Leadership							
a	Serve as an exemplary role model	❑	❑	❑			
b	Motivate and encourage staff	❑	❑	❑			
c	Remain aware of public issues	❑	❑	❑			
d	Tolerate ambiguity in the organization and community	❑	❑	❑			
e	Appreciate and actively support diversity in thought and deed	❑	❑	❑			
f	Lead strategic planning efforts	❑	❑	❑			
g	Develop and articulate a vision for the workforce development effort	❑	❑	❑			
h	Articulate values and guiding principles for the workforce development effort	❑	❑	❑			
i	Build enthusiasm for the workforce development mission	❑	❑	❑			
j	Set policy	❑	❑	❑			
k	Arbitrate disputes and conflicts	❑	❑	❑			
l	Form coalitions with others in the college and community	❑	❑	❑			
m	Lead continuous quality improvement efforts	❑	❑	❑			
n	Develop and maintain "content expert" status	❑	❑	❑			
17. Personal and Professional Development							
a	Establish personal and professional goals	❑	❑	❑			
b	Read broadly and remain aware of events affecting goals	❑	❑	❑			
c	Attend conferences and training programs relevant to goals	❑	❑	❑			
d	Participate in professional organizations relevant to goals	❑	❑	❑			
e	Pursue advanced degrees and professional certification or licensure	❑	❑	❑			
f	Conduct research on issues relevant to goals	❑	❑	❑			

Coaching Checksheet for Community College Workforce Developers (cont'd)						
Column 1	**Column 2**					**Column 3**
Have you, the mentor, coached the mentee on:	Yes ☒	No ☒	N/A ☒	Mentor's Initial	Mentee's Initial	Comments
17. Personal and Professional Development (cont'd)						
g	Make presentations relevant to goals	❑	❑	❑			
h	Publish on issues relevant to goals	❑	❑	❑			
i	Mentor others whose personal and professional goals coincide	❑	❑	❑			

Note: Adapted from *Hierarchy of Competencies for Continuing Education Professionals*, unpublished manuscript (Rothwell, 1997). For more information, contact William J. Rothwell, PhD, Pennsylvania State University, College of Education, Department of Learning and Performance Systems, Workforce Education and Development, 305C Keller Building, University Park, PA 16802, Phone: 814-863-2581.

APPENDIX F

Templates for Community College Workforce Developers

A s we assembled this book, we realized that many newcomers to workforce development might find themselves overwhelmed. So much needs to be done. And there is always so little time to do it. How could we help?

The answer was to provide templates and other resources at the back of the book. Instructional designers have long used templates to accelerate the course development process. Lawyers use templates of contracts and other legal documents to reduce their time drafting such documents and thereby enhance their productivity. The templates provided here offer structures or examples for approaching a task related to the administration of workforce development, which you can adapt to meet the needs of a specific situation.

In offering these templates, we also want to promote the sharing of best-practice examples. We encourage you to give us feedback on these examples and provide other best-practice examples that could be used in subsequent editions of this book or possibly made available online. Please e-mail comments to William J. Rothwell at wjr9@psu.edu.

TEMPLATE 1: STRATEGIC PLANNING CHECKLIST

How do you know whether your workforce development organization's strategic plan covers the bases it needs to cover? This checklist gives you a quick and useful tool to use in assessing the quality of your institution's strategic plan for workforce development.

For each item shown in the left column of the checklist, place a check in those items that are covered or addressed by the plan. Leave blank those items that are not covered. When you are finished assessing the comprehensiveness of your institution's strategic plan for workforce development, pay close attention to those items that were not checked. Decide whether they need to be addressed in a revision.

Source: Eric Bergstrom

Strategic Planning Checklist	
The term *outreach* is used throughout the checklist, but you may substitute the term *workforce development* if you prefer.	
Activity	☑ **Completed**
1. Identify the mission of the academic institution; align outreach strategies with the mission	❑
2. Contact key community workforce development leaders/organizations who can help explore community needs and opportunities for the outreach organization	❑
• Obtain community demographic information	❑
• Identify existing community workforce development strategies	❑
• Identify industry cluster groups	❑
• Identify major employers	❑
• Identify known area education and training needs	❑
3. Identify organizations already providing education and training programs to address training needs	❑
4. Create an advisory group to assist the outreach organization's market exploration and program planning processes	❑
• Group is comprised of representatives from a cross-section of industries and workforce development organizations (all major industry clusters represented)	❑
• Group meets 1–2 times/year	❑
• Specific activities assigned to the advisory group:	❑
• Identification of needs in the community	❑
• Evaluation of the outreach organization's reputation	❑
• Communication of the outreach organization's existence to other community members	❑
• "Sounding board" for new programs and services	❑
• Sponsor of new programs and services	❑
5. Identify niche opportunities to be addressed by the academic institution	❑
• Identify specific program needs	❑
• Develop marketing strategies for each program	❑
• Define program delivery requirements	❑
• Target population	❑
• Schedule requirements	❑
• Instructor/facilitator	❑
• Cost	❑

Strategic Planning Checklist (cont'd)	
The term *outreach* is used throughout the checklist, but you may substitute the term *workforce development* if you prefer.	
Activity	☑ **Completed**
• Links to other programs	❑
• Access to facilities	❑
• Access to specialized technology	❑
• Access to faculty	❑
• Resource for obtaining local, state, and federal workforce development funds	❑
6. Assess the ability of the staff to address niche opportunities; make adjustments to staff in order to address niche opportunities	❑
• Hire individuals with specialized skills and backgrounds to build and deliver programs	❑
• Utilize part-time professionals with a single-program focus to develop, to market, and to launch programs	❑
7. Create a marketing plan to communicate the outreach organization's programs and services; market the organization's programs and services in the following ways:	❑
• Create a power point presentation as a flexible document to communicate programs and services at formal presentations	❑
• Participate in career fairs, education fairs, etc.	❑
• Create a web site for the outreach organization	❑
• Volunteer to speak at programs and for organizations where the outreach organization's programs, services, and staff can be profiled	❑
• Meet one-on-one with leaders of organizations to assess their organizational needs and to describe the outreach organization's programs and services partner with other outreach organizations to provide a nonredundant, broader, comprehensive portfolio of programs and services	❑
• Open house events to profile programs and services	❑
• Advertisement of programs and services	❑
• Radio spots	❑
• Newspaper advertisements	❑
• Sponsor of events	❑
• E-mail	❑
• Brochures (production, mailing, etc.)	❑
8. Create a budget for the outreach organization	❑
• Facilities	❑
• Staff	❑
• Instructors/facilitators	❑
• Materials/supplies	❑
• Marketing/advertising expense	❑
• Technology	❑
• Outreach expense (meals, travel, etc.)	❑

TEMPLATE 2: STRATEGIC PLAN FOR A COMMUNITY COLLEGE WORKFORCE DEVELOPMENT EFFORT

What should be included in a strategic plan for a workforce development effort? Sometimes the process of thinking through the structure or organizational scheme of the plan can be difficult in its own right. By using a template, you have a place to start and can focus more time and attention on issues rather than organizing the plan. Form a committee that represents the institutional effort and key stakeholders. Then begin the process of thinking through the key issues raised in the template. As with any template, you will need to adapt it for your organization's uses.

Source: Elaine A. Gaertner

Strategic Plan for a Community College Workforce Development Effort

Executive Summary

In September 2000, the Office of Economic Development of the XYZ Community College District revised its strategic plan to focus the direction of the department. In that plan, the district stated that it wished to achieve the following:

- A surplus in the budget
- A stable, thriving department work team
- A new industry-driven regional collaborative grant
- An increased awareness of the services we provide among both the communities that we serve and the district of which we are a part
- A significant number of new customers from the manufacturing sector

As of December 2001, four of our five goals have been met.

- Contract Education (renamed: "Training and Development Solutions") continues to be self-funded and has generated an $18,000 surplus.
- Our work team has increased to four full-time staff persons with two full-time consultants providing assistance with projects.
- We applied for and received an industry-driven regional collaborative grant for $600,000 (to be distributed over two years) to upgrade the skills of incumbent workers and help create employment opportunities in the machine technology industry.
- Due to significant marketing consisting of new printed materials and staff interaction with clients and district personnel, we are not only raising consciousness internally within the district by clarifying the department's role, but also expanding our visibility externally in the business and economic devel-

opment community.

- We have penetrated the manufacturing industry with only a handful of new clients. Although much of this lack of response can be attributed to the economic downturn, we recognize a need for further growth in this area, and focusing on this sector as a source of clients will continue to be a priority for the department.

As the department comes out of a period of financial turnaround, we are now committed to aggressive growth and expansion, while maintaining our dedication to quality instruction and service delivery. However, this growth and expansion must be seen in the larger context of Economic Development. Although *contract education* and *economic development* have often been used interchangeably, there is a need to differentiate between the terms.

Economic development refers to the overall status of the regional economy, incorporating the employers, the local labor force, funding sources and economic trends regarding attracting and retaining business and industry to the area. The Office of Economic Development participates in a multitude of opportunities to respond to and influence the economic development within the district's service area. These range from vocational/occupational and apprenticeship programs to certificate degree programs to special grant-based projects.

Contract education, on the other hand, is the provision of services (on a contractual basis) to the service area's businesses. There is a historical trend within the department to narrowly define Contract Education with a focus on training as *the* solution to businesses' needs. There has been a shift in the marketplace from training solutions to measurable performance improvement, and

Strategic Plan for a Community College Workforce Development Effort (cont'd)

the department is aligning itself to this new dynamic by offering a more comprehensive approach. The Office of Economic Development's Contract Education department, or Training and Development Solutions, now has a broader perspective, as the "provision of services to proactively identify business goals, agree on a desired performance, and partner with clients and others to implement solutions to improve performance." These services are provided to public, private and non-profit entities within the XYZ Community College District service area, and are but one aspect of the Office of Economic Development.

In addition to Training and Development Solutions, the Office of Economic Development also has a Strategic Economic Development Initiatives department. This department encompasses those areas of the Office of Economic Development that go beyond contract education, which include researching and applying for collaboration and grant opportunities, and involvement in district-wide, regional and statewide organizations dedicated to economic development and policy making. At this time, the district dean is responsible for the Office of Economic Development's Strategic Economic Development Initiatives, employing two full-time contractors to work with specific projects.

Departmental Principles

As was stated in the last revision of Office of Economic Development's Strategic Plan (*date*), the department continues to be committed to the following guiding principles:

Systematic growth. Limited resources and an aggressive growth plan demand that we approach our Training and Development Solutions business systematically. This approach encompasses researching and approaching industries (such as manufacturing), as well as prospecting and cultivating a relationship with named companies, in a two-pronged drive. The two areas are distinct enough in their requirements to warrant separating them, both from an organizational standpoint, as well as when looking at staffing requirements.

Additionally, through the creation of the Strategic Economic Development Initiative, we can determine which collaborations would be appropriate to participate in, and which grants and other funding opportunities to pursue.

Inter- and Intradistrict cooperation. As first steps toward a more comprehensive Office of Economic Development for the XYZ Community College District, we have invited key players from the two colleges to explore the opportunities and hurdles facing the colleges and district within the economic development arena. The intention of nurturing collaboration with the colleges is to have district-wide understanding and approach to economic development, rather than separate approaches, as was the practice in the past.

Quality. We are strongly committed to the highest quality of instruction and service delivery, to superior customer service for both our external and internal customers, and to a quality work experience for all those in the department.

Summary of Expected Results

At the end of the district's fiscal year, the department should display results that include

- An expanded approach to economic development
- The further development of the Strategic Economic Development Initiative
- Staffing to meet the expanded role of the Office of Economic Development

- A significant number of new customers from the manufacturing sector (carried over from the previous year's goals)
- A broader awareness of the Office of Economic Development's role, both internally within the district, as well as externally in the business community
- A stable, thriving, department work team

Vision, Mission, and Value Statements

Vision

To become a vital part of a national network of community college districts systematically assisting companies to solve business problems and take advantage of untapped opportunities, and to be a participant in the economic development conversation in the region.

Mission

The Economic Development/Contract Education department of the XYZ Community College District exists to help companies and organizations resident in the district's service area solve business problems and take advantage of untapped opportunities; and to par-

Strategic Plan for a Community College Workforce Development Effort (cont'd)

ticipate in, and contribute to the economic development policymaking for the district, region, and state.

Core Values

1. Superior quality in everything we do
   - Instruction/training
   - Professional services
   - Customer service
   - External customers
   - Internal customers
2. Collaboration, not competition
   - District campuses

- Regionally
- Statewide
- Other service providers
3. Profitablility
   - Internal pricing/costing policies
   - Negotiations
   - Funding
4. Healthy, happy work environment
   - Physical space
   - Empowered workforce
   - Career advancement
   - Compensation

Situation Analysis

Organization [*Insert organization chart here*]

Current Staffing

District Dean—1. As *Department Manager* for the Office of Economic Development, the District Dean is responsible for the overall management of the department, including staffing/performance, quality assurance and policy and procedures, strategic planning, budget development and management, marketing and technology. Additionally, the District Dean acts as *Project Director* in developing and managing ED>Net grants and maintaining local, regional and statewide organizations, and as *District Coordinator* to coordinate the application of policy, procedure and practice with the colleges, as well as participating routinely in district-wide planning committees to the colleges occupational/vocational programs.

Program Manager—1. The Program Manager is responsible for marketing, promotion and source opportunities for the Business Development area of Training and Development Solutions. Additionally, the Program Manager develops and maintains partnerships with training, consulting and materials vendors, delivery and assessment of services for public, private and nonprofit businesses within the district's service area.

Program Coordinator—1. The Program Coordinator serves as the support staff for the Program Manager, in the areas of project management, marketing and sales.

Administrative Assistant—1. The Administrative Assistant is responsible for departmental operations, such as payroll, A/P, A/R, purchasing and HR, as well as being responsible for the master calendar, scheduling meetings, instructors and the two computer labs. The Administrative

Assistant also serves as the district receptionist.

(Near) Future Staffing Requirements

Program Director—1. District Dean is currently serving in multiple roles and utilizing contractors to administer and manage specific projects for the department. With the clarification of the division between Training and Development Solutions and Strategic Economic Development Initiative, there is the requirement for a staff position to focus solely the Strategic Economic Development Initiative. This role would encompass researching and application of grant opportunities, including regional collaboratives, ED>Net, the Department of Education, and the Department of Labor prospects.

Program Manager—1. An additional Program Manager, for Strategic Accounts in Training and Development Solutions who will focus on strategic (or "named") major accounts is required to expand the department, and to respond to growth in our service area. This staff person will be responsible for researching, contacting and nurturing relationships with major accounts to secure large, long-term contracts.

Program Coordinator—1. While the current Program Coordinator will be able to assist both of the Program Managers in the initial start-up phase for the new Program Manager in charge of Strategic Accounts, as growth and expansion in both areas occurs, and additional support person will be required to manage the workload.

Financial

The department has become a viable part of the district's services. Training and Development Solutions, our contract education department has become self-funded and

Strategic Plan for a Community College Workforce Development Effort (cont'd)

generated a $18,000 surplus over the last year. We intend to continue this growth trend over the next few years, in spite of the regional economic downturn. The current budget projects revenue for the year at_____, with expenses at _____.

Contracts

As of June 30, XXXX, the department held the following open contracts:

Client	Remaining Contract Value
The Alliance	$46,195
Federal Corrections Inst.	$7,560
OPEIU	$11,621
PTC	$30,000
Shade Foods	$105,825
Total	*$201,201*

Strength/Weakness/Opportunity/Threat (SWOT) Analysis

This analysis is designed to highlight the department's strengths upon which to build, and the perceived weaknesses that require attention. In addition, based on those strengths and weaknesses, the opportunities for growth and success, as well as what threats exist that have the potential to harm or slow business growth.

Strengths

- Department's commitment to quality customer service
- Commitment of the college district administration to the department's success
- Quality department staff and contracted professionals
- Department is growing and expanding in all areas, including contract education which has become self-funding.
- Initial steps have been taken toward districts' and colleges' joint goals and objectives in the area of economic development for the region.
- Better visibility both internally (within the district and colleges) and externally (within the business community)
- More targeted approach to business development
- Department is embracing performance consulting as a tool to better serve our clients
- Good instructor pool
- Good relationships between department and instructors
- Solid infrastructure to support the delivery of quality instruction and professional services
- Ongoing commitment to staff growth and development opportunities, including ED>Net courses

Weaknesses

- Need for further communication and collaboration between the campuses and the district in the area of Economic Development for the region
- Need for further training in the area of performance consulting to better serve our clients
- Lack of office space restricts staffing abilities
- Lack of depth in service providers
- Lack of computer-based or distance-learning solutions

Opportunities

- Marketplace shift from focusing on "training solutions" to embracing "performance improvement" and the many options that can entail.
- Research continues to support the need for basic skills to address the problem of "insufficiently literate" employees
- Training delivery method of choice is still live classroom instruction
- Growth in investment in computer-based training
- Manufacturing industry's continued investment in training and services
- Manufacturers need of a skilled workforce is the most significant barrier to technology adaptation.
- Continued outsourcing of training departments

Threats

- Businesses may want to go with more experienced performance consultants
- Campuses are reluctant to break isolationistic tendencies and work with district and each other in the area of Economic Development
- Bureaucratic delays with government projects make projections difficult
- Competition from larger consulting firms like Accenture
- Competition from smaller, specialized consulting firms
- Internal conflict between district function of contract education and individual campus
- Corporate interest in non-instructor led training
- Corporate Universities or Internal Training Departments

Strategic Plan for a Community College Workforce Development Effort (cont'd)

External Environmental Assessment
(Economic State of the Region)

- Booming economy in *(insert name of region)* Service Region.
- Median household income in the *(area)* exceeds $70,000
- Mean household income in the *(area)* exceeds $55,000
- More than half of adults with household incomes of

- $50,000 or more participate in continuing education
- Regional unemployment at record low of 4.2%
- High tech companies moving into region at rapid rate
- Manufacturing firms still primary employers throughout region
- Tight labor market

Objectives

Expand Approach to Economic Development

- Work with the chancellor to create a district economic development team (EDT), consisting of representatives from the campuses and the district.
- Explore with the EDT ways in which the district and campuses can work together on grants and other regional opportunities.
- Document the plan and get sign-off from key players.
- Pursue prospects as appropriate.

Develop a Strategic Economic Development Initiative

- Deliver verbal and written department summary reports to the chancellor, vice chancellors, and college presidents on a quarterly basis.
- Submit summary reports to the board on a quarterly basis.

Measure the Impact of Programs and Services

- Use and document participant evaluations and conversations with the customer.
- Measure the impact of services provided on the identified performance needs of the customer.
- Offer ways for the company to measure its return on investment.Have students complete evaluations at the end of training.
- Administer pre- and post-tests or performance demonstrations to determine what was learned.
- Deliver impact data to instructors that allow them to make appropriate changes to training content and delivery.
- Measure incidence of repeat customers and referrals.

Develop Strong Partnerships and Alliances

- Develop partnerships with companies that offer capabilities or competencies that the department is

unable to provide to its customers.
- Solicit and receive training grants from the state.
- Advise state and regional agencies on the design of industry training and assistance policies to the competitiveness of local companies.

Optimize Department Management and Operations

Optimize department financial performance:

- Develop financial analysis and projections for the year.
- Develop long-term, repeat customers.
- Develop and manage department budget.
- Design a systematic way to track costs and determine price based on comprehensive cost of delivery.
- Expand methods of raising funds, charging fees, paying staff, and using consultants
- Reinvest a portion of revenue in the development of new products and services.
- Establish department control over a portion of the budget surplus.
- Pursue opportunities to acquire flexibility and control over the budget.

Manage human resources:
- Establish human resources plans that include performance goals in staff preparation and development, staff recruitment, compensation, promotion, and benefits.
- Develop pool of part-time consultants to meet fluctuating customer demand.
- Develop the department pay scale based on market value.
- Create opportunities and initiatives for self-directed responsibility.
- Develop a compensation, promotion, and recognition system that reinforces high performance.
- Have department staff participate in training and

Strategic Plan for a Community College Workforce Development Effort (cont'd)

workshops that help to meet department and personal objectives.

- Offer professional development opportunities to all staff.
- Ensure that the work environment is safe and healthful.
- Monitor staff-related and department performance data to adjust work flows and staffing patterns.
- Locate and hire qualified individuals for service delivery.

Apply strong strategic and organizational planning:
- Conduct extensive research on trends and events in the external environment.
- Conduct internal performance audits using institutional research data and program information.
- Develop a planning committee (advisory committee) of faculty, staff, board members, students, and community residents.
- Use listening sessions for community members, business, government, and other providers.
- Update the strategic plan on an annual basis.
- Monitor financial progress monthly.
- Join a planning committee for the two campuses.

Maintain responsive operational processes:
- Document all processes from the sales call to the termination of the contract.
- Assign department staff to each step of the process.

- Conduct periodic reviews of process flow documentation.
- Continually evaluate and upgrade systems.
- Provide training on system and other procedural changes within the department to affected staff.
- Communicate changes and rationale for changes directly to staff.
- Hold staff meetings monthly.
- Use appropriate technology for the information, planning, and service delivery needs of the center.

Establish and maintain a productive relationship with the colleges:
- Deliver verbal and written department summary reports to the chancellor, vice chancellors, and college presidents on a quarterly basis.
- Submit summary reports to the board on a quarterly basis.
- Ensure that the chancellor, vice chancellors, college presidents, and vice presidents publicize the activities of the department.
- Ensure a cooperative relationship regarding the sharing of facilities, instructors, curriculum, grant leads, and other resources
- Provide professional development for the college faculty.
- Ensure that the campuses are marketing the services of the department and that the department is marketing the services of the campuses.

Marketing Plan

Develop Printed Materials
- department logo and identity
- case study examples related to customer
- performance requirements
- presentation folder
- brochure
- price sheet
- services fact sheet
- sales support tools including evaluation forms, surveys, etc.

Develop Web Presence
- Web site content and layout
- Web site marketing
- Web advertising

Promotion in Development
- new department strategy launch
- internal customers
- district support staff
- campus administration and faculty
- external customers
- Chambers of commerce
- Manufacturing roundtables and associations

Advertising
- College campus catalog ads
- Chamber of commerce directories

Direct Mail
- Joint mailer with Manex, Inc.
- Joint mailer with Ed>Net

Template 3: Job Profile of a Workforce Development Dean or Director

Mac McGinty is associate vice president for business development and corporate training at Thomas Nelson Community College in Hampton, VA. In May 2001, he gathered a "subject matter expert" panel of Virginia Community College System (VCCS) workforce development (WFD) coordinators. This is the prioritized task list that came out of that activity, which you can use to prepare a job vacancy notice.

Job Profile of a Workforce Development Dean or Director

1. Creates innovative programs to meet the needs of clients.

2. Reads professional materials, reviews Web-based information, and networks in the community to stay abreast of current theories, trends, best practices, and programs to provide workforce training and retraining.

3. Represents the college at various meetings involved in virtually every aspect of the community—ranging from chambers of commerce, to economic development, to jurisdictional organizations, to educational organizations, to develop partnerships.

4. Conducts numerous telephone conversations and e-mail communications while marketing training opportunities to potential clients.

5. Identifies opportunities to create new training and education programs to serve the community and support the business plans of the center.

6. Evaluates ongoing and established programs to ensure that there is indeed value being added and that the community and the college is achieving an appropriate return on investment.

7. Manages, identifies sponsors, and places candidates into programs such as apprenticeship, tech prep, internships, coops, and other entrepreneurial programs designed to meet specific needs.

8. Serves on various boards (e.g., WIB), partnerships (e.g., planning districts), and advisory groups (e.g., WFD Council) to influence issues relative to WFD.

9. Attends community, governmental, civic, and political events in support of college business or social networking.

10. Handles complaints from dissatisfied clients, staff, and students.

11. Makes face-to-face contact with area clients or potential clients and internal customers.

12. Manages departmental budgets using paper printouts and computer-based programs.

13. Conducts public presentations to make the service-area business community aware of programs and opportunities available through the WFD Center.

14. Directs staff to follow-up on all client requests, including classroom arrangements, book sales, registrations, assessments, and numerous other activities involved in the delivery of services.

15. Makes recommendations to the president, the board, and other leaders of the college to support the mission of workforce development and continuing education.

16. Facilitates discussions in conjunction with WFD program development and training.

17. Produces numerous marketing materials such as ads, brochures, Web-related materials, etc.

18. Markets college programs that may not be a specific part of WFD or not a primary program to this director, to clients, and to the community in general.

19. Provides training feedback to clients to build and sustain new and existing relationships.

Job Profile of a Workforce Development Dean or Director (cont'd)

20. Works with other educational institutions, creating memorandums of understanding, developing partnering opportunities, and watching for market competition.

21. Attends staff meetings to disseminate WFD activities to campus/college administrators.

22. Conducts contract negotiations with client companies to come to agreement on training to be offered, costs, numbers of participants, credits to be awarded, location of training, and many other aspects relative to training programs.

23. Creates materials for publishing/disseminating to professional community to further WFD issues and programs.

24. Locates and identifies business/industrial small and medium-sized enterprises to develop and deliver current, state-of-the-art, workplace programs for retraining and retooling.

25. Prepares and edits reports to higher authorities.

26. Sees to the professional development of assigned WFD staff and self through appropriate conferences, workshops, seminars, the WFD academy, etc.

27. Creates a long-term business plan for the department or center aimed at supporting the college's mission, vision, and strategic plan.

28. Scans professional materials to locate articles and information of interest to college, WFD centers/departments, or clients.

29. Works in teams with college adjunct or full-time faculty to develop programs and procedures that support delivery of training to client companies and individuals.

30. Works with other college departments, administrators, faculty, and VCCS staff to promote mutually acceptable solutions between established policies and changing needs of clients.

31. Writes articles, class schedules, Internet materials, and program advertisements to promulgate WFD opportunities.

32. Conducts WFD staff meetings to plan, organize, and prioritize center activities.

33. Conducts staff performance expectations and evaluation discussions with assigned classified staff, administrators, faculty, and adjunct faculty.

34. Conveys college and client expectations and guidelines to assigned adjunct faculty.

35. Initiates cold-calls to prospective/potential clients with the aim of making them aware of all services/programs available through the college.

36. Operates equipment such as scanning machines, overhead projectors, computers, computer projection equipment.

37. Uses various tools such as, flip charts, white boards, multimedia, conference calls, compressed video, and others.

38. When necessary, refers to college and VCCS policy manuals to determine requirements for various programs.

39. Conducts tours of campus, buildings, and facilities.

40. Sets up rooms for training.

41. Inventories assets of the department/center ranging from costly equipment to on-hand assessment materials.

42. Uses the VCCS FRS to enter or retrieve client and student information.

43. Assigns rooms and labs to various activities involved with WFD.

44. Handles money, checks, and vouchers relative to course expenses.

45. Registers students for credit or noncredit courses.

TEMPLATE 4: JOB PROFILE OF A WORKFORCE DEVELOPMENT COORDINATOR

Mac McGinty is associate vice president for business development and corporate training at Thomas Nelson Community College in Hampton, VA. In May 2001, he gathered a "subject matter expert" panel of Virginia Community College System (VCCS) workforce development (WFD) coordinators. This is the prioritized task list that came out of that activity, which you can use to prepare a job vacancy notice.

Job Profile of a Workforce Development Coordinator

1. Looks for opportunities for, and participates in, the creation of innovative programs to meet the needs of clients and works with other college departments to facilitate the administration of these programs.

2. Conducts numerous telephone conversations and e-mail communications while marketing training opportunities to potential clients, answering questions, replying to issues, or answering enquiries.

3. Develops open-enrollment courses, schedules, and marketing strategies.

4. Drafts contracts for presentation to client companies, including such information as training to be offered, costs, numbers of participants, credits to be awarded, location of training, and many other aspects relative to training programs.

5. Helps in the locating of adjunct faculty to develop and deliver current, state-of-the-art workplace programs.

6. Makes face-to-face contact with area clients or potential clients and internal customers.

7. Negotiates pricing for noncredit courses, fees, and other services.

8. Works with other college departments, administrators, faculty, and VCCS staff to promote mutually acceptable solutions between established policies and changing needs of clients.

9. Coordinates with other staff personnel to follow-up on all client requests, including such things as classroom arrangements, book sales, registrations, assessments, and numerous other activities involved in the delivery of services.

10. Works with other educational institutions, creating memorandums of understanding, developing partnering opportunities, and watching for market competition.

11. Writes articles, class schedules, Internet material, and program advertisements to promulgate workforce development opportunities.

12. Participates in various boards (e.g., WIB), partnerships (e.g., planning districts), and advisory groups (e.g., WFD Council) with which the college may be connected.

13. Produces numerous marketing materials such as ads, brochures, Web-related materials, etc.

14. Represents the college at various meetings ranging from chambers of commerce, economic development, jurisdictional organizations, educational organizations, and development partnerships.

Job Profile of a Workforce Development Coordinator (cont'd)

15. Evaluates on-going and established programs to ensure that there is indeed value being added and that the community and the college is achieving an appropriate return on investment.

16. Compiles, stores, and retrieves management data, using PC-based programs, such as Microsoft Office and the VCCS FRS.

17. Participates in WFD staff meetings to plan, organize, and prioritize center activities.

18. Provides inputs to the business plan for the department or center aimed at supporting the college's mission, vision, and strategic plan.

19. Facilitates discussions in conjunction with WFD program development and training.

20. Handles complaints from dissatisfied clients, assigned faculty, or individual participants and ensures that complaints are addressed in an appropriate manner to optimize overall customer satisfaction.

21. Organizes, plans, and executes events, such as conferences, seminars, and board meetings in support of college business or social networking.

22. Attends staff meetings to disseminate WFD activity information to other campus/college departments.

Template 5: Job Description for a Contract Education Sales/Account Manager

Developing a job description can be difficult. Here is an example of a job description for a contract education sales/account manager in a community college that you can use as a starting point for developing a comparable job description for your institution. Of course, as always, you will need to modify it to meet the unique requirements of your institution.

Source: Elaine A. Gaertner

Job Description for a Contract Education Sales/Account Manager

General Description
Under direct supervision of the District Dean of Economic Development, the Contract Education Sales/Account Manager plans and directs all aspects of a self-supporting performance improvement center that markets, sells, and delivers training and consulting services for public and private sector organizations in the *[name of community college or district]* service area. The position is charged with generating revenue in excess of the department's operating expenses.

Start Date of Employment
Start date will be as soon as possible upon completion of search process.

Annual Salary Range
$58,000–$65,000 plus benefits. Actual placement is nonnegotiable and is based on applicant's verified education and experience.

Note. This position is a funded by a special program. The incumbent must generate revenue sufficient to cover operating costs of department including salary and benefits for department staff.

Representative Duties and Responsibilities
The Contract Education Sales/Account Manager will carry out the following representative duties and responsibilities:
1. Assume management responsibility for all services and activities of Contract Education department.
2. Interview, select, train, motivate, and evaluate assigned personnel, including contracted instructors and consultants.
3. Plan, apportion, and direct employees' and contracted employees' work.
4. Develop and maintain a working knowledge of the business climate and economic/workforce development trends in the district and the region.
5. Using a variety of data sources, analyze, evaluate, and identify market segments that hold the highest potential for success in matching department services offering to employer needs. Include a feedback and evaluation mechanism to assist in adjusting target markets or services offering.
6. Using a consultative selling approach with an emphasis on business performance improvement, sell appropriate services to clients.
7. In response to client needs, develop training/services proposals for current and prospective clients.
8. Negotiate and secure agreements/contracts with clients and instructors/consultants.
9. Working collaboratively with district marketing functions, provide strategic direction and oversight for new and continuing marketing activities to business, industry, and government clients.
10. Establish and maintain collaborative working relationships with college departments, other community colleges in the region, other educational institutions, community-based organizations and workforce development agencies.

Job Description for a Contract Education Sales/Account Manager (cont'd)

11. Monitor and evaluate ongoing training and services activities to ensure program quality.
12. Provide oversight in the organization and coordination of the various elements associated with training/services delivery including but not limited to tasks such as: scheduling facilities, confirming instructors, identifying needed training materials, taking care of registration procedures (if applicable), and ensuring that program evaluations are completed.
13. Maintain accurate records of activities to ensure program quality. Such records include but are not limited to: business expenses, sales call logs, weekly activity reports, and monthly sales reports.
14. Perform other duties assigned by the district dean of economic development.

Qualifications
1. Successful candidates will demonstrate the following:
2. Ability to provide administrative and professional leadership and direction for the department.
3. Ability to perform responsibilities and duties in a fast-paced, entrepreneurial environment.
4. Experience in leading, managing, and coordinating training programs or consulting services.
5. Knowledge of and experience with the principles, methods, and practices of
    a. staff selection, supervision, training and evaluation
    b. budget preparation and administration
    c. research, analysis, and evaluation of service delivery methods, procedures, and techniques
    d. research techniques to acquire information concerning the performance improvement needs of business and industry in the District service area as well as public agencies such as cities, special districts and the county
    e. marketing and consultative sales, public relations
    f. contract management
    g. program development and evaluation
5. Experience negotiating contracts/agreements.
6. Ability to learn, interpret, and apply district policies and procedures.
7. Ability to communicate clearly and concisely, both orally and in written work.
8. Knowledge of adult learning theory.
9. Computer literacy, skilled in the operation of commonly used software, including Internet communication skills.
10. Organizational, time management, and problem-solving abilities.
11. Knowledge of pertinent federal, state, and local laws, codes, and regulations affecting a contract education unit of a community college.

Minimum Education and Experience:
1. Understanding of, sensitivity to, and respect for the diverse academic, socioeconomic, ethnic, cultural, disability, religious background and sexual orientation of the community college system.
2. Bachelor's degree in a related field.
3. Three years sales/marketing experience.

Preferred Education and Experience:
1. Master's degree.
2. Experience in marketing and sales of educational or performance improvement services to industry.
3. Work experience in industry, business, or government.

License:
Possession of a valid California driver's license is required. Contract Education Sales/Account Manager must be able to use his/her personal automobile to perform work-related duties.

TEMPLATE 6: INTERVIEW GUIDE FOR AN INITIAL MEETING WITH A CLIENT

You are sitting at your desk and the phone rings. A local businessperson wants to ask your institution to design and deliver some training to meet a need that is being experienced by his or her organization. Does that sound familiar? Use the template to plan what questions you will ask a prospective client when you are asked to collect enough information to write a proposal. Leave space under your questions to jot answers during the interview.

Source: William J. Rothwell

Interview Guide for an Initial Meeting With a Client
Script for Opening the Interview: "I would like to thank you for taking time to meet with me today. What I need to do is gather some information so that I can craft a good proposal. I would like to ask you some specific questions about the issue/problem you have previously shared with me."

[date]	[name of person interviewed and his or her job title]
1. Could you tell me about the issue that brought us together today?	
2. How would you concisely state the problem or issue in a sentence or two?	
3. Who is involved with this issue, to the best of your knowledge? In other words, how many people are affected?	
4. What have you already tried to do, if anything, to address this issue? What happened as a result?	

Interview Guide for an Initial Meeting With a Client (cont'd)	
[date]	*[name of person interviewed and his or her job title]*

5. When did the problem first come up, and where (what geographical location) seems most affected?

6. How do you know that you have a problem or issue?

7. How could you measure the cost of the problem or issue on the organization? In other words, what metrics could be used to measure its impact?

8. What do you want to do to solve the problem or address the issue, and what leads you to believe that is the most appropriate approach to addressing it?

9. When do you wish to begin taking this corrective action, and do you have a budget

10. What other information would help me understand this problem or issue better? Could you give it to me?

Script for Closing the Interview: "Thank you for taking the time to share this information with me. It will take me about [*how long?*] to prepare a proposal. To whom should I send the proposal? How would it be best to do that? Thanks again."

TEMPLATE 7: WORKSHEET FOR DRAFTING PROPOSALS TO CLIENTS

Where and how do you start to prepare a proposal for a client? What follows is a worksheet that poses the basic questions that your proposal should address. Your answers to those questions will provide you with a draft proposal.

Source: William J. Rothwell

Worksheet for Drafting Proposals to Clients
Use this template to begin the process of preparing a first-rate proposal to help a client meet a business need, solve a business problem, or address a pressing issue. Use the six subheads that begin each question as subheads on your final proposal. Answer each question as fully as possible. If you lack sufficient information from the client to complete this template, you may have to phone him or her and pose follow-up questions.

[date]	*[name of person preparing the proposal]*

1. The Issue: What is the problem to be solved, the issue to be addressed, or the business need to be met? (*State it succinctly in one or two sentences.*) (*Note: It is desirable to indicate here any measures you may have obtained from the client that would indicate how much money the problem or issue is costing the organization and how that amount was determined.*)

2. The Recommended Solution: What should be done to help the client address the issue, and why is that probably the best approach? (*State it succinctly in two or three sentences.*)

3. The Project Steps: What steps should be taken, and in what sequence, to implement the solution? (*Begin each task step with a verb describing an action. If you wish, indicate what deliverables will be provided upon completion of each step and who bears accountability for doing what.*)

4. The Timeline: What is the timeline? (*Create a Gantt chart that shows the project steps along the left column and the timeline along the top. Then draw bars to show how long it will take to finish each step in the project.*)

5. The Budget: How much will it cost to carry out the project, and what are the predicted costs and benefits of performing the project? (*Use the steps of the project to estimate labor hours, travel expenses, and other costs. Then roll up the costs of each step into a budget for the total project. If you wish, give the client a flat cost and benefit figure rather than a detailed breakdown of expenses.*)

6. Qualifications of the Project Staff: Who will be involved in the project team, and what qualifications make them the best choices? How do their skills relate to the project?
(*Provide narrative sketches, resumes, or vitae pertinent to the project.*)

TEMPLATE 8: CONTRACT TRAINING BUSINESS PLAN

This template will help you think through how to prepare a business plan to conduct contract training for a local employer. Of course, the outline provided can also be useful to consider for other business plans—from contract training to strategic plans to marketing or program plans. Simply identify the parts of this template you want to include in your plan, delete those that are not appropriate, and add those that are appropriate.

Source: Elaine A. Gaertner

Contract Training Business Plan

A. Title Page
   Name of program and names, addresses, telephone numbers, and facsimile numbers of principal staff.
B. Executive Summary (to be completed *after* all other sections)
   1. Vision/Mission and Goals
      - Two to four paragraphs (minimum) to four pages (maximum) detailing vision/mission and goals of business.
   2. Overview
      - Brief summary of the business/program, including current position, development strategies, financing required, potential return on investment, profitability evaluation methods, and schedules and timetables for implementation.
C. Business Description
   1. History
      - How long have the program been in business?
      - Who are the program leaders and their contributions to the college/district?
   2. Type of Business
      - Name of your program.
      - What product or service will you supply?
D. Marketing Plan
   1. Niche Identification
      - Describe your niche or special competitive position. Be especially careful to distinguish your services from those offered by other departments/programs at your college/district.
      - Describe how you will capture, hold, and expand your market share over a five-year period.
   2. Customer Identification
      - Who are your customers?
         - List at least five customer groups who have identifiable characteristics that would be possible users of your product or service.
         - Know the difference between users and purchasers.
      - Where are your customers?
         - Determine the general geographical location of each customer group.
   3. Competition
      - List at least four competitors and why customers buy from them. Include any internal competitors you may have.
      - Explain why you think you can compete with them.
   4. Location
      - What is the address of your location?
      - Does your location assist or diminish sales? Why?
      - Will you pay lease/rent or is the space provided? If you pay rent/lease, list the approximate square footage and the cost per square foot plus other lease arrangements (i.e., percentage of gross sales, duration, etc.)

Contract Training Business Plan (cont'd)

- What types of businesses are located next to you?
- What are the traffic flow patterns for this location?
- What future development will take place in the near future around your location (i.e., housing, new stores, industry, etc.)?
- Is there convenient transportation, parking, and ease of entry and exit?

5. Promotion
   - What methods or media will you use to reach each customer group identified?
   - Describe the frequency, duration coverage, and cost of your total advertising program.
   - What types of promotional or public relations activities will you conduct (include costs)?
   - To what extent will your suppliers help with your promotion and advertising?
   - How do your competitors advertise and promote their businesses?
   - Prepare one or more of the following: a flyer, a brochure, newspaper advertisement, direct mail piece, radio commercial, personal sales call outline, or a yellow-page ad.

6. Pricing/Sales
   - What will be your pricing? What is your mark-up? Will you offer discounts or specials?
   - Define your pricing image: cheap versus high class, discount, inverse price demand.

E. Financial Plan
   1. Sources of Capital
      - How much capital will be supplied by the college/district and what are the sources (general fund, PFE, grants, other)?
      - State the sources and terms of both your short-and long-term payback expectations.
   2. Capital Equipment
      - List the equipment, machinery, fixtures, decorations, signs, and so forth that will be needed.
   3. Balance Sheet
      - Prepare an opening day balance sheet.
   4. Income Statement
      - Prepare a projected five-year income statement.
   5. Breakeven Analysis
      - Prepare five-year breakeven analysis projection. Be sure to include any contributions to college, departments, etc.
   6. Recordkeeping Plan
      - Describe or develop recordkeeping system to cover sales, inventory, accounts receivable, cash, payroll, expenses, and accounts payable using one of the following methods:
         - Self-developed with journals, ledgers, and so forth. List costs.
         - College/district supplied fiscal systems.
         - An accountant or bookkeeping service. List the services you will require from them and their fees.
         - An onsite computerized system. List type, costs, and backup system.
      - Are your college/district fiscal system reports timely enough to enable effective program management?
      - Are your college/district fiscal systems timely enough to manage cash flow?

F. Operational Plan
   1. Opening Requirements
      - What opening promotion, public relations or advertising will done? What will be done in the short term?
      - Are there any requirements for insurance will you need to carry?
      - What types of utilities will you require?
      - What legal and professional fees will be paid for from income generated?
      - List any installation, decoration, or remodeling needed and the permits required.
   2. Physical Layout (if you will move into an off-campus site that your program revenue must support)
      - Draw a diagram of
         - Entrances, exits, signs, windows, and parking facilities.

Contract Training Business Plan (cont'd)

- Storerooms, restrooms, and office space.
- Locations of fixtures, equipment, and machinery.
- Location of supplies, inventory, and merchandise displays.
- Traffic or workflow within the establishment.

3. Suppliers
   - List the names of your suppliers of merchandise, materials, supplies, and services. What will each supply?
   - List the names of your suppliers for fixtures, equipment, and machinery and whether you will lease or buy. What will each cost?
   - For each supplier, list their terms, methods of delivery, dependability, and promotional or start-up services available.

G. Management
   1. Objectives, Policies, and Procedures
      - Write policies or procedures for the following areas:
         - Pricing (mark-up, discounts, specials)
         - Quantity (variety)
         - Quality (high, average, low)
         - Customer relations (service, delivery)
         - Supplier relations (terms, services, delivery)
         - Personnel (wages, selection, training, benefits, promotions)
         - Image (service, fairness, quality)
         - General (policies and procedures specific to type of business or those items not previously covered but unique to the business)

   2. Management and Organization
      - What background and personal qualifications do you have for this program?
      - Write a functional job description for each key position.
      - Draw an organizational chart.

H. Summary
   - Write a brief (two to four paragraphs) conclusion that ties together all information.

I. Attachments (include as appropriate)
   - Resumes of leadership, beginning management team, and staff members
   - Job descriptions
   - Organizational chart
   - Sample ads, promotional pieces
   - Contracts, partnership agreements
   - Policy and procedure outline or brochure
   - Leases or property purchase agreements
   - Legal documents (professional certifications and licenses; state or federal taxpayer ID certification)

TEMPLATE 9: ACTION PLANNING WORKSHEET

After training, how do you apply what you have learned to your job, and how do you balance tactical plans (actions taken daily, weekly, or monthly) with strategic plans (actions taken for a specific project)? To begin planning both your daily workload and your project plans, first, make a list, in numerical order, of your project or performance goals. Then describe each goal in detail and describe the results you expect. Remember to set SMART goals—goals that are specific, measurable, achievable, relevant, and timely. Review your goals with your supervisor or manager, sign them, and give copies to your supervisor or manager and to the development manager, if applicable. Second, use this action planning worksheet to help you plan how you will apply what you have learned to your day-to-day tasks and to your project plans. You may use the worksheet as a to-do list for yourself or for staff.

Source: Wesley E. Donahue

Action Planning Worksheet			
To get the greatest return on investment from your workforce development training, you need to apply what you have learned to your job. Use this worksheet to describe your goals as on-the-job applications for the ideas and skills that you learned from your WFD training (column 1). In the remaining columns, list the specific actions or steps needed to accomplish your goals (what is needed and when, how will the action be carried out, who will take the action?), the resources you require to achieve your goals, and potential barriers to achieving your goals. Your completed worksheet will enable you to draft an action plan that you can discuss with your supervisor.			
Goals	**Actions Needed**	**Resources Needed**	**Potential Barriers**

Template 10: Interview Guide for Mandated Training Program Planning

Sometimes decision makers want to give people training even when they do not necessarily need it. In such real-world cases in which trainers cannot argue because the training is going to be given anyway, it may be best to create a specification for training that clarifies exactly what decision makers want that training to be. Use this program planning interview guide with decision makers when they demand that training be given. Ask one or more decision makers for information to complete the interview guide, and use their answers to prepare a detailed description of the training. Then feed it back to decision makers, verify that is what they want, and use the description for program planning.

Source: William J. Rothwell

Interview Guide for Mandated Training Program Planning
Directions to the Workforce Developer: Use this template to help you collect information from one or more decision-makers who have mandated that training be conducted. For each question appearing in the left column below, provide an answer in the right column. Then type up the results, feed them back to decision-maker(s), and verify that the program plan matches up to the client's expectations.

[date]	[name of person interviewed]
The Purpose: What is the purpose of the training? (*State it succinctly in one or two sentences.*)	
Objectives: What should the trainees know or be able to do when the training is finished? (*Provide a list of objectives. Begin each one with an action verb.*)	
The Outline: What key topics should be covered in the training? (*Try to get the interviewee to give you an outline of topics to be covered.*)	
The Medium or Media: How should the training be delivered? (*Onsite, online, or blended? Why?*)	

Interview Guide for Mandated Training Program Planning (cont'd)

Directions to the Workforce Developer: Use this template to help you collect information from one or more decision-makers who have mandated that training be conducted. For each question appearing in the left column below, provide an answer in the right column. Then type up the results, feed them back to decision-maker(s), and verify that the program plan matches up to the client's expectations.

[date]	*[name of person interviewed]*

Targeted Participants: Who exactly should participate in the training? (*Give job titles or categories or locations.*)

Materials: What special materials from the organization should be used in the training? (*For instance, if the course is about the company's performance evaluation program, one answer might be the company's performance evaluation forms.*)

Methods: What approaches should or should not be used in the program? (*For instance, if managers do not like to role play, the interviewees might say: "Let's avoid role play." If managers do like case studies or hands-on experiences, the interviewees might list them.*)

Instructor(s): What special qualifications, if any, are essential for instructors who deliver the training? Do they need special preparation? If so, what kind?

Evaluation Methods: How will the success of the training be measured? What metrics should be used? How should participant success be determined?

Template 11: Training Agreement

I f your college does not have a standard boilerplate document to use to for contracting for train-ing services with a faculty member or an outside vendor, you can use this template to draft one. Fill in information indicated in brackets. Review the draft with your college's legal department and with the vendor you plan to use for services. Negotiate which terms need to be included, omitted, or reworded.

Source: William J. Rothwell

Training Agreement

Agreement Between [Company Name], [Vendor Name], and [College Name]

This Agreement is entered into on this [date] day of [month] in the year [year], by and between [Vendor Name], [Company Name], and [College Name].

[Company Name] engages American business professionals to conduct various professional services. [Trainer's Name] of [Vendor Name] is a leading [training specialty] consultant. [Company Name] engages [Vendor Name] to conduct [programs] for [Company Name]. The programs shall [purpose of programs]. [College Name], through its Division of Continuing Education, awards Certificates of Completion and Continuing Education Units for University-recognized programs.

In consideration of the premises, and for other good and valuable consideration, the receipt and sufficiency of which is acknowledged, the parties hereto hereby agree as follows:

I. Obligations of [Vendor Name]
    1. [Trainer's Name] will prepare and facilitate two programs to be delivered and conducted in [location] on the following dates of the year: [day, month, and year]. These programs shall be on the topics of [topics]. The agenda and content of each program is set out in outline form in Appendix [or Appendixes A, B, C, etc.], attached hereto and incorporated by reference.
    2. One month before the course, [Trainer's Name] shall prepare and electronically transmit to [Company Name] all materials that will be used in the programs. These materials include the outlines and the content of the programs along with all handouts and material to be presented to the attendees.
    3. Whenever on the premises in [Location], [Trainer's Name] will ensure that his or her employees and agents will obey all reasonable instructions and directions issued by [Company Name], and will comply with all applicable safety and security regulations.
    4. [Vendor Name] will provide [Company Name] with receipts and other forms of documentation evidencing the out-of-pocket expenses, e.g., local phone bills, meals, and laundry with the hotel up to USD [$] per day.

II. Obligations of [Company Name]
    1. [Company Name] shall reimburse [Trainer's Name]'s round trip airfare to and from [Location] by econo my class.
    2. [Company Name] shall pay for [Trainer's Name]'s hotel accommodations during his or her stay. His or her hotel will be at least of four-star quality and should include broadband computer access so that [Trainer's Name] may remain in touch with the U.S.A.
    3. [Company Name] shall make available to [Trainer's Name] working space, facilities, data, and any docu-mentation required by [Trainer's Name] in [Location] to complete his or her obligations under this contract.
    4. [Company Name] shall pay for the following expenses:
        a. Any currency conversion fee.
        b. Any applicable local taxes.

Training Agreement (cont'd)

    c.   All travel-related expenses and all lodging and meal expenses during the trip.

    d.   Any translation and translator-related expenses.

    e.   The cost of photocopying all handouts.

    f.   The cost of procuring a PowerPoint video projector.

    g.   Any necessary expenses related to the programs.

5. [Company Name] shall reimburse [Trainer's Name] for all reasonable out-of-pocket expenses (e.g., travel, reproduction, telephone, etc.) incurred in [Location] or with [Location] for the performance of his or her obligations under this contract.

6. Payment for Services

    a.   [Company Name] agrees to pay [Vendor Name] the following within 30 days of each program's completion: USD [$] per day net for [programs].

    b.   [Company Name] agrees to pay [College Name] the following administrative fees within 30 days of each program's completion: an administrative fee of USD [$] per participant.

III. Obligations of [College Name]

1. [College Name] will issue Certificates of Completion to the [Company Name] participants who successfully complete each program.

2. [College Name] will award the appropriate Continuing Education Units (CEUs) to the participants for each successfully completed program.

IV. Provisions

1. Ownership of Work Product

    [Either Trainer's Name or Vendor Name] shall retain the copyright of all intellectual property that he or she produces, which constitutes the contents of the programs covered under this contract.

2. Warranties

    Both [Trainer's Name] and [Vendor Name] warrant and affirm that [Company Name]'s receipt and use of services and deliverables provided under this agreement will not violate or in any way infringe upon the rights of third parties, including property, contractual, employment, trade secret, proprietary information and nondisclosure rights, or any trademark, copyright, or patent rights.

3. Reciprocal Covenant Not-to-Solicit Personnel

    For a period of one (1) year after this Agreement terminates for any reason, none of the parties to this Agreement nor any of their affiliates, employees, or agents shall directly or indirectly, individually or on behalf of any person or entity:

    a.   Recruit, solicit or encourage any person to terminate his or her relationship with the other parties, or

    b.   Recruit, solicit or hire any of the other party's then current or former (within 12 months) employees, independent contractors, or agents. In each case, this restriction shall be limited to the other party's employees, independent contractors, or agents who are or were previously involved with performing services relating to [Company Name], [Vendor Name], or [College Name].

4. Hold Harmless/Limitation of Liability

    Each party to this Agreement will be responsible for, and to the extent of, its own actions, omissions, or negligence. None of the parties to this Agreement shall be liable to the others for the payment of any consequential, indirect, or special damages, including lost profits. Nevertheless, if one of the parties fails to provide any of the material provisions of the Agreement without sufficient notice and without good cause, then the breaching party will be liable for all damages arising from its failure to provide the agreed-upon services.

5. The Relationship Between the Parties

    In all matters relating to this Agreement, [Vendor Name] shall be acting as an independent contractor. Neither [Trainer's Name] nor his or her employees are employees of [Company Name] or [College Name] under the meaning or application of any federal or state employment or insurance laws, or otherwise. All parties shall assume all liabilities or obligations imposed by any one or more of such laws with respect

Training Agreement (cont'd)

to their employees, agents, or contractors, if any, in the performance of this Agreement. This Agreement does not create a joint venture or partnership.

6. Governing Law

   This Agreement shall be governed and construed in accordance with the laws of the state of [State Name] without regard to the conflicts of law principles thereof. Each of the parties hereto consents and agrees to the jurisdiction of any state or federal court sitting in, or with jurisdiction over, the County of Centre, the State of [State Name], and waives any objection based on venue or *forum non conveniens* with respect to any action instituted therein, and agrees that any dispute concerning this Agreement or any matter related to this Agreement shall be heard only in the courts described above.

7. Notice

   Any notice or other communication required or permitted under this Agreement shall be given in writing and delivered by hand or by registered or certified mail, postage prepaid and return receipt requested, to the following persons (or their successors pursuant to due notice):

   If to [Company Name]:
   Attention: [Contact Name]
               [Company Name]
               [Address]

   If to [Vendor Name]:
   Attention: [Trainer's Name]
               [Vendor Name]
               [Address]

   If to [College Name]:
   Attention: [Contact Name]
               [College Name]
               [Address]

8. Assignment

   None of the parties has the power or the right to assign any of the rights under this Agreement or to dele gate any of the duties under this Agreement without the expressed written consent of the other parties.

9. Arbitration

   Any controversy or claim arising out of or relating to this Agreement, or the breach thereof, shall first be submitted to arbitration and administered by the American Arbitration Association under its Commercial Arbitration Rules then in effect at the time a demand for arbitration is filed with the Association. All arbitration shall take place in [County], [State]. Any award rendered by the arbitrator(s) may be entered as evidence in any legal proceedings initiated if the arbitrator(s) ruling is not acceptable to all involved parties.

10. Attorney's Fees

    If any legal action or proceeding arising out of or relating to this Agreement is brought by any party to this Agreement, the prevailing party will be entitled to receive from the other party or parties, in addition to any other relief that may be granted, the reasonable attorneys' fees, costs, and expenses incurred in the action or proceeding by the prevailing party.

11. Merger and Modification

    This written Agreement constitutes the entire Agreement between the parties, and any prior or contemporaneous representations or warranties are not considered as part of the parties' Agreement. No modification of this Agreement shall be effective unless in writing and signed by both parties.

12. Survival of Enforceable Provisions

    If any provision of this Agreement is invalid or unenforceable under any statute or rule of law, the provision is to that extent to be deemed omitted, and the remaining provisions shall not be affected in any way.

Training Agreement

13. Waiver

No waiver by one party of any breach by another party of any of the provisions of this Agreement shall be deemed a waiver of any preceding or succeeding breach of the same or any other provisions hereof. No such waiver shall be effective unless in writing and then only to the extent expressly set forth in writing. This Agreement will inure to and be binding on the heirs, executors, administrators, successors, and assigns of the parties to this Agreement. However, nothing contained in this paragraph will constitute consent to the assignment or delegation by either party of any rights or duties under this Agreement.

14. Cancellation

If any party cancels for good cause any of the engagements contained in this Agreement, the cancelled engagement shall be rescheduled to another date to be mutually agreed upon by all parties. Nevertheless, the rescheduled engagement must occur within six weeks of date of specification. If cancellation occurs within one month of the scheduled program delivery by either [Vendor Name] or [Company Name], USD [$] will be paid by the canceling party to the other party.

IN WITNESS WHEREOF, and in acknowledgment that the parties hereto have read and understood each and every provision hereof, the parties have executed this Agreement on the date first set forth above.

[Company Name]:
By: Approval
          Signature:
          Approval date:
          Printed name [Contact Name]:
          Printed title:

[Vendor Name]:
By: Approval
          Signature:
          Approval date:
          Printed name [Contact Name]:
          Printed title:

[College Name]:
By: Approval
          Signature:
          Approval date:
          Printed name [Contact Name]:
          Printed title [President]:

TEMPLATE 12: CONSULTING AGREEMENT

Use this template to draft an agreement with an outside consultant to your college. As with any legal document, you will need competent legal advice to customize this agreement for your college.

Source: Larry Michael

Consulting Agreement

Agreement

AGREEMENT effective [Date], by and between [College Name], and [Consultant Name, Consultant Organization Name], hereinafter ("Consultant), with an office and principal place of business at [Consultant Address], for project named [Project Name], for [Client Name, if applicable].

Recitals

WHEREAS, Consultant is experienced in the delivery of [subject/content area]; and

WHEREAS, [College Name] which provides organizations within its service area with assistance and information in improving their competitiveness; and

WHEREAS, [College Name] desires to secure the benefit of Consultant's expertise and Consultant desires to so consult for [College Name].

The parties, intending to be legally bound, therefore agree as follows:

1. Consulting Arrangement. Consultant will consult for [College Name], and [College Name] will receive the benefit of Consultant's services.

2. Term. The term of the Consulting Agreement shall be for services, commencing [start date], and ending [end date].

3. Duties. During the term of this Consulting Agreement, Consultant shall perform the work and services contained in Exhibit A described as attached hereto and incorporated herein by this reference.

4. Extent of Consulting Services. During its term, Consultant shall devote his or her best efforts and such amounts of time and attention as are required to adequately discharge his or her duties under this Consulting Agreement.

5. Compensation.
   a. [College Name] shall pay Consultant for the services and shall reimburse Consultant for expenses in accordance with Exhibit B, attached hereto and made a part hereof.
   b. Payment to Consultant will be subject to meeting milestones established in the Schedule of Services contained in Exhibit A.

6. Suspension or Termination. [College Name] may suspend performance or terminate this agreement effective upon written notice to Consultant in the event of a termination of grant, a withdrawal or shortage of funding, or in the event that Consultant is convicted of a criminal act, becomes insolvent, has a petition in bankruptcy file by or against it, has a receiver appointed, makes an assignment for the benefit of creditors, or is otherwise in breach of this agreement or its agreement with any Client.

7. Relationship Between the Parties. Consultant is retained only for the purposes and to the extent set forth in this Consulting Agreement, and his or her relationship to [College Name] shall be that of independent contractor

Consulting Agreement (cont'd)

and not an employee. as such, Consultant shall not be entitled to any pension, health insurance, or any other employee benefit offered by [College Name] to its employees.

8. Notice. Any notice required or desired to be given pursuant to this Consulting Agreement shall be in writing and mailed by certified mail to the parties at the following addresses:

[College Name]:   [Name of College Representative]
                      [Title]
                      [College Name]
                      [Address]
Consultant: [Consultant Name]
                      [Title]
                      [Consultant Organization]
                      [Address]

9. Confidential Information. Consultant agrees to treat any confidential and proprietary information ("Trade Secrets") that it receives from [College Name] or any Client with the highest degree of confidentiality, and agrees not to disclose same to any other person or use such Trade Secrets for any purposes other than contemplated by this Agreement. Consultant agrees to have his or her employees sign individual confidentiality agreements if so requested by [College Name] or Client.

10. Entire Agreement. This Consulting Agreement constitutes the entire understanding and agreement between [College Name] and Consultant with regard to all matters herein. There are no other agreements, conditions or representations, oral or written, express or implied, with regard thereto. This Consulting Agreement may be amended only in writing, signed by both parties.

11. Governing Law. This Consulting Agreement shall be construed and enforced in accordance with the laws of the Commonwealth of Pennsylvania.

12. Headings. Headings in this Consulting Agreement are for convenience only and shall not be used to construe or interpret its provisions.

13. Counterparts. This Consulting Agreement may be executed in two or more counterparts, each of which shall be deemed an original but all of which together shall constitute one and the same agreement.

IN WITNESS WHEREOF, [College Name], by its appropriate officers, and Consultant have signed this Consulting Agreement.

Witness: [College Name]
By: [Name of College Representative]
Signature: [Signature]
Date: [Date]

Witness: Consultant
By: [Consultant Name]
Signature: [Signature]
Date: [Date]

Exhibit A: Schedule of Services

Project Name:
Project Description
    A.   Services to be provided: [insert description]
    B.   Schedule of services: [insert timeline for deliverables]

Witness: [College Name]
By: [Name of College Representative]
Signature: [Signature]
Date: [Date]

Witness: Consultant
By: [Consultant Name]
Signature: [Signature]
Date: [Date]

Exhibit B: Compensation

Project Name:

    A. Fees: [insert fee structure]
    B. Billing and Payment: [insert specifics]

Witness: [College Name]
By: [Name of College Representative]
Signature: [Signature]
Date: [Date]

Witness: Consultant
By: [Consultant Name]
Signature: [Signature]

TEMPLATE 13: LETTER OF UNDERSTANDING BETWEEN WORKFORCE DEVELOPMENT ORGANIZATIONS AND CONTRACT INSTRUCTORS (PROFESSIONAL ASSOCIATES)

Use this form as a template to begin preparing a letter of understanding with a contract instructor (known in workforce development circles as professional associate). Be sure to have the letter approved by the legal counsel for your college.

Source: Wesley E. Donahue

Letter of Understanding Between Workforce Development Organizations and Contract Instructors (Professional Associates)

Letter of Understanding Between
[College Name] and [Instructor Name]

This Letter of Understanding serves as a set of principles to cover the basic terms and conditions under which instructional services provided by [Instructor Name], as a professional associate, are made available to [College Name]. These terms and principles will remain in effect unless terminated by either party with 30 days prior written notice.

[College Name] offers confidential [type of training] and services of a wide-ranging nature to its clients. [College Name's] obligations require employees and professional associates to maintain high standards of professional ethics and to be discreet, trustworthy, and fully committed to our organization and our clients.

Therefore, in consideration of your association with us, it is understood and agreed that:

1. [College Name] may offer your instructional services as appropriate, to [College Name's] clients.

2. You will keep confidential, and not divulge to others, information regarding the business and activities of current, past and potential clients of [College Name] that may come into your possession as a result of the association with [College Name].

3. The use of [College Name's] materials will be only for those organizations authorized by [College Name]. Further, it is understood that requests by organizations for similar service will be referred to [College Name] for appropriate action.

4. Intellectual Property Rights: All rights to materials produced by or developed for [College Name] prior to or during the performance of work assignments shall be owned by [College Name]. You shall be deemed to possess an implied license for the use of these rights solely for the purposes of [College Name] assignments.

5. As a professional associate, your instructional skills and services shall be available to [College Name] on a reasonable, mutually-agreeable schedule, at a fee of [$] plus all related, prior-approved travel and extraordinary expenses.

6. As a professional associate, you agree to abide by the copyright laws and provide service in the highest professional manner consistent with the full-time employee(s) of [College Name].

7. As a professional associate, you shall hold [College Name], its trustees, officers, employees, agents, and contractors harmless of any claims or damages arising out of your performance for [College Name].

Letter of Understanding Between Workforce Development Organizations and Contract Instructors (Professional Associates) (cont'd)

8. Governing Law and Jurisdiction: If any disputes arise related to your performance for [College Name], they shall be governed and construed in accordance with the laws of [State Name] and each party submits to the jurisdiction of the [State Name].

Please indicate your understanding and agreement by signing and returning one copy of this letter to the Director of [Workforce Development Organization, College Name, Address].

ACCEPTED:
By: [Instructor Name]   SSN: [SSN]
Signature: [Signature]
Date: [Date]

By: Director of [Workforce Development Organization, College Name]
Signature: [Signature]
Date: [Date]

TEMPLATE 14: DEBARMENT FORM

In this day of sensitivity to ethics and conflicts of interest, how sure are you that your employees or contractors have met all legal requirements? Use this form to ensure that you have documented evidence of legal compliance. (Of course, you should ask your institution's legal counsel to review and approve the form.) To ensure compliance, have workers complete the form at time of hire, and have contractors complete the form as they review and sign a contract or letter of agreement with your organization.

Source: Larry Michael

Debarment Form

Subcontractor Certifications

Certifications Regarding Lobbying; Debarment & Suspension; Drug-Free Workplace; Delinquent Federal Debt; Compliance with Clean Air and Water Pollution Acts; and Procurement Integrity

The following certifications/compliance requirements are made by checking the appropriate boxes and verified by the signature of the Authorized Representative of the Subcontractor:

1. Delinquent Federal Debt. ❑ No ❑ Yes (If yes, explanation attached)

2. Debarment and Suspension. ❑ No ❑ Yes (If yes, explanation attached)

3. Drug-Free Workplace. ❑ No ❑ Yes (If no, explanation attached)

4. Clean-Air Act and the Federal Water Pollution Control Act, as amended.

5. Contract Work Hours and Safety Standards Act

6. Procurement Integrity. I, the undersigned, am the officer or employee responsible for the preparation of this offer and hereby certify that, to the best of my knowledge and belief, with the exception of any information described in this certificate, I have no information concerning a violation or possible violation of subsections (a), (b), (d) or (f) of the Office of Federal Procurement Policy Act, as amended (41 U.S.C. 423), (hereinafter referred to as "the Act") as implemented in the FAR, occurring during the conduct of this procurement.

As required by subsection 27(e)(1)(B) of the Act, I further certify that to the best of my knowledge and belief, each officer, employee, agent, and representative of the Subcontractor who has participated personally and substantially in the preparation of submission of this offer has certified that he or she is familiar with, and will comply with, the requirements of subsection 27(a) of the Act, as implemented in the FAR, and will report immediately to me any information concerning a violation or possible violation of subsection 27(a), (b), (d) or (f) as implemented in the FAR pertaining to this procurement.

Violations or possible violations: ❑ No ❑ Yes

Any Further Violations Will Be Reported as Required by the Act.

I agree that the certifications required by subsection 27(e)(1)(B) of the ACT shall be maintained in accordance with paragraph (f) of FAR 52.203.8.

7. Lobbying: The undersigned certifies, to the best of his or her knowledge and belief, that:

No Federal or Public appropriated funds have been paid or will be paid, by or on behalf of the undersigned, to any person for influencing or attempting to influence an officer or employee of any agency, a Member of Congress,

Debarment Form (cont'd)

an officer or employee of Congress, or an employee of a Member of Congress in connection with the awarding of any Federal or Public contract, the making of any Federal or Public grant, the making of any Federal or Public loan, the entering into of any cooperative agreement, and the extension, continuation, renewal, amendment, or modification of any Federal or Public grant contract, loan, or cooperative agreement.

If any funds other than Federal or public appropriated funds have been paid or will be paid to any person for influencing or attempting to influence an officer or employee of any agency, a Member of Congress, an officer or employee of Congress, or an employee of a Member of Congress in connection with this Federal or Public contract, grant, loan, or cooperative agreement, the undersigned shall complete and submit the Standard Form-LLL, "Disclosure Form to Report Lobbying" in accordance with its instructions.

The undersigned shall require that the language of this certification be included in subawards at all tiers (including subcontracts, subgrants, and contracts under grants, loans, and cooperative agreements) and that all subrecipients shall certify and disclose accordingly.

This certification is a material representation of fact upon which reliance was placed when this transaction was made and entered into. Submission of this certification is a prerequisite for making or entering into this transaction imposed by section 1352, Title 31, U.S.C. Code. Any person who fails to file the required certification shall be subject to a civil penalty of not less than $10,000 and not more than $100,000 for each such failure.

By: [Employee/Subcontractor Name]
Signature: [Signature]
Date: [Date]

TEMPLATE 15: FINANCIAL INTEREST DISCLOSURE FORM

How do you know when the potential for conflict of interest that exists? Use this form as a template to work with your institution's legal counsel to develop a financial interest disclosure form that is appropriate to your college. Have new hires and contractors sign this form.

Source: Larry Michael

Financial Interest Disclosure Form

[College Name]
Significant Financial Interest Disclosure
(as referenced in Policy and Procedure III 3.05.11)

Faculty/Staff Name:
School/Department:
Job Component Involved (e.g., assignment, project, etc.):
Outside Activity Involved (e.g., business, financial interest, etc.):

I am disclosing the following significant financial interests (check all that apply) and attaching supporting documentation that identifies the business enterprise or entity involved and the nature and amount of the interest:

_____ Salary or other payment for services (e.g., consulting fees or honoraria).

_____ Equity interest (e.g., stocks, stock options, or other ownership interests).

_____ Intellectual property rights (e.g., patents, copyrights, and royalties from such rights).

_____ Other significant financial interest of the employee that possibly could affect or be perceived to affect the results of the research, educational, or service activities of the college.

_____ Gift(s) with a value in excess of $100.

Further I agree:

1. To update this disclosure as new reportable significant financial interests are obtained.
2. To cooperate in the development of a conflict of interest resolution plan and reduce it to a Memorandum of Understanding (MOU) for my personnel file.
3. To comply with any conditions or restrictions imposed by the College to manage, reduce, or eliminate actual or potential conflicts of interest.
4. To have a fully executed MOU in place prior to undertaking activities deemed potential conflicts of interest by my supervisor.

[Employee/Contractor]:
Signed: [Signature]   Date: [Date]

Endorsements:

_____ I have reviewed the significant financial interest disclosure and believe that it will be possible for the above individual to execute an MOU to reduce or eliminate any conflict of interest.

_____ I have determined that no conflict of interest exists.

Supervisor:
Signed: [Signature]   Date: [Date]

Superior:
Signed: [Signature]   Date: [Date]

TEMPLATE 16: TRAINING EVALUATION FORM

This template includes basic questions you may want to include on an evaluation form. Use the form as is, or modify it to meet the needs of your college. Template 17 offers another format for you to consider in developing a customized form, and Template 18 lists some additional questions you may want to add.

Source: Wesley E. Donahue

Training Evaluation Form

1. Please rate the overall impact of the program.　**Low　Average　High**
　　　　　　　　　　　　　　　　　　　　　　1　2　3　4　5　6　7

2. What is your overall rating of the instructor?　**Low　Average　High**
　　　　　　　　　　　　　　　　　　　　　　1　2　3　4　5　6　7

3. What did you like best about the program?

4. What did you like least?

5. Which exercise or activity did you find most helpful?

6. What do you recommend to strengthen the program?

7. What do you plan to do differently as a result of this program?

8. Write additional comments here:

_____

College:　　　　　　　　　　　Course #:
Name (optional):　　　　　　　Date:

Thank you for your participation and comments!

TEMPLATE 17: COURSE EVALUATION FORM

Like Template 16, this template provides examples of the kinds of questions you may wish to ask students at the end of a training course. Use the form as is, or modify it to meet the needs of your college. Template 18 illustrates other questions you may wish to add.

Source: Larry Michael

Course Evaluation Form

Instructor: _____ **Course:** _____

Student Name: _____ **Phone:** _____ **E-mail Address:** _____

Please check the appropriate box

	Strongly Agree	Agree	Neutral	Strongly Disagree	Disagree	Not Applicable
Relevancy:						
1. Overall, I was satisfied with the knowledge gained from this course.	☐	☐	☐	☐	☐	☐
2. The topics included were valuable to me.	☐	☐	☐	☐	☐	☐
3. The information that I learned will help me in my job.	☐	☐	☐	☐	☐	☐
Course Content:						
4. The examples and demonstrations were appropriate.	☐	☐	☐	☐	☐	☐
5. The practice exercises reinforced the course material.	☐	☐	☐	☐	☐	☐
6. The amount of information was adequate for the length of the course.	☐	☐	☐	☐	☐	☐
7. The course materials were effective in the classroom.	☐	☐	☐	☐	☐	☐
8. The course materials will be useful as a reference.	☐	☐	☐	☐	☐	☐
Facility and Administration:						
9. The classroom environment was conducive to learning.	☐	☐	☐	☐	☐	☐
10. The registration process was efficient and timely.	☐	☐	☐	☐	☐	☐
11. The vehicle parking was convenient.	☐	☐	☐	☐	☐	☐
Instructor:						
12. The instructor presented the course material in a logical manner.	☐	☐	☐	☐	☐	☐
13. The instructor presented the material clearly and understandably.	☐	☐	☐	☐	☐	☐
14. The instructor demonstrated a good knowledge of the subject matter.	☐	☐	☐	☐	☐	☐
15. The instructor encouraged student participation and questions.	☐	☐	☐	☐	☐	☐
16. I would take another course with this instructor.	☐	☐	☐	☐	☐	☐
Overall:						
17. Overall, I was satisfied with the quality of the course.	☐	☐	☐	☐	☐	☐
18. I would recommend this course to others.	☐	☐	☐	☐	☐	☐

Information:

	TTC Catalog	Newspaper Ad	Web Page	Direct Mailing	Through Work	Other
19. How did you hear about this course?	☐	☐	☐	☐	☐	☐

Course Evaluation Form (cont'd)

Comments:

20. What was the most important thing you learned as a result of this course? _____

21. Was there anything that you particularly liked about this course? _____

22. Was there anything that you particularly disliked about this course? _____

23. What other courses would you be interested in taking? _____

24. Other comments: _____

TEMPLATE 18: QUESTIONS TO ADD TO A TRAINING EVALUATION FORM

Nearly all training concludes with an evaluation form that asks participates to rate the quality of the instructor, training material, facilities, refreshments, and other relevant issues affecting the training experience. Although such forms measure the reaction level, they may be a starting point for collecting additional information. Adding the questions recommended should not be too difficult, and the information gathered from these questions may be helpful in providing a foundation for subsequent measurement.

Source: William J. Rothwell

Questions to Add to a Training Evaluation Form

To evaluate reaction, add
- What is the one thing about this training program that you liked the most, and why did you like it?

To evaluate learning, add
- What is the most important thing that you learned from this training program, and why do you think that it was important?

To evaluate on-the-job behavior change, add
- What did you learn in this training program that you plan to take back to your job and apply?
- To evaluate results or return on investments, add
- In what ways do you think that the organization will save money or increase revenues based on the results of the training that you have received? Please answer that question and then explain it briefly.
- Decision makers will want to know how to measure increases in productivity or reductions in cost that resulted directly from the training you have received. How do you think that the results of this training could be measured financially in terms of increased job productivity, reduced expenses, or other measures? What measures are most appropriate to use for this program, and how do you think that the financial results of the training should be measured?

State-by-State Electronic Resources for Workforce Development Strategic Plans and Customized Job Training Grants

Michael J. Brna Jr.

State-by-State Electronic Resources for Workforce Development Strategic Plans and Customized Job Training Grants		
State	**Workforce Development Strategic Plans**	**Customized Job Training Grants**
Alabama	Alabama Department of Economic and Community Affairs http://www.adeca.alabama.gov	Alabama Industrial Development Training http://www.aidt.edu/index.html
Alaska	Alaska Workforce Investment Board abor.state.ak.us/awib/home.htm Alaska Department of Labor & Workforce Development http://www.labor.state.ak.us	The State Training and Employment Program (STEP) Alaska Workforce Investment Board http://www.labor.state.ak.us/awib/home.htm
Arizona	Governor's Council on Workforce Policy Arizona Department of Commerce Arizona Office of Workforce Development http://www.commerce.state.az.us/Workforce/default.asp	Arizona Workforce Connection Arizona Job Training Program http://www.arizonaworkforceconnection.com
Arkansas	Arkansas Workforce Investment Board http://www.arworks.org/statcon.html	Arkansas Department of Economic Development Existing Workforce Training Program (EWTP) Business and Industry Training Program http://www.1-800-arkansas.com/home.cfm
California	California Workforce Investment Board (CalWIB) http://www.calwia.org	California Employment Training Panel http://www.etp.cahwnet.gov

State-by-State Electronic Resources for Workforce Development Strategic Plans and Customized Job Training Grants		
State	**Workforce Development Strategic Plans**	**Customized Job Training Grants**
Colorado	Colorado Office of Workforce Development http://www.state.co.us/owd	Colorado Office of Workforce Development Workforce Development Council http://www.state.co.us/gov_dir/wdc/council/council.htm
Connecticut	Connecticut Employment & Training Commission (CETC) http://www.ctdol.state.ct.us/rwdb/cetc.htm	Connecticut Department of Labor http://www.ctdol.state.ct.us
Delaware	Delaware's Workforce Investment Board http://www.delawareworks.com/wib	Delaware Economic Development Office Workforce Development Training http://www.delawareworkforce.com/trainglance.htm
Florida	Workforce Florida, Inc. http://www.workforceflorida.com	Workforce Florida, Inc. Incumbent Worker Training http://www.workforceflorida.com
Georgia	Georgia Department of Labor http://www.dol.state.ga.us	Office of Economic Development Georgia Department of Adult and Technical Education QuickStart program http://www.dtae.org/quickstart/menu.html
Hawaii	Department of Labor and Industrial Relations dlir.state.hi.us Workforce Development Division http://www.dlir.state.hi.us/wdd	Department of Labor and Industrial Relations Employment and Training Fund Program (ETF) http://www.dlir.state.hi.us/wdd/etf/ETF%20Home.htm
Idaho	IdahoWorks http://www.idahoworks.org	Workforce Training Program http://www.idahoworks.com/E1.training.htm
Illinois	Illinois Workforce Development http://www.ilworkforce.org Illinois Workforce Investment Board http://www.ilworkforce.org/IWIB/IWIB.shtml	Illinois Department of Commerce and Economic Opportunity Employer Training Investment Program (ETIP) http://www.illinoisbiz.biz/bus/employ_ind_training.html
Indiana	Indiana Department of Workforce Development http://www.in.gov/dwd/workforce_serv/wia/plan	Indiana Department of Workforce Development http://www.in.gov/dwd/education

State-by-State Electronic Resources for Workforce Development Strategic Plans and Customized Job Training Grants		
State	**Workforce Development Strategic Plans**	**Customized Job Training Grants**
Iowa	Iowa Workforce Development Board Division of Policy and Information http://www.iowaworkforce.org/policy	Iowa Department of Economic Development http://www.iowasmart.com/services/work force/training.html
Kansas	Kansas Department of Human Resources Employment and Training http://entkdhr.state.ks.us/WIA.htm Workforce Network of Kansas http://www.workforcenetworkkansas.org	Kansas Department of Commerce http://kdoch.state.ks.us/ProgramApp/ program_grant.jsp
Kentucky	Strategic Workforce Development Plan Kentucky Workforce Investment Board http://kwib.state.ky.us	KY Department for Training & ReEmployment http://dtr.state.ky.us
Louisiana	Louisiana Workforce Commission http://www.laworkforce.net	Louisiana Economic Development http://www.lded.state.la.us/businessresources/ workforcetraining.asp
Maine	Maine Jobs Council http://www.state.me.us/labor/mjc	Maine Jobs Council Maine Workforce Investment Boards http://www.state.me.us/labor/mjc/dynamic-frameset.html?lwib.html
Maryland	Governor's Workforce Investment Board http://www.mdworkforce.com Maryland Workforce Development Association http://www.mwda.org	Customized Workforce Development Training Programs http://www.choosemaryland.org/business/ workforce/training.asp
Massachusetts	Department of Labor and Workforce Development http://www.state.ma.us/dlwd	Massachusetts Division of Employment and Training Massachusetts Workforce Training Fund http://www.detma.org/workforcehome.htm
Michigan	Strategic Workforce Development Plan Michigan's Workforce Investment Board http://www.michigan.gov/mdcd/0,1607,7-122-1683_18969—-,00.html	Michigan Department of Career Development http://www.michigan.gov/mdcd
Minnesota	Governor's Workforce Development Council http://www.gwdc.org	Minnesota Department of Trade and Economic Development Workforce Development Division http://www.dted.state.mn.us

State-by-State Electronic Resources for Workforce Development Strategic Plans and Customized Job Training Grants		
State	**Workforce Development Strategic Plans**	**Customized Job Training Grants**
Mississippi	Mississippi Development Authority http://www.mississippi.org/jobs_training/wia_overview.htm Workforce Investment Network http://www.mississippi.org/jobs_training/win_in_ms.htm	Mississippi Development Authority Employment Training Division http://www.mississippi.org/jobs_training/etd_overview.htm
Missouri	Department of Economic Development Division of Workforce Development http://www.ded.mo.gov/employment/workforcedevelopment/default.shtml	Department of Economic Development Division of Workforce Development Customized Training Program http://www.ded.state.mo.us/business/expandrelocate/customizedtraining.shtml
Montana	Governor's Workforce Investment Board http://www.state.mt.us/gov2/css/boards/workforce/minREG040302.asp	Montana Department of Commerce http://www.commerce.state.mt.us
Nebraska	Nebraska Department of Labor Nebraska Workforce Development http://www.dol.state.ne.us/nwd	Nebraska Department of Economic Development http://www.neded.org
Nevada	Department of Employment, Training, and Rehabilitation Employment Security Division http://www.detr.state.nv.us/wia/wia_index.htm	Nevada Commission on Economic Development Workforce Training Programs http://www.expand2nevada.com/newsite/workforce/training.html
New Hampshire	Workforce Opportunity Council, Inc. NHWorks http://www.nhworks.org	Custom Workforce Opportunity Council, Inc. NHWorks Customized Training Programs http://www.nhworks.org/employers.cfm?page_number=44
New Jersey	New Jersey Department of Labor http://www..nj.gov/labor Workforce Investment Boards http://www.state.nj.us/njbiz/s_wib.shtml	New Jersey Department of Labor Customized Training Program http://www.nj.gov/labor/bsr/custrain.html
New Mexico	New Mexico Workforce Connection http://www.wia.state.nm.us/map.html New Mexico Economic Development Department http://www.edd.state.nm.us/index.html	New Mexico Economic Development Department http://www.edd.state.nm.us/PROGRAMS/pr_train.html

State-by-State Electronic Resources for Workforce Development Strategic Plans and Customized Job Training Grants		
State	**Workforce Development Strategic Plans**	**Customized Job Training Grants**
New York	Workforce New York Strategic Five Year State Plan http://www.workforcenewyork.com/stateplan/ stateplantoc.html	Workforce New York Funding Opportunities http://www.workforcenewyork.org/funding.htm
North Carolina	North Carolina Department of Commerce North Carolina Commission on Workforce Development http://www.nccommerce.com/workforce	North Carolina Department of Commerce Incumbent Worker Development Program http://www.nccommerce.com/workforce/ incumbent_worker
North Dakota	North Dakota Department of Commerce Economic Development and Finance http://www.growingnd.com	Job Service North Dakota New Jobs Training http://jobsnd.com/employers/workforce.html
Ohio	Bureau of Workforce Services www.ohioworkforce.org http://www.ohioworkforce.org	Ohio Department of Development Office of Investment in Training Ohio Investment in Training Program http://www.odod.state.oh.us/OITP.htm
Oklahoma	Oklahoma Workforce Investment Board http://www.oklahomaworkforceboard.com	Oklahoma Employment Security Commission Employment Services http://www.oesc.state.ok.us/ES/default.htm

Oregon	Department of Community Colleges and
	    Workforce Development
	WorkSource Oregon
	http://www.workforce.state.or.us/workforce.htm
		Oregon Economic and Community
		    Development Program
		Workforce Development Assistance
		http://www.econ.state.or.us/BIAworkforce.htm

Pennsylvania	Pennsylvania Workforce Investment Act Website http://www.paworkforce.state.pa.us/pa_ workforce/site/default.asp	Pennsylvania Department of Community and Economic Development http://www.inventpa.com/search.aspx WEDnetPA Guaranteed Free Training Program http://www.wednetpa.com
Rhode Island	Rhode Island State Workforce Investment Office http://www.dlt.ri.gov/webdev/WIO/default.htm	Rhode Island Human Resources Investment Council Grant Programs http://www.rihric.com/grantprogramshric.htm

South Carolina	South Carolina Employment Security
	    Commission
	http://www.sces.org
		State Board for Technical and Comprehensive
		    Education
		Special Schools Program
		http://www.sctechsystem.com

State-by-State Electronic Resources for Workforce Development Strategic Plans and Customized Job Training Grants

State	Workforce Development Strategic Plans	Customized Job Training Grants
South Dakota	South Dakota Department of Labor http://www.state.sd.us/dol/dol.asp South Dakota Workforce Development Council http://www.state.sd.us/dol/WIA/WDC.html	South Dakota Governor's Office of Economic Development Workforce Development Program http://www.sdgreatprofits.com/labor/training.htm
Tennessee	Tennessee Department of Labor & Workforce Development http://www.state.tn.us/labor-wfd	Tennessee Department of Economic and Community Development Industrial Training Service http://www.state.tn.us/ecd/its.htm
Texas	Texas Workforce Commission Strategic Plan http://www.twc.state.tx.us/twcinfo/stratplan/stratplan03.html	Texas Workforce Commission http://www.twc.state.tx.us
Utah	Department of Workforce Services http://www.jobs.utah.gov/StateCouncil/dwsdefault.asp	State of Utah Training and Events http://www.utah.gov/textonly/business/training.html
Vermont	Vermont Human Resource Council http://www.det.state.vt.us/~hric Vermont Department of Economic Development http://www.thinkvermont.com/workforce/index.cfm	Vermont Department of Employment and Training http://www.det.state.vt.us
Virginia	Virginia Workforce Council http://www.vec.state.va.us/vwc	Virginia Department of Business Assistance http://www.dba.state.va.us/workforce
Washington	Workforce Training and Education Coordinating Board State Unified Plan for the Workforce Development System http://www.wtb.wa.gov/uni-plan.html	Washington State Board for Community and Technical Colleges Workforce Education http://www.sbctc.ctc.edu/workforce/default.asp
West Virginia	West Virginia Development Office Governor's Workforce Investment Division http://www.wvdo.org/workforce/index.html	West Virginia Development Office Governor's Guaranteed Workforce Program http://www.wvdo.org/business/training.html

State-by-State Electronic Resources for Workforce Development Strategic Plans and Customized Job Training Grants		
State	**Workforce Development Strategic Plans**	**Customized Job Training Grants**
Wisconsin	Wisconsin Department of Workforce Development Governor's Council on Workforce Investment http://www.dwd.state.wi.us	Wisconsin Department of Commerce http://www.commerce.state.wi.us
Wyoming	Wyoming Department of Workforce Services http://dwsweb.state.wy.us Wyoming Workforce Development Council http://dwsweb.state.wy.us/councils/wdccouncil.asp	Wyoming Department of Workforce Services Workforce Development Training Fund http://dwsweb.state.wy.us/employers/trainingfund.asp

Note. Some links for the strategic workforce development plans take you directly to the strategic plans, whereas others require contact with the listed agencies to access their strategic plans. Also note that there may be customized job training grant programs other than those listed, but they are readily identifiable by contacting the listed agencies.

Eric Bergstrom is director of the Pennsylvania State University's Lancaster Center and professional associate of Penn State's Management Development Programs and Services. For the past six years, he has taught credit and noncredit business management courses, as well as training and development and organizational development courses. He is a regular presenter at conferences on training and development, organization development, and leadership, and he has facilitated programs for government, nonprofit, professional association, and manufacturing organizations to enhance their strategic planning process, continuous improvement processes, human resource development, and organization development.

Prior to joining Penn State, Bergstrom served for more than 20 years in a variety of human resources and manufacturing management positions including as division human resource manager and organization development manager. While in those positions, he led organization transformation efforts, established multi-plant, divisionwide training organizations, institutionalized an open-book management environment, developed and implemented comprehensive management development programs, and led the redesign of a large human resource organization. Bergstrom earned a BS and an MEd in training and development from Penn State and is currently completing coursework for a PhD in workforce education and development. ❉

Dennis Bona is currently the vice president for instruction at Kellogg Community College (KCC) in Battle Creek, Michigan. He has been involved in workforce education since 1979, and perhaps his greatest contribution to date has been the development and direction of KCC's nationally recognized Regional Manufacturing Technology Center. This center continues to deliver instruction to local business and industry through an open entry/exit, individualized, and self-paced instructional format and houses one of the most successful customized training programs in the country. He is currently challenged with transferring the customer service principles gained from working with employers to the academic division of his institution. ❉

Michael J. Brna Jr. is executive director of the Mon Valley Renaissance economic/workforce development program at California University of Pennsylvania. Brna

earned a BS degree in finance and an MBA with honors from California University of Pennsylvania and is currently an honors PhD candidate enrolled in Pennsylvania State University's Workforce Education and Development Program. He has appeared before the Pennsylvania House of Representatives Intergovernmental Affairs Subcommittee for Workforce Development and served as a member of the Pennsylvania State System of Higher Education's Science and Technology Task Force. Brna wrote the inaugural WEDnetPA Guaranteed Free Training grant in the Commonwealth of Pennsylvania in 1996. ❉

Wesley E. Donahue is director and associate professor with Pennsylvania State University's management development organization, a self-supporting provider of education and training services to business and industry clients around the world. Before joining Penn State, he was regional sales vice president for Mar-Kay Plastics in Kansas City, Missouri; co-founder and executive vice president of Leffler Systems of New Jersey, a manufacturing company; and manager of technology for Brockway, Inc., a Fortune 500 company now part of Owens Illinois. Donahue also co-owned and operated a retail business for 10 years. Among other publications, he coauthored *Creating In-House Sales Training and Development Programs—A Competency-Based Approach to Building Sales Ability* (with Rothwell and Park, 2002). ❉

Karen A. Flannery has been in the continuing education field for 23 years and is currently the associate dean of continuing education at Luzerne County Community College in Nanticoke, Pennsylvania. Her current assignment includes managing the credit-free operation, which has an ACT Center, and serving as ACT 48 Coordinator. Flannery works with area businesses to custom design training programs to achieve their business goals and employees' training needs. Flannery is a certified WorkKeys job analyst. She holds national certification as a Certified Meeting Professional from the Convention Liaison Council, Washington, DC, and international certification in program planning from LERN, Manhattan, Kansas. She has been recognized both regionally and nationally for outstanding achievement in program development. She earned a PhD in workforce education and development from Pennsylvania State University and an MPA from Marywood University. She is currently enrolled in the Human Performance Improvement Certificate program through the American Society for Training and Development (ASTD). She is a member of ASTD, National Council for Continuing Education and Training, and International Society for Performance Improvement. ❊

Elaine A. Gaertner is working on assignment with the Business Relations Group in the Employment and Training Administration of the U.S. Department of Labor, on capacity-building efforts to enhance the publicly funded workforce system's outreach and response to high-growth industries. She also serves as statewide director of organizational development with the California Community Colleges' Economic and Workforce Development Program, where she provides technical assistance to the 106 community colleges. She maintains a private consulting practice specializing in organizational development, performance consulting, and program evaluation for higher education and public sector workforce and economic development organizations. She has worked with training departments throughout Silicon Valley, including Apple Computer, IBM, Pacific Bell, Hewlett-Packard, Kaiser-Permanente, and Westinghouse Corporation.

Gaertner is prominent nationally as a subject expert and master trainer in performance consulting to higher education and workforce development programs. She has consulted with state systems in five other states and was instrumental in working with the Ohio Board of Regents to develop its research and development report *Organizing for High Performance in the Delivery of Business and Industry Services.* This benchmark report, the only one of its kind, has since been used to assess the effectiveness of corporate training units nationwide.

Gaertner is recognized as a thought leader in transforming higher education business and industry outreach units beyond training to performance improvement. She has been a major contributor to the following publications: *Maximizing Your Impact in Contract Education: A Handbook for Community Colleges* (1996); *Performance Technology: Its Application for Community Colleges* (1997); *Using a Collaborative Performance Improvement Process in Service Partnerships: A Process Guide* (1997); *Organizing for High Performance in the Delivery of Business and Industry Services* (1998); *Best Practices of College Business and Industry Centers: A Self-Improvement Guide* (1998). She was also a recipient of the National Council for Continuing Education Training Regional Leadership Award in recognition of her work in helping higher education implement and infuse the concepts of human per-

formance technology into their corporate and continuing education programs. ❊

Patrick E. Gerity is currently the executive director of Slippery Rock University's Office of Corporate Partnerships. In this position, Gerity is the project manager of the Regional Learning Alliance Project, charged with developing a 75,000-square-foot regional Workforce and Economic Development Center. He formerly worked for the State System of Higher Education's Educational Resources Group, where he was empowered to work with the 14 state-owned universities to establish a rapid response team to address corporate training and development needs across the commonwealth. In this effort he worked with university presidents, provosts, and deans to develop strategic plans and assist in the development of corporate relations.

Gerity was responsible for the successful writing of a $9 million grant, which the State System of Higher Education received from the Pennsylvania Department of Community and Economic Development. He directed the development of an agreement between the Pennsylvania Community College Commission, representing the 15 public community colleges, and the State System of Higher Education and its 14 public universities to collaborate in using the grant funds to make the Guaranteed Free Training Program available to new and expanding manufacturing and technology-based businesses in Pennsylvania. On his recommendation, these 29 collaborating public institutions became known as the Workforce and Economic Development Network of Pennsylvania (WEDnetPA), which is in its fifth year and has trained more than 400,000 Pennsylvania employees.

While he was a director of workforce development for 12 years at the Community College of Allegheny, Gerity also served on the American Association of Community Colleges (AACC) Commission for Workforce and Economic Development, as the first AACC state liaison for Pennsylvania, on the Board of Directors for the National Council for Continuing Education and Training, and as a member of a number of civic and professional associations. He has also served on state advisory committees for the Pennsylvania Department of Education, the Pennsylvania Department of Community and Economic Development, and the Pennsylvania Workforce Investment Board. He has received three degrees from the Pennsylvania State University—most recently a PhD in workforce education and development with a special emphasis in training and organization development. ❊

Mary Gershwin, of the Colorado Community College System, has led multicollege initiatives over the last 15 years to improve opportunities for the 110,000 students in the Colorado system. Gershwin currently serves as executive director of system advancement, providing statewide leadership for resource development for the statewide system of 13 community colleges. She is vice president for collaboration for the National Council of Workforce Development and president of the Colorado Partners of the Americas. She has written for a wide variety of publications and speaks throughout the United States on workforce development, resource development, and collaborative leadership. She holds a PhD in communications and a BA in economics from the University of Denver. ✳

James Jacobs is the associate director for community college operations at the Community College Research Center at Columbia University and director of the Center for Workforce Policy at Macomb Community College. He specializes in the areas of occupational change and technology, suburban economic development, occupational education, retraining of displaced workers, and needs assessment of occupational programs. He has also been a tech prep director and was responsible for developing a machinist training program at Macomb. He is a national expert on workforce development and community colleges and advisor to a number of national foundations on workforce development policy. Currently, he is the president elect of the National Council for Workforce Education, a national postsecondary organization of occupational education and workforce development specialists. He also serves on the advisory board of the congressionally mandated National Assessment of Vocational Education.

Jacobs has conducted many specific examinations of community college programs. He is a coauthor of a statewide assessment of tech prep programs in Michigan and has conducted major studies on the impact of new manufacturing technologies on skill requirements of firms both for the U.S. Department of Education and the U.S. Department of Labor. In addition to consulting for many community colleges in the United States on the development of workforce and economic development programs, he has written numerous technical articles and papers for community college journals and is a regular presenter community college conferences and meetings. ✳

Marsha King is the director of human resources for Capital One Financial. In this role, she partners with senior executives in the areas of performance management,

talent development, succession planning, and change management. She is also an adjunct professor of organization development at Johns Hopkins University and George Washington University. She spends her free time doing public speaking and writing in the field of human resources. ✳

Rebecca Klein-Collins has managed best practice studies, data collection and analysis, and other research projects on behalf of Council for Adult and Experiential Learning (CAEL) and its public sector and corporate clients, first as an employee of CAEL and then later as an independent consultant. Her clients include the Ohio Board of Regents, Levi Strauss & Company, the Levi Strauss Foundation, the State of Indiana's Department of Workforce Development, and Chase Manhattan Bank. Her projects have included research and survey design, data analysis, and qualitative data collection and analysis through interviews and focus groups. She holds a BA from Grinnell College and an MA in public policy from the University of Chicago's Harris School of Public Policy. ✳

Frederick D. Loomis is associate professor of workforce education and development in the Department of Learning and Performance Systems in the College of Education on the University Park campus of the Pennsylvania State University. He also holds an affiliate appointment with Penn State's School of Information Sciences and Technology. He leads the Penn State Workforce Education and Development Outreach Initiative, a strategy designed to focus resources to identify best practices and performance indicators and to respond to the critical policy issues and professional development opportunities of the commonwealth's workforce development system.

Loomis received a BA in political science from Temple University and an MPA and a PhD in higher education from Penn State University. He has served in a variety of administrative and management roles, including special assistant to executive vice president and provost for Web strategy development, director of strategic planning and information technology for Penn State's outreach organization, and director of the Solutions Institute, the outreach arm of the School of Information Sciences and Technology.

From 1998 to 2000, Loomis served with the Governor's Office for Information Technology as executive director of Pennsylvania's Y2K outreach program and was responsible for assisting local governments, schools, businesses, and community organizations on Y2K compliance, emergency preparedness, and contingency planning. Loomis also served for more than 10 years with the federal government's Office for Civil Rights, conducting compliance reviews of colleges and universities. His research and teaching have focused on strategy, planning, negotiation theory, educational equity, change management, information policy, and the impact of technology on society. He has consulted with education institutions, governments, and nonprofit organizations in the United States and abroad. Most recently, Loomis coauthored a chapter on e-government with Pennsylvania's chief information officer in *Pushing the Digital Frontier* (2001). He also wrote the "Contingency Planning Guide for Year 2000," sponsored by the Information Technology Association of America and the United Nations Y2K Task Force. ❋

Cheryl A. Marshall is the director of the Center for Business Performance & Training, a community college–based consulting program at Mt. Antonio College in Walnut, California, that targets business clients who want to improve performance and productivity. The purpose of her consulting is to give organizations a number of options for enhancing performance, including performance-based training or other nontraining solutions. Since joining the center in 1999, Marshall has completed more than a dozen performance analyses for business clients, conducted more than 25 performance-based workshops, and facilitated numerous strategic planning and team-building sessions.

Prior to joining the center, Marshall worked as a project manager and senior organization development and learning officer at Sanwa Bank. One of her major clients included the Information Services Department, where she conducted numerous team-building seminars and was project lead for redesigning its career development and performance management systems. While partnering with the commercial banking executives, she helped develop a strategic plan that was integrated into the sales training program. She has also worked as an independent consultant with clients including Boeing, Southern California Edison, TRW, and Avon. She has facilitated numerous sessions with managers on topics such as strategic planning, competency development, and customer service.

During her tenure as a consultant, Marshall taught more than 60 graduate and undergraduate courses including organization behavior, training and development, and management. She recently completed her doctoral degree in education at the University of Southern California, specializing in human learning and performance. She received her MA in industrial-organizational psychology from California State University, San Bernardino. ❋

Larry Michael is the associate dean of the Technology Transfer Center (TTC) and of Continuing Education for Pennsylvania College of Technology. The TTC provides noncredit training and consulting services to business and industry. The center trains more than 5,000 students annually and coordinates more than $3 million of federal and state grant-related training and consulting services to business and industry. Before joining the college in 1991, Michael spent more than 20 years in manufacturing, retailing, and government in various technology-related disciplines. He holds an MS in workforce education and development from Pennsylvania State University and a BS in computer science from Virginia Commonwealth University. ❋

John E. Park is associate director and assistant professor with Pennsylvania State University's Management Development Organization, with special interests in sales, marketing, and strategic planning. Prior to joining Penn State, he was assistant vice president of Glenn Insurances, Inc., in New Jersey; a senior casualty underwriter with Commercial Union Insurance, Mechanicsburg, Pennsylvania; and commercial underwriter with Pennsylvania National Insurance in Pittsburgh. Park was also involved in all facets of a family business for more than 25 years. Among his many publications is *Creating In-House Sales Training and Development Programs—A Competency-Based Approach to Building Sales Ability* (with Rothwell and Donahue, 2002). ❋

Paul Pierpoint is dean of the Division of Community Education at Northampton Community College (NCC) in Bethlehem, Pennsylvania, which had contracts with more than 200 employers and served more than 17,000 individuals in 2002. He has also been NCC's dean of business, technology, and allied health and was responsible for most of the for-credit occupational programs offered at the college. Before joining NCC, he was chair and director of the Community College at West Virginia State College in Institute, West Virginia, where he was also an associate professor of management and marketing for 12 years. He earned an EdD in higher education administration from West Virginia University, an MBA in management and marketing from the University of Pittsburgh, and a BA in journalism from the Pennsylvania State University. Pierpoint has served as the chair of the Pennsylvania Statewide Occupational Deans Group, member of the statewide Workforce and Economic Development Network of Pennsylvania (WEDnetPA), and member of the Economic Development Council of the Lehigh Valley and other business and economic development groups. He has testified multiple times before various Pennsylvania congressional panels and committees and was active at the statewide level with Pennsylvania's early implementation of the Workforce Investment Act. He is on the board of directors for the National Coalition of Advanced Technology Centers. ❊

Leslie Roe is dean of economic development and contract education for the Chabot-Las Positas Community College District. Her responsibilities range from strategic planning, budget development, and supervision of staff and overall department management; to developing and administering workforce development grants; to interacting and coordinating with the district's colleges, regional occupational organizations, and state agencies. In this position, she combines her understanding of the business climate, the need for flexible, dynamic solutions to workforce development issues, and strong marketing skills to position and promote the community college system as an integral part of the regional workforce development system. Her business development skills were critical in the successful turnaround of her department, taking it from a deficit position to one of the highest-performing centers in the state in a little less than three years.

In her previous position, she served as executive director with a local education foundation, where she was highly involved in the development of a program that supported the national School-to-Career initiative. Prior to her work with the foundation, Roe worked in the private sector as a business development and marketing executive in the Silicon Valley with Hewlett-Packard and Tandy Corporation, before starting her own marketing consulting firm and working with companies such as Hewlett-Packard, Palm Computing, 3Com, Ingres, and Computer Associates. Roe graduated from California State University, Sacramento, with a BA in liberal arts and received her MA in organization development from the University of Phoenix. She is a requested speaker for many venues, including workforce development–focused conferences such as those held by the California Community College Association for Occupational Education and ED>Net. She currently holds leadership positions for the Bay Region Contract Education Professionals organization and the Statewide Contract Education Executive Advisory Committee. ❊

William J. Rothwell is a professor of workforce education and development in the Department of Learning and Performance Systems in the College of Education on the University Park campus of Pennsylvania State University.

He leads a graduate emphasis in workplace learning and performance. He is also president of Rothwell & Associates, Inc. (www.rothwell-associates.com), a full-service private consulting firm that specializes in all facets of human performance improvement. Before entering academe in 1993, Rothwell had 20 years of experience as a practitioner, serving first as training director for the Illinois Office of Auditor General and later as assistant vice president and management development director for the Franklin Life Insurance Company, at that time a wholly owned subsidiary of a Fortune 500 multinational company.

Rothwell holds a BA in English from Illinois State University, an MA in English from the University of Illinois at Urbana-Champaign, an MBA from the University of Illinois at Springfield, and a PhD with a specialization in employee training from the University of Illinois at Urbana-Champaign. Best known for his extensive and high-profile work in succession management (see *Effective Succession Planning*, 2000), Rothwell has many publications to his credit. Among the most recent are *What CEOs Expect from Corporate Training: Building Workplace Learning and Performance Initiatives that Advance Organizational Goals* (with Lindholm and Wallick, 2003), *Planning and Managing Human Resources*, 2nd ed. (with Kazanas, 2003), *Creating Sales Training and Development Programs: A Competency-Based Approach to Building Sales Ability* (with Donahue and Park, 2002), *The Workplace Learner: How to Align Training Initiatives with Individual Learning Competencies* (2002), and *Building Effective Technical Training: How to Develop Hard Skills Within Organizations* (with Benkowski, 2002). Rothwell is also a coeditor of two Wiley/Jossey-Bass/Pfeiffer book series: *Practicing Organization Development and Change Management* (with Sullivan and Quade) and *Using Technology in Training and Learning* (with Richey and Spannaus). ❊

Ethan S. Sanders is president and CEO of Sundial Learning Systems. Before founding this company, Sanders was manager of instructional design for the American Society for Training and Development (ASTD). While at ASTD, he led the research and writing of two major competency studies and redesigned several of ASTD's courses. Before joining ASTD, he was a senior instructional designer of management development courses in the banking industry and a training manager in the transportation industry. He is the coauthor of numerous publications, including *Models for Learning Technologies*; *Models for Workplace Learning and Performance*; *Performance Intervention Maps: 36 Strategies* *for Solving Your Organization's Problems*; *HPI Essential*; *ASTD Distance Learning Yearbook*; and the ASTD course "Human Performance Improvement in the Workplace." Sanders is also the author and one of the primary evaluators of ASTD's e-learning certification standards. He teaches several of ASTD's courses, which are offered through public and corporate seminars. He holds a master's degree in applied behavior science from Johns Hopkins University. Sanders can be reached at Sundial Learning Systems, 113 North Henry St., Alexandria, VA 22314; phone: 703-739-4344; e-mail: esanders@sundial-learning.com ❋

Michael Taggart has served as director of workforce development for the Ohio Board of Regents since 1995. A primary responsibility has been providing leadership for the EnterpriseOhio Network, a statewide alliance of 53 two-year campuses that work collaboratively to provide workforce development services to Ohio employers. Before joining the Board of Regents staff, Taggart served as executive director of the Unified Technologies Center of Cuyahoga Community College in Cleveland and as director of the Private Industry Council of Cleveland. He holds an MBA from Baldwin Wallace College and a master's degree in social service administration from Case Western Reserve University. ❋

Pamela Tate is president and CEO of the Council for Adult and Experiential Learning (CAEL). She is nationally and internationally recognized for her work in facilitating workforce education and training programs among educational institutions, business, labor, and government. Her efforts in assisting colleges and universities to develop systems of Prior Learning Assessment and systems of quality assurance in adult learning programs have earned ample

attention. Tate has been directly involved in the design and implementation of CAEL's tuition assistance management and workforce learning programs since 1986, when CAEL designed the PATHWAYS program for Qwest and the Communications Workers of America. As a presenter, she is regularly sought for her insight into adult learning and workforce development and their vital relationship to the future of the economy. Tate graduated from the University of Illinois at Champaign with an MA in English and an MA in journalism. She completed her doctoral coursework at the Annenberg School of Communications, University of Pennsylvania. In 1996, Tate was acknowledged for a career devoted to expanding lifelong educational opportunities for adults with the Doctor of Humane Letters honoris causa, conferred by SUNY Empire State College, Saratoga Springs, New York. ❋

Laurance J. Warford is currently project manager for the College and Career Transitions Initiative (CCTI), a cooperative grant awarded by the U.S. Department of Education, Office of Vocational and Adult Education, to the League for Innovation in the Community College Consortium. The purposes of CCTI are to improve student transitions between secondary and postsecondary education and careers and to improve scholastic achievement at both levels. Prior to joining CCTI, he was a community college administrator in Iowa and Oregon who served in various capacities and provided leadership in workforce education both locally and nationally. He is recognized as a national leader in workforce training through his seminal research in the area of customized contract training in the community college and his writing on the need for comprehensive workforce training. He earned a PhD from the University of Oregon and a BA and an MA from the University of Northern Iowa. ❋